THE EVIDENCE FOR THE
SIXTH SENSE

THE EVIDENCE FOR THE
SIXTH SENSE

Amazing insights into:

Life after death • Re-incarnation

The science of enlightenment

Spiritual emergency • Spontaneous healing

Masters of the self

And how miracles are made

HAZEL COURTENEY

CICO BOOKS

LONDON NEW YORK

First published in this revised edition in 2011 by CICO Books
an imprint of Ryland Peters & Small Ltd

20–21 Jockey's Fields, London WC1R 4BW
519 Broadway, 5th Floor, New York, NY 10012

www.cicobooks.com

10 9 8 7 6 5 4 3 2 1

A CIP catalog record for this book is available from the Library of
Congress.

ISBN: 978-1-907563-51-5

Other books by Hazel Courteney
Divine Intervention
Countdown to Coherence
500 of the Most Important Ways to Stay Younger Longer
500 of the Most Important Health Tips You'll Ever Need
Mind and Mood Foods
Body and Beauty Foods

For more information on Hazel's work, log on to her website:
www.hazelcourteney.com

Cover design: Jerry Goldie Graphic Design

Printed in the USA

Contents

Acknowledgements

When I began this book, I had no idea of how this journey would unfold. And yet thanks to all of you who have given such tremendous amounts of help, knowledge and wisdom. I believe that something special has been created.

Firstly I offer a heartfelt thank you to my husband Stuart, whose patience, unconditional love and support has truly kept me on an even keel during the last year whilst I have researched and written this book.

My deepest gratitude goes to Gary Schwartz for not only writing a wonderful Foreword, but also for listening, sharing and trusting. Thanks a million, Gary.

To Laurie Campbell, Allison Dubois and Sally Morgan – all great mediums who helped me find Diana once more, thank you all.

To Professor Stanislav Grof, Christina Grof, and Emeritus Professor William A Tiller, I salute your patience and thank you for your valuable contributions and wisdom.

A big hug for biophysicist Harry Oldfield and his ex-wife Eileen, two people with very big hearts.

To Isobel and Chris Clarke, I thank you both not only for your valuable contribution, but also for your healthy hospitality on a winter's day.

Dr David Simon at the Chopra Center in California granted me a personal interview – even though his schedule was packed. Thank you, David.

Also to Dr Michael Newton in California for your insightful books and for allowing me to quote from them.

Huge amounts of gratitude I send to Professor Frederick Travis based in Fairfield, Iowa. Fred, your patience was awesome.

Thank you also Vianna Stibal, Christine Holohan, Julie James and Janice Hartley for sharing your truly magical and courageous stories.

For a real English gentleman, scientist Rupert Sheldrake – my eternal respect. The same to Dr Serena Roney-Dougal for once again helping to clarify so many subjects with such patience and grace. Thanks Serena.

To Swamiji Shivkrupanandji goes my gratitude, for sharing your love and light and for being who you are. Emma, Sirla and Jaya – thank you for all your support.

I cannot allow this section to pass without also saying a huge thank you to Veronica Keen and Dr Sangeeta Sahi, for sharing your contacts and asking nothing in return. I owe you girls a big lunch.

Grateful thanks to my editor Liz Dean, for making the process of editing my manuscript pain-free. Thanks, Liz.

Finally, to my true friend Lindsay Ross Jarett: thank you for working your fingers to the bone transcribing all the tapes. Thank you one and all – I could not have done it without you.

An eye for an eye leaves everyone blind.
Gandhi

For Diana and the spirit realms

Foreword

by Professor Gary E. Schwartz

There are numerous books linking science to spirit, but they are either too technical for the layman or too light for the serious researcher. Although not an academic herself, Hazel manages to truly bridge the gap between science and spirit in this riveting story that grows as it goes and, most importantly, it can be understood by anyone.

Hazel has managed to weave a huge amount of information into her story that will make you laugh, but also make you think. Whether you are interested in enlightened masters, enlightenment itself, spiritual emergency, evidence of life after death and the myriad extraordinary phenomena associated with them – and you want to know how they are possible in everyday terms and in science – this book is for you.

As a Harvard-trained scientist, a former Professor at Yale University, and a Professor of Psychology, Medicine, Surgery, Neurology, and Psychiatry at the University of Arizona, I approach claims such as spiritual emergency, energy healing and afterlife communications from a strictly scientific research point of view. Sure, swamis or their followers sometimes claim that their particular swami experiences phenomena such as materialization of objects and 'bilocation' (being in two places at once) and everyday people sometimes claim to experience strange phenomena such as near-death out-of-body experiences and communication with deceased family and friends. *The question is, are such claims real? Can they be established scientifically?*

As you will read in *The Evidence For the Sixth Sense*, it appears that genuine spiritual emergencies and transformations of consciousness such as Hazel experienced in 1998, are happening more frequently, worldwide – to housewives, businessmen, physicians and even scientists. Not only are their experiences consistent with contemporary scientific theory, but the phenomena can be brought into the laboratory and put to experimental test.

I have had the privilege to evaluate scientifically one of the most remarkable and controversial experiences associated with Hazel's personal spiritual emergency – her belief that Diana, Princess of Wales communicated with Hazel after Diana's death in August 1997.

In Chapter 4 you will read the results of a controlled experiment we performed in Tucson, Arizona, in which Hazel participated as a secret research 'sitter' (someone who wants to hear from deceased relatives, friends or colleagues) with two highly experiences research mediums. Neither medium knew Hazel, nor she them. Neither medium was told who they were going to be reading for, nor were they told what country Hazel was from or whom she was hoping to hear from in the spirit world. And most importantly during the readings, Hazel was not allowed to utter a word or make any obvious facial expressions. The evidence from these readings was surprising, highly emotional and extremely convincing. From my perspective – playing devil's advocate and remaining the sceptical scientist – these experiments with Hazel and the mediums were jaw-dropping.

Even more remarkable was a follow-up experiment we completed just a few weeks before Hazel finished writing this book. The experiment involved Sally Morgan, a celebrity British medium who was staying in Westport, Connecticut, at the time we tested her in June 2004. This experiment was run 'double-blind' (which is fully explained on page 252). At the time, Hazel was in London when this test took place. As you will read in Chapter 16, the results from this experiment were even more extraordinary. I present additional information from this experiment in my book *The Sacred Promise*.

The 'big picture' that Hazel paints in this book is one of wonder, joy, humility and hope. She reveals the profound power of the human mind – as expressed by swamis, scientists, psychics and everyday people – to ultimately discover its true potential.

If Hazel's overall vision is correct – and I have become convinced that it is – then we are approaching a paradigm shift of monumental proportions. Like many other scientists, I believe the time has now come for us all to let go of some of our old cherished beliefs, be they scientific or religious, and see the world through new eyes.

The Evidence For the Sixth Sense is like a beautiful garden that has been put together by a visionary artist. It is a carefully selected collection of extraordinary stories, experiences, scientific findings and take-home messages about the reality of spiritual transformation, physical healing and human evolution, magically arranged so that the grandeur of the whole book – the 'big picture' – can be clearly understood by anyone who has the wisdom to read it.

Once you have walked in this enthralling garden, you will never be the same again. For the sake of humanity I hope you are ready and willing to be transformed

Gary E. Schwartz

Professor Gary Schwartz
January 2011

– dynamically vibrates as instruments in a cosmic orchestra playing music we are just beginning to hear. Like many other scientists, I believe the time has now come for us all to let go of some of our old cherished beliefs, be they scientific or religious, and see the world through new eyes.

The Evidence for the Sixth Sense is like a beautiful garden that has been put together by a visionary artist. It is a carefully selected collection of extraordinary stories, experiences, scientific findings and take-home messages about the reality of spiritual transformation, physical healing and human evolution, magically arranged so that the grandeur of the whole book – the 'big picture' – can be clearly understood by anyone who has the wisdom to read it.

Once you have walked in this enthralling garden, you will never be the same again. For the sake of humanity I hope you are ready and willing to be transformed.

Gary E. Schwartz

1

Back to the Future

After the ecstasy, the laundry.
ZEN SAYING

September 21, 2000 – Knightsbridge, London

It was a crisp, autumn morning, with clear blue skies. It felt good to be alive. I had a business meeting at 9.30am, and knew I would be sitting in a stuffy office most of the day. What a waste. Hyde Park, with its sea of golden leaves beckoned. Walking to my meeting would increase my circulation, give me some much-needed air and sunlight and help burn off a few of the calories that would be served over lunch.

With my high heels in a carrier bag and wearing my trendy J. P. Tod walking shoes, I set off at a brisk pace with my head buzzing, mentally preparing for the meeting ahead. Don't ask me why, but I did not immediately cross over Knightsbridge Road and into the park – instead I walked down Knightsbridge and into the morning rush hour.

As I passed Harvey Nichols, the fashionable London store, I decided to cross the busy road opposite the French Embassy at the pedestrian lights, and head off across the park. The traffic fumes were dulling my buoyant mood.

Unfortunately, the pedestrian lights were out of order, and on the central reservation stood four laughing young, Far Eastern tourists, wearing the trendiest of clothes and sporting designer shoulder bags. I made a mental note to make time to look for some fashionable clothes. After all, I silently reasoned, at 51 – and just about to film a TV health show – I had better update myself.

A black taxi suddenly appeared as if from nowhere. The group moved forward. The scream in my throat made no sound. They had looked to their right before stepping into the road, but the traffic was coming from the left. They didn't see the cab – to them the road was clear. The taxi hit one of the girls with a dull thud and her body flew into the air like a rag doll and slammed back onto the road.

Screams filled the air, traffic stopped. Her three stunned companions tried to drag her lifeless body towards the kerb. The shocked driver screamed at them to stop and leave her where she lay – in the centre of a busy road in the rush hour.

I reached for my mobile, as did many others, and dialled 999. It seemed like an eternity until the emergency operator answered. They put me through to the ambulance service. The man was calm: 'Is she conscious, which side was she hit, are there any obvious injuries?' I answered in a daze as best I could, feeling totally useless, staring at the unconscious figure before me. Thankfully, the paramedics arrived quickly and feverishly worked on her for over two hours. I stood transfixed, willing her to live.

Meanwhile, the traffic around Knightsbridge came to a standstill. Dozens of large red buses were left abandoned in Belgrave Square, drivers swore at the inconvenience, other pedestrians stared and moved on. The Prada bags the tourists had carried were abandoned in the road, as suddenly being in fashion no longer mattered to the woman fighting for her life, to her distraught companions – or to me. The police eventually told me to go home as there was nothing more I could do. I subsequently learned that the stranger died later that day from massive internal injuries.

I thought about Princess Diana - how she too had died from massive internal injuries, happy one minute and gone the next. Feeling sick to my stomach I turned and walked the few hundred yards back home, my important meeting forgotten. I was shaking like a leaf as I turned the key in the door.

I was in shock, of course. I made some camomile tea and stirred in a spoonful of honey. When your brain is shocked it uses up more fuel – glucose – and after 12 years as a health writer, I knew that the honeyed tea would help calm me down. Then I took some homeopathic Bach Rescue Remedy under my tongue. Finally, I let my emotions out and wept for the young stranger who had been so carefree one minute and dead the next. How life hangs by a thread.

A voice that was not mine spoke in my head. 'Don't worry, you of all people *know* that we go on. She, like you is shocked, but she is being helped during her transition. Remember, *remember* what you *know.*' Those words bought a brief, sad smile to my lips, and I pulled myself together. When I finally looked at the clock, I felt as though only an hour or so had passed since I left home, but it was midday – time to call my 9.30 appointment and apologize. Life goes on.

It was also hard to believe that two and a half years had passed since I had gone through an incredible near-death experience over Easter 1998, and yet on many days I had felt as though I had lived several lifetimes since then. But yes, the voice was right. I knew better, though my knowing did not make my sadness any easier to bear.

That night, as we took our daily evening walk, I shared what had happened with my husband, Stuart. He was sympathetic, but to him it was just another tragic story, like the ones we see on TV and in the newspapers every day. After all, he said, 1.2 million people die every year on the roads around the world and merely suggested that this incident should make me even more careful when crossing the street. How, I wondered, could he be so unaffected? And yet, when I told him that I had briefly heard the voice again, he stopped in his tracks. A look of fear flashed across his face and he asked, 'I hope all *that* is not starting again?'

We hugged and I laughed. Of course it wasn't, I assured him. But secretly I wished that *some* of it was. Witnessing the accident that morning had triggered memories I had thought were better forgotten. As I lay in bed that night, waiting for sleep to come, I said a prayer for the stranger and her family, and thanked the universe for my safe, warm bed. As the minutes turned to hours, I began mulling over the events of 1998 that had left an indelible mark on my life.

Before it had all begun, I had been an award-winning health columnist with *The Sunday Times*. Hundreds of letters arrived weekly asking for my health advice. Following more than three decades of illness and surgery, I had become well by changing my diet and using alternative therapies – and in doing so, had become quite knowledgeable about health matters.

During the first three months of 1998, I had never been so happy, and felt that I was truly living my purpose for this lifetime. But in early April, everything had changed overnight.

Whilst shopping in Harrods that fateful week before Easter, I had begun hearing voices, become telepathic and incredibly psychic, and had affected electrical equipment; I had levitated, begun making 'ash', and could see and hear other dimensions – and if that, and more, wasn't enough, I had also experienced a 'walk in'. In other words, a person who had physically died seemed to be inside me, communicating through me, controlling many of my thoughts as well as numerous paranormal events.

And as I remembered how I had left my physical body on that Easter Saturday – witnessed by a medical doctor – I thought again of the young woman I had last seen lying in a pool of blood in the road. It's a fact that not one of us is going to leave this world alive, yet death remains one of mankind's greatest mysteries. It had been so easy for me to pass from this world to the next; in one second I was watching my bedroom fill with a whitish mist whilst the doctor held my hand and stroked my forehead, and in the next I was watching the scene from the bedroom ceiling. There was no fear, just a mild surprise as I realized that the shrivelled mess below me was me! I felt no panic as I observed the doctor's tears; I had become a detached observer in the drama unfolding below me, and had no wish to return to my body.

Years earlier I had heard a medium say that the last breath you take on earth is the first breath you take in the next dimension – and during those timeless moments I knew this to be true. I was free, and it felt completely blissful. Needless to say, I did return to my physical body and during the months that followed, hundreds of strange events set me on a journey to discover what was happening to me. By interviewing numerous scientists I realized that I had gone through a major spiritual emergency – when spiritual transformation becomes a crisis – and mine sure had become a crisis.

During the following year I wrote the story of what had happened to me in 1998 and beyond in *Divine Intervention*, which was first published in December 1999. It caused quite a furore. Why? Because I claimed to have been in direct contact with none other than Diana, Princess of Wales. My credibility as a health journalist was virtually destroyed overnight. And yet I knew with my whole heart that my experience had been real, and many phenomena had been witnessed by credible people. As time passed my amazing psychic abilities, plus the phenomena, faded away. At the height of my experience I had prayed for them all to stop, but once they had I desperately wanted them back. It's human nature: most of us don't appreciate what we have until it's gone.

In order to try to somehow 'switch' myself back on, in July 1999 I travelled to Charlottesville in America to meet the spiritually enlightened Indian yoga master Swami Satchidananda at his ashram. He was wonderful, full of compassion and wisdom, and told me that my constant wanting for something to happen was preventing any return to such a heightened spiritual state. He suggested that I start from scratch on my journey by living a pure, loving life, helping others, eating a healthy diet, meditating regularly

– and dedicate myself to the spiritual path. In this way, he said I would not harm my body and mind as my sudden awakening had during 1998. But I was looking for a single magic bullet, someone, or something, that could 'switch me on' just as it had in 1998. And yet in my heart I knew that if my physical body was not prepared, then such an incident a second time could prove fatal.

And so, in between writing health features for various newspapers, feeding my husband, looking after our homes and getting on with life, I chanted, I meditated and along the way met others who to varying degrees had also been through spiritual awakenings and emergencies. It's comforting to know that so many people are also going through their own unique awakenings at this time. Some of their stories appear later in this book.

I attended courses with spiritual teachers such as Dr Deepak Chopra. I studied the ancient geometry Flower of Life courses devised by American scientist Drunvalo Melchizedek, and attended his Mer-Ka-Ba meditation classes. If friends told me that an enlightened person such as John de Ruiter from Canada, Sri Chinmoy or Shri Mataji Nirmala Devi from India were in the UK, I would make the effort to go and see them. I attended a briefing on peace by His Holiness the Dalai Lama – what a magical soul he is. These people are 'on line' as I had been – people who have integrated huge amounts of spiritual energy and knowledge into their everyday lives. Some have attained mastery over their physical bodies and minds through their connection to the 'all that is' – what most of us refer to as God.

A few 'masters of self', such as Sai Baba in India, are capable of incredible feats, or tricks, as I used to call them: appearing in several locations at the same time, healing, manifesting objects including ash, telepathy and so on – which can in many cases now be explained by science. And surely, I thought, if I could see someone like Sai Baba face to face, he could switch me back on. Couldn't he? But I did not have time to fly half-way around the world for a magic bullet, and my husband, Stuart, desperately wanted me just to forget the whole experience.

During my search at times I became more psychic, and once in a while I received fleeting messages that I thought might be from Diana, attempting to get through again. But the more desperate I became to return to that heightened, awesome, blissful state, any peace continued to elude me. One scientist suggested the easiest route back to enlightenment would be to go and live in an ashram for a few months! It took me all of five seconds to consider his suggestion – and then I laughed. Of course, I have free will and I could choose what I wanted to do. But my wonderful husband had already put up with enough goings on to wreck most marriages and he had truly been my rock. I could not ask for more. And the thought of living in India for months was not high on my, or his, wish list. After all, I love my food, I love shopping and hot showers ... I just wouldn't fit in. For now I needed just to be 'normal' for his sake. And yet, during the previous two years, there were many times when I had felt just like the character ET in Spielberg's magical film – who was *desperate* to reconnect and go 'home', just as I had during 1998.

Imagine that you had climbed Mount Everest and from the top you can see and understand everything so clearly – you really can see the bigger picture. And then you come back down the mountain, and can only see a small, restricted view that is shrouded in fog – and so you longingly and lovingly look back from whence you have come, wondering how you ever achieved such an amazing feat. My sense of loss and disconnection during 1999 is almost impossible to put into words. For a time during 1998, I had truly understood what Jesus meant when he said, 'I and my father are one.' But over time, I had simply become *only* Hazel again. Or so I believed ...

Eventually, I concluded that I was simply meant to teach others that such experiences are real, valid, have huge growth potential and are explainable in science – and how to cope with them, which would not be so simple at all.

Then there had been the Diana problem. After *Divine Intervention* was published I received hundreds of letters from people who were claiming to have also received messages from the Princess. What was I supposed to reply? In many cases, I had felt like saying, 'Your letter is outrageous – I believe she would never have said such a thing.' But then I chided myself, who am I to judge? Other letters, however, were magical and I believe that Princess Diana is indeed coming through to many wonderful people to let the world know that we do indeed go on.

But neither they, nor I, could verify what I had heard.

Back then, little did I know that Diana and the higher realms were setting events in motion that would not only help verify my experience, but also some of the information I had received.

Rather than remembering day after day what I had known, and talking on and on about my experience, by September 2000 I eventually forced myself to completely let go and surrender, and trust that if those in the spirit world had a meaningful job for me to do, they would let me know. While I waited for any signs, I returned to what I knew best: writing about health. And yet, to have gone through so much and to have known so many answers and universal truths, the thought of returning to writing about irritable bowel or eczema horrified me! Then I reminded myself that we are all very special beings in a physical body and if we don't look after it, then we become ill. My knowledge had served me well in the past, so perhaps it would work again. It felt as if I were going backwards towards my future.

By the spring of 2000, I had already returned to *The Sunday Times* writing health features, plus a small column called 'Witch Hazel' in which I wrote about scientific research into the power of the mind, reincarnation and various other spiritual subjects. After several months, I realized there was such a wealth of information available on both esoteric and health subjects that deserved more space than any newspaper or magazine could ever give them. So I decided to devote my time to writing books.

And so as I lay in bed on that September evening my thoughts returned to the health book I was in the middle of writing, and to the TV series I was making – I needed to stop remembering 'all *that*' stuff I had gone through, as my husband had asked, and simply get on with my work.

The universe, meanwhile, had additional ideas.

When sleep finally came I dreamed about Sai Baba the Indian enlightened spiritual teacher. I had not given him too much thought for almost two years – since I had stopped materializing ash – which he has done since childhood. Yet the dream, in which he was calling my name from afar, was so profound that I made a note of it the next morning in my spiritual diary.

As the days passed I focused intently on getting on with my book. It took every waking moment. There was no time to ponder what the dream might have meant.

October 5, 2000

As I sat typing the heading 'Depression' for the book, my mood truly matched the subject. I was desperate to throw my computer out of the window and to go and live on chocolate biscuits for the rest of my life. Yes, even health writers love some treats.

The phone on my desk rang. I answered it sharply as the last thing I needed was yet another interruption. It was a friend calling from Ireland, to say that her 92-year-old boss was flying to India on a private jet on November 12 to visit Sai Baba and, as they had heard me mention him on several occasions, would I like to join them? I was speechless. Ever since I had first become interested in spiritual issues so many people had mentioned Sai Baba.

I knew from what I had been told and had read that he could materialize objects, including Holy ash; that he was a great healer and teacher and that thousands of people visited his ashram in Puttaparthi near Bangalore every day just to be in his presence and receive his blessings. But what about my health book? Also, on Remembrance Sunday I was due to give a lecture on health in London. Yet I had always believed that when the universe sends you a signal, you need to take notice. Such a chance I knew would never come again in this lifetime. I said yes immediately.

Suddenly I felt like Cinderella, and I was going to the ball.

Worlds Collide

The chances of someone awakening without a teacher are like the chances of getting pregnant without a partner. The spiritual teacher is the partner that is necessary for spiritual birth. Not too many immaculate conceptions happen.

ROBERT ENNIS

November 12, 2000 – Biggin Hill airfield, Kent

The Chinese have a saying, 'the journey is often better than the arrival.' Little did I know how my journey would shake many of my spiritual beliefs to the core.

On that cold, damp Remembrance Sunday, as the royal family and members of government paid sombre homage to the men and women from the armed services killed or wounded in battles during the past decades, I said farewell to my husband Stuart. I watched from my taxi as he waved me off, looking pensive and sad. He was not keen for me to go to India, and yet he knew that my host, James, and his people would take care of me. My childish enthusiasm had finally won over his reticence, and he had given his blessing to my adventure.

We drove to Biggin Hill, a small airfield in Kent. To my amazement, we drove straight through the barrier and out to the aircraft. There were no check-in queues, no belligerent children and – joy upon joys – no struggling to lift the luggage. Just a small jet – a Falcon 900 – with its beckoning steps. Even Cinderella would have been surprised.

There were just five of us in the party, but enough seats for eight passengers, plus a full-sized single bed turned down in readiness for our elderly host, who was ill and in pain with shingles. As I gawped at the luxurious pale cream leather, the walnut panelling and the gold taps in the toilet, my expressions brought a smile to James's tired face.

During my twenties I had worked for several years for British Airways as a stewardess on Boeing 747s, and it was truly hard work. On an LA flight, for instance, I would walk upwards of 24 Kilometres (15 miles), accompanied by dozens of heavy smokers puffing away for hours on end. My diet in those days had been a disgrace, all white bread, full cream milk and snacks – anything just to keep going. No wonder I developed varicose veins, a chronic cough and continuous health problems. Cause and effect.

Today, as we turned east towards our first refuelling stop of Dubai, a single stewardess in her thirties served us eggs on wholemeal organic bread, accompanied by Earl Grey tea in bone white china, on a silver tray. By the look of her perfect legs, I should have worked on private jets instead.

I certainly did not envy James's wealth or lifestyle and after all, he was being truly generous by sharing his costly pilgrimage with others. Millions of people at all levels of society act generously every day, doing what they can where and when they can to help others, and in that way the world could – and is – becoming a happier place. Our thoughts, words and deeds accumulatively really do create our reality – at every level. Also, I reminded myself of what the spirit of Diana had said to me during 1998 when I began emptying all my wardrobes to send most of my clothes to charity: 'If you give it all away, then you become part of the problem rather than part of the solution.' Balance, I thought, we just need more balance.

Feeling altogether brighter, I wondered if Diana had enjoyed travelling on private jets. And in my head I immediately heard a light-hearted voice say, 'Peace of mind would have been preferable.'

Now was this really Princess Diana making contact again – or was it just me talking to myself? Does it matter? To me it does, and I asked the universe if one day I might receive some verification that the voice I had heard so clearly during 1998 really had been Diana's. My wish would take three years to be granted.

In the meantime, the comment made me think about my marriage, and how during 24 years together Stuart and I have hardly ever had a cross word – we are true soul mates. I looked around the plane and thought that of course it would be great if we could all win the lottery and hire private jets and eat only the best foods. But I already had so many things to be grateful for. And you cannot share your dreams with a private plane or a diamond ring. They won't cuddle you when you're ill or dry your tears – but they are still fun!

It's human nature to desire a soul mate or companion, a place to live that's safe, food for our physical bodies, to live without violence and fear, hopefully to have sufficient money to pay our bills and so on. Yet most people on their death beds – as did I during my near-death experience over Easter 1998 – think about those they love and leave behind. George Harrison said as he lay dying in November 2001 that we simply need to love each other more. If only we would.

Thousands of feet below me was Tel Aviv and I thought of all the hatred and bigotry being acted out daily – mostly in the name of religion. Such a waste. If only we could all grasp the ultimate reality that *we are all part of God – the 'all that is' – and all parts make the whole.* And numerous scientists are now beginning to truly understand this concept, some of whom I have interviewed for this book.

In the meantime, Dubai was fabulous – decadence with bells on. I had not been there for over 20 years since my flying days, and how it has changed. Modern architecture, tons of marble and granite, fantastic gold souks alongside famous brand-name shops and five-star hotels, and all surrounded by the timeless grandeur of the desert. We stayed one night and ate as though it was our last supper.

As I chose from a fantastic buffet, I recalled the extreme poverty I had witnessed in India two decades earlier – the dreadful stomach bugs, the flies and the heat – and wondered where I might be eating the next day. Typical of me, thinking of my stomach. How many times had I suggested to people that we need to eat to live – and not live to eat!

The next morning we headed for Bangalore, a huge sprawling city in southern India. Before landing I changed into the local dress of a salwar kameez – the dress code at Sai Baba's ashram, which we hoped to visit before nightfall. When the aircraft doors were opened, the heat hit us like a furnace and the distinct aroma of India filled our senses. We had entered another world.

Our passports were checked on board, we refuelled and then took off on the remaining short 25-minute flight to Puttaparthi. The airstrip is small, set in a dry, arid valley and is used by visiting dignitaries, rock stars and royalty who are coming to visit Sai Baba. This is where he was born – where he grew up and, apart from a brief journey to Africa in his youth, where he has remained.

As we taxied to a halt, myriad porters in rags and bare feet helped us unload the luggage in the searing mid-afternoon sun. Cabs that in the West would have been scrapped decades earlier transported us into the small town of Puttaparthi. I use the term 'town' loosely; the main street is simply dust, lined on either side with small bazaars, shops and a couple of cafés. It reminded me of how Hollywood portrayed pioneering townships in western films. But this wasn't Hollywood, it was real – and worlds apart from where we had come.

Beggars of all ages, some with horrendous deformities, sat in the dust, virtually oblivious to the flies that hovered around their faces. I could hardly imagine living in such hardship, yet millions of people in places such as India, South America, parts of Russia and Africa live like this every day. Their lives are just one big grind for survival. Yet people come from all walks of life, rich and poor, peasants and scientists, kings and queens – and often from great distances – to see one man. Most come wanting something from Sai Baba, and I was one of them.

We checked in to the only decent hotel in the township and the owner, Mrs Jaishree Menon, a Sai devotee and scientist, who also runs a local orphanage, suggested that if we left our bags in reception we would just make it for the afternoon *darshan*, when Sai Baba appears to give his blessings.

With mounting anticipation we followed her through the dust and ran the gauntlet of shop owners pleading for us to buy their goods. In the gutter I spotted a small child, no more than a year or so old. She was playing with a handful of dirt and as I stroked her head she turned. Her eyes were enormous and she smiled the most stunning smile. She was happy with her handful of dirt and yet with all I already had, I had come wanting more. Suddenly I felt very humbled.

Finally we walked under the archway and into the ashram, which is huge. Exploring would have to wait. Our hostess hurried towards an enormous square-shaped, low-level, open-air building. Ladies were shown to the right and men to the left. We left our shoes outside and quietly found a space to sit. I was incredulous at the numbers inside the temple – a sea of maybe 15,000 people squatting with their knees tucked under their chins on concrete floors, in neat rows – so that we resembled a large fan shape. At the front was a low-set podium with a throne-like chair and at the back, various small doors. Hoards of temple helpers walked back and forth, watching us carefully to make sure that our heads remained covered and that we were respectful in our silence. The waiting seemed interminable.

After about an hour, suddenly, without any fanfares, 74-year-old Satya Sai Baba, the avatar, slipped quietly and gently into the temple on the red carpet, way, way in front of us, looking like a tiny orange dot in the distance. Avatars are rare beings, and yet he looked so ordinary. The tension was palpable as we all craned our necks to try and catch a glimpse of this small man with a mass of hair in his long orange robe.

We think in terms of being born and then ascending to 'heaven'. But avatars are born with a *full knowing* of who they (and we) really are. They are able to effect numerous and virtually limitless miracles. They have mastery and transcendence of the physical world – including the ability to materialize objects at will, to affect physical matter, to appear at various locations at the same time, to give healing when it's appropriate, and on rare, medically corroborated occasions (in Sai Baba's case) to bring the dead back to life, and so on.

Many people dismiss such claims and stories as poppycock, yet numerous scientists, doctors and psychiatrists have consistently witnessed hundreds of Sai Baba's 'miracles' that challenge the current framework of science; Baba's 60 years of spiritual work have been documented in the dozens of books written about him. Today, quantum and material physicists are finally beginning to comprehend how such feats are possible – and whilst researching this book I met several, whose theories have enormous implications for how we view ourselves and our place in the universe.

I believe that Mohammed, Buddha and Krishna, amongst others – and possibly Jesus – were avatars. But over the centuries there have been, and still are, hundreds of fully self-realized beings who became, or become, enlightened after years of self-discipline and training. Depending upon their specific purpose for returning, they have the capability to do some of the things that Sai Baba does, but they may not be required to or choose to. Going public with their potential capabilities may not be their way of doing things. We are all unique drops from the whole – to an extent we have free will and choice, and we all have our own individual ways of expressing who we are.

Jesus once said, 'God's house has many mansions,' and in this day and age we would say 'many dimensions'. Even scientist Stephen Hawking acknowledges the probable existence of 11 dimensions. But let's begin in the third dimension, which is our physical world, then move on to the fourth, where most of us go when we leave the physical body. Moving onwards and upwards through even higher vibrations, we reach the masters of light and time in the twelfth dimension and beyond. Keep in mind that many people on this planet today can already see and access other dimensions that don't have concrete barriers between them. One dimension simply merges into another – much like the colours of a rainbow, which co-exist although each is on a different wavelength.

I believe that the specific work on earth chosen by an avatar or enlightened being depends upon the dimension from which they have incarnated, plus their chosen blueprint for this lifetime. For a brief moment in time during 1998, I had been truly blessed when I experienced an enlightened state and was able to effect a few of the 'miracles' and abilities of such people. And at some level I still have those potential capabilities; we all do.

Meanwhile, many of us believe that the spiritual, non-physical parts of ourselves – call it your higher self, spirit, soul or whatever, is 'out there' somewhere. Some teachers state that when we reincarnate into our present bodies, a small facet of us – whether you call it your spirit self, soul, higher self or just energy – remains in the higher dimensions, and I believe this to be correct. Also, you can leave an energy imprint from previous lifetimes in that time/space moment.

But when you become enlightened, *all* the parts come together from everywhere, and in every sense of the word you become whole, or 'holy'. This is when you are totally existing, 'wholly in the moment', and there is truly no separation. There is nothing left 'out there anywhere'; no karma, nothing – you just are! You and your mother-father God become as one, for I understood that God is neither masculine nor feminine. God simply *is*.

We also tend to think of ourselves as being fairly solid, but in reality we are mainly 'space'. The small physical me is a fraction of matter – Hazel is maybe one percent matter – but 99 percent of me is space, which contains infinite numbers of frequencies that contain and transport information.

My quixotic thoughts and my aching back brought me back into the moment, and thinking about light reminded me of the stories surrounding Sai Baba's birth. Legend has it that Sai Baba's menopausal mother was struck by a ball of light, knocked unconscious, and nine months later he was born. In his early teens his parents, who were illiterate, superstitious peasants, became afraid of the range of poems and philosophy that their son quoted – which were way beyond the scope of any education he had received. They presumed Satya was possessed by a devil and eventually took him to a local medicine man, who cut crosses into his scalp and then poured a caustic-like acid into the wounds. His parents were horrified. And yet their son bore such treatment without complaint and was free from pain, even though his head was dreadfully swollen and blistered.

In May 1940, his father watched as his son manifested sweets and fresh fruit out of thin air – and a crowd began to gather. As his father raised a stick to beat his 'magician' son, he demanded to know, 'Who are you?' His son calmly told his father and the crowd that he was the reincarnation of a respected Moslem Holy Man called Sai Baba of Shirdi who had died eight years before Satya was born – and from that day he was to be known as Satya Sai Baba.

He told his incredulous parents that his time had come to go out and teach, and so he left home at just 13. As news of his 'miracles' spread, people began to follow him and asked him to become their guru, their teacher, just as they had with Jesus and other great sages thousands of years before. Work began on his now world-famous ashram and, as I sat on that hard floor with thousands of others from all religions and all countries, I knew that I was seeing a part of mankind's evolving understanding of our true spiritual nature unfold before me.

But it sure didn't feel like it. If I was hoping for some magic bullet spiritual re-awakening inside me, apart from the pain in my backside from sitting on such a hard floor, I was sorely disappointed. Perhaps I would see Sai Baba more closely tomorrow.

Dusk fell, and we returned for our shoes. They were gone. We walked home in the dust praying that not too many parasites were underfoot, waiting to permeate our soft, spoiled skin.

Mrs Menon told us to be up by 4am ready for morning *darshan*. Cinderella was back from the ball with a bang.

November 13, 2000

Before dawn we retraced our steps to the ashram in the crisp morning air. In a side area of the temple, we were asked to simply sit in great long lines. After an hour, the helpers then choose the lines randomly, and we started filing in to the main temple area. My line was twentieth to go, and once we found places we were about 20 rows from the front.

At 7am, Sai Baba reappeared. He is so tiny. But the depth in his eyes is incredible to see. Behind him was a stand in which all the VIPs sat, including Princess Beatrice of the Netherlands and other notables. I smiled; Sai Baba needs lots of donations to keep the ashram running. Mother Teresa was famous for getting people to part with their money, but it all went to the poor. Sai Baba does the same; the donations buy food that feeds the poor daily in several surrounding villages, and there is also a huge state-of-the-art hospital not far from the ashram, which gives free treatment to rich and poor alike.

By 8am all I could think about was my rumbling stomach and I headed off to the Western canteen, a huge marquee in the grounds. It is an amazing feat to feed up to 15,000 people twice daily. And yet dozens of helpers from around the world with seemingly infinite patience serve delicious vegetarian food. My porridge and fruit were fabulous – and cheap. And being in such a spiritual hot house, I thought it best to stay as grounded as possible – and porridge certainly achieves this aim.

Polite notices reminded us not to waste food and I thought of how much we throw away at home. When I was young my mother used to say 'Eat what's on your plate – think of the starving in India,' and I would sarcastically reply, 'I don't live in India, mother.' Little did I know then how lucky I was. These days, India is becoming a far richer country, but the divide between rich and poor remains a huge chasm that has yet to be bridged.

On a nearby table I noticed a group of about 12 young people gathered around a young man who looked like a 70s hippy. He was about 28. They seemed to be deferring to him, and laying food before him.

Immediately I knew that he was in the midst of a serious spiritual awakening. It was his eyes – they were huge and full of light and knowing – just as mine had been. Luckily, they spoke English, so I went for a chat. His friends told me that they had been living in the ashram for several months and that this young man, David, from Bristol, in the UK, had become an enlightened person like Sai Baba, except that he was the reincarnation of Jesus. I kept a straight face. He was the second Jesus I had met that day. The other was a young man from Australia who said that his hands were the hands of Jesus and he could effect similar 'miracles' of healing.

The problem is that when you go on line to the 'all that is', your brain can become very overloaded. And once you believe a fact 100 percent with your mind and body, it tends to happen. But it's important to remember that *your* reality during a spiritual awakening process may not be the ultimate truth that you think it is in *that specific moment* – and most importantly, it might not be another person's reality either.

Other than that, the young Australian was perfectly lucid and very humble and we chatted amiably. He had come to the ashram to try to work his way towards an ultimate answer. He had done well to have got as far as Jesus – with just one step to go. And that step would be to think, 'If I am the reincarnation of Jesus and I and my father are one, *who am I?*' And eventually you come to the realization that *you are God. We all are.* But you are a part of God, from your unique perspective as a human being. It's a very important distinction to make.

It seems very soul-destroying to suggest to someone in these heightened states that they need to write down their insights, but not necessarily to always act upon them, until you come through the experience. That's why it's so important to have grounded friends around you who can help you through the experience. And as UK-based parapsychologist Dr Serena Roney-Dougal once warned me, if ego comes into play, and those around you do not fully comprehend what is happening, then the situation can become dangerous. Why? Because the underlying personality of the person does not necessarily change as they go through their enlightenment process – and for some they never fully integrate the knowledge that becomes available to them, which can take 20 years.

The Australian was obviously coming along nicely on his spiritual journey and had no ego, but the guy from Bristol had gone into overdrive. David's friends were deferring to him, and kneeling to receive the divine light pulsing through his eyes, and he truly believed he was the reincarnation of Jesus and, more importantly, his friends did too. He even looked a little as you would imagine Jesus to look. And because he believed it 100 percent, it had become his reality.

It's hard to explain in limiting words how incredibly powerful you feel during a kundalini energy type awakening that forms a bridge from our third-dimensional physical world to the higher realms of super-consciousness. A kundalini-type awakening can happen in seconds, as mine did, but it's how your physical body and mind integrate what is happening that determines whether you might end up in an institution – or are able to learn and grow from the experience and then help teach others. It's a very fine tightrope to walk.

In March 1997, Herff Applewhite, who was often referred to as 'the One that was Jesus' and 39 members of his Heaven's Gate movement, killed themselves in America's largest mass suicide. Here was a man – who had once been diagnosed as being psychotic – hearing 'inner' voices giving him instructions. And because he believed totally that he was in the right, and was convincing, many innocent people died. This is an extreme example of what can happen if a spiritual awakening goes way out of balance and becomes a tragedy.

I knew that I should try to help David. I had a chat with his friends and told them briefly about my experience – how I too during 1998 had given *darshan* through my eyes, how I was manifesting ash like Sai Baba, and how I had managed to manifest the occasional object and so on. They looked highly sceptical, but thankfully I had a copy of *Divine Intervention* with me and when they saw the pictures of my purple auric field as it had been during 1998, a flicker of 'Oh, this happens to other people, does it?' crossed their faces.

I suggested that they should support David, allowing his experience to unfold, but to stop worshipping him. Yes, he was full of divine light, but the body can only hold so much and he badly needed grounding. They needed to encourage him to eat more grounding foods, with plenty of vegetables, rice, potatoes and of course porridge – all earthy, stodgy, grounding foods. Also to give him some sugar if the experience became too heightened. I explained that in these states, the brain burns lots of energy and, that while sugar is not normally a healthy food, in these states it can become a life-saver. Everything is indeed a paradox.

One of them suggested that they would try to make an appointment for David to meet Sai Baba, and I wished them well.

In many ways, I felt a little envious of David. To be in such a heightened state can be terrible if you don't know what's happening. But once (and if) you can sort things through, it can be beyond bliss. In a perfect world, the obvious conclusion would be for a person undergoing a full kundalini awakening to learn how to hold and integrate this state of bliss – which is what masters of the self and avatars can do – without burning out their physical bodies and minds. But to do this takes discipline. As I have already said, you would need to truly 'walk your walk' every day of your life – that is, through your thoughts, what you eat, how you take care of your body, regular spiritual practices, to eliminate ego, and so on. You literally need to live the light.

'Oh well,' I mused, 'at least I have known such a state of being, at total oneness with everything, which very few people ever experience, and even if I don't meet Sai Baba (which I knew was a rare event) it really doesn't matter now.' We were leaving in 48 hours anyway ...

But within two hours of having that thought, everything changed.

That afternoon, as I queued again for *darshan*, a helper appeared from nowhere and motioned me towards the front row. Apparently James's godson, Charles, had met one of Sai Baba's senior aides who had arranged for us all to sit in the front. I felt sure that James had perhaps given a large donation to the hospital, but he was sitting across on the men's side and I knew it would be considered impolite for me to pry.

Whatever, it was fine with me. Alongside me were beggars, plus the rich and famous. As I sat down right in front of the red carpet, I allowed myself a brief feeling of superiority – after all, the front would guarantee me the best view. Big mistake.

As Sai Baba appeared, he began throwing free saris into the crowd as part of his forthcoming 75th birthday celebrations. The word quickly went out into the town and within minutes the entrance to the temple area was swamped with local beggar women. The guards could not halt the surge, and as they tried to push people back, the women began falling on us. Suddenly, as panic rose in my throat, I wished I had remained at the back. Sai Baba, meanwhile, had moved on to the men's side to repeat the process – seemingly oblivious to the mayhem that was unfolding before me.

Just as the tourist had died in front of me in the road in Knightsbridge just two months earlier, I too was about to be taught another valuable lesson. It's amazing how one's life or outlook can change in a few moments.

Lessons and Miracles

Men are disturbed not by things that happen,
But by their opinions of the things that happen.
EPICTETUS (55–135 BCE)

There is a school of thought in so-called New Age philosophy suggesting that every single event that happens to us is perfect in the grand universal scheme of things. It has a purpose or a reason. Indeed I believe that we should all try to learn positive lessons from negative situations, but my argument is that if every single thing that happens is supposedly perfect for each unique life's purpose, what about free will? When people say absolutely everything is as it should be, to my mind this is one way of passing the buck.

For instance, if you were to freely choose to eat several hot fried doughnuts every day for many weeks without doing any exercise, would you be surprised if your cholesterol and blood sugar levels climbed too high – increasing your risk of obesity, stroke, heart disease and late onset diabetes? Neither would I.

And as millions of people live to eat, obesity now affects more than 50 percent of people in the Western world. Late onset diabetes costs the NHS more than £5 billion a year to treat. Is that 'perfect' or as it should be? Of course not: it's cause and effect. What goes around comes around.

Every one of us individually and collectively contributes and co-creates every aspect of our lives and our world today. So I prefer to say that everything is as *it is in this moment* – because of our thoughts and actions, plus the accumulation of our thoughts and actions since mankind has been on the planet.

I also believe that we come with specific life lessons carried forward from previous lifetimes, which we choose to learn prior to each incarnation. But the paths we travel are, to a large degree, under our control. It's the choices we make every day, at every level, that affect possible outcomes and possible futures.

I had made the choice to come to India, where the poverty is overwhelming; so when Sai Baba handed out the saris, why was I surprised that poor people came rushing in, desperate to grab the clothes? Cause and effect. Shit happens. But shit can teach you valuable lessons.

November 13, 2000 – 6pm

As the guards tried to control the avalanche of humanity pouring into the temple, my heart felt as though it was in my mouth and tears of frustration welled in my eyes. Desperately I tried to move, but the weight of women falling on those of us in the first few rows left me paralysed. I fought to control my rising fear and panic by saying to myself over and over, 'Stay calm, stay calm, it will be okay' – but it was hard to think positively in that moment.

After what seemed like an eternity, but in reality was only a minute or two, I heard voices of reason and authority nearby and felt the weight gradually being removed from above and around me. A few women sitting in the VIP stand to my right had forced their way into the crowd, and began helping to free those of us that had so quickly become trapped.

As they half dragged and carried me back towards their area, someone pushed a clove between my lips. The explosion of the spice's flavour on my tongue prevented me from fainting, and suddenly I felt embarrassed for being so tearful – but during the preceding few moments I had truly believed that I might never see my family again.

My back was pressed to the temple's outer walls and I tried to pull myself together as the guards locked the doors in an effort to restore order. My lesson for that day was surely never to allow myself feelings of superiority over another person based upon where I might be sitting, and not to pre-judge a situation without knowing the whole story. Anyway, is there ever a 'whole, complete and finished' story when considering the enormity of our never-ending journey? Not really.

The universe and everything in it, to my mind, is an infinite continuum in which we keep playing out our roles and learning from our experiences, both good and bad. Everything, including us, keeps going around in circles until we come to an absolute truth – which has the potential to set us free. But to do what?

I believe that our purpose is to live consciously, truly *knowing* who we all are and opening to our fullest potential capabilities. And then, if we choose to incarnate and remain in this dimension in a physical body, to consciously make more right choices. If we were to have a total understanding of cause and effect (karma) at every level, whilst serving humanity without ego, then everything could indeed have the *potential* to be perfect.

Then you might say, 'Well, what is perfect?' It depends upon our *perception* and *judgement* of perfection in each moment and in all situations. For some people, winning the lottery is their idea of perfection. To others it's being healthy, or having a roof over their heads, clothes on their backs, food to eat, living in peace – or looking like their favourite Hollywood star.

To me perfection would be having the ability to remain in a constant state of bliss connected to the 'all that is', to go beyond karma and ego, to once again have the ability to manifest my reality instantly, to be telepathic, psychic and a good healer – whilst maintaining the ability to hold and integrate the divine light in my physical body without causing the havoc that it did back in 1998 – plus sufficient money and common sense to help keep me grounded!

Then you might ask, 'But would that serve your soul purpose for this lifetime?' Or think, 'We need the bad stuff to truly appreciate the good stuff' – and our discussion could go on into infinity. Once you start thinking multi-dimensionally, believe me, everything becomes a paradox.

Meanwhile, back in the ashram, feeling *very* grounded and humble, I slowly began to calm down.

Sai Baba returned from the men's side and continued offering his blessings. The westerners who rescued me, many of whom have lived in the ashram for years, said that such an incident had never before happened. But I had heard reports of various controversies surrounding Sai Baba, such as the purported story about a family that had committed suicide because they had not managed to meet him, and some serious charges of possible sexual misconduct brought against him by a family in Canada, detailed in a TV documentary.

There is a theory that whenever you have a powerful spiritual being, there will always be a few who will try to bring them down, either through jealousy or a misunderstanding. Or, you might consider that the controversy surrounding Sai Baba might be his way of reminding us not to worship him, but simply to find the God within and worship yourself. Yet to my mind, a truly and fully enlightened being would not cause harm to anyone or anything. Overall, however, I do not know if the allegations are true, and therefore I do not judge either Sai Baba or his accusers. What I do believe is that during more than 60 years, Sai Baba has done great good.

I discussed some of the negative accusations against Sai Baba with Jacqueline Young, a psychologist who has spent many of her Christmas holidays treating the poor in India, as a volunteer with one of Sai Baba's Seva (service) organizations. She has also visited Sai Baba's ashram on many occasions and has worked with Sai Baba in his ashram.

She says, 'Because the ashram is indeed a spiritual hothouse, and can be an endurance test at every level – I have witnessed on several occasions that people's *perception* of what happens during meetings with Baba, when one's senses can become heightened and adrenalin is pumping, may not in every case be what *actually* happened.

'For instance, one time seven of us were granted an interview with Baba and when we came out, as we sat excitedly discussing the meeting, one woman started saying things like, 'How could he have said such things and why did he touch me like that?' Six of us sat listening to her, open-mouthed. Her perception of what had actually happened was completely at odds with what the other six of us had seen and heard. The woman's perception of events in fact related to her own problems and issues. It's important for people to keep in mind that whatever issues they come to resolve, situations will tend to occur within the ashram that will bring everything to the surface, which enables people to deal with them and then move on. It's also important to note that of all the millions of people that have visited Sai Baba, the negative testimonies have only come from a very small number of people – about five. Maybe such testimonies are inevitable, for wherever you have good, evil will come up to meet it.'

Maybe she is right. I remember when some people questioned the motives of Mother Teresa, an amazing woman who devoted her life to the poor and dying in Calcutta. At every opportunity she graciously prised money out of those who could afford it and gave all of it to the poor. No matter how pure or saintly you live your life, you can never please all of the people all of the time. None of us can, and people often make themselves sick trying.

As I listened to Jackie, I thought it's no wonder that enlightened beings such as Mother Meera, based near Thalheim, Germany, give their blessing, their light, in total silence; words are so open to misinterpretation. At *darshan*, you kneel before Mother (she is very tiny) to allow her to pulse the divine energy emanating from her eyes and energy field into yours, thus increasing the amount of pure frequencies in and around you – which can then trigger changes necessary for your highest good. Back in January 1998 as I knelt staring into Mother's eyes, I had wished for an acceleration in my spiritual awakening. Three months later, my spiritual emergency began so be careful what you wish for.

Back in the ashram, as I looked across at the hundreds of women gazing adoringly at Sai Baba and saw the sheer desperation in their faces – praying that he might stop and bless them or take their letters – I knew that I had no real need to be here. Why, I asked myself, would anyone travel so far at such expense to go through all this – the hard floors, the heat, the flies, the sickness and poverty, and little or no water or electricity at various times during the day?

Because we choose to.

I had come, hoping to somehow become 'enlightened' again by being in an enlightened person's energy field – which is extremely powerful. I had gone backwards, thinking of myself as the subject seeking an external object – enlightenment - and in doing so I had created a separation in my mind. And it's this concept and belief of being separated that has kept us from claiming our birthright and understanding our true nature and abilities for thousands of years.

Also, I thought, if Sai Baba or any other totally enlightened man or woman made everything easy for us all by answering every prayer, how would we learn or grow?

As I sit writing (March 2004) I have just seen the film *Bruce Almighty*, which illustrates this point brilliantly. Hollywood star Jim Carey plays a highly dissatisfied TV reporter living in Buffalo near New York. He blames everyone and everything, but never himself, for all his problems. Morgan Freeman plays a very modern God. Jim Carey chooses to ignore the helpful signals that the universe sends him, and his life goes from bad to worse. Eventually he meets Freeman (God), who tells Carey's character that He is getting rather tired of listening to all Carey's moans and groans and asks

Carey, 'How many people have you helped this week?' Sheepishly, Carey admits: 'None!'

The upshot is that 'God' tells Carey's character that if he thinks he could do his (God's) job any better, then He will confer all His powers upon the reporter for a week whilst He enjoys a well-deserved vacation. 'But,' says God, 'with my power comes responsibility – and there are just two conditions. Firstly, don't tell anyone you're God, as you don't want that kind of attention. Secondly, you cannot interfere with free will.'

And so Carey's character goes off and begins practising at being God. Firstly, he takes revenge on some colleagues who he believes are responsible for his problems by playing cruel tricks on them – and continues to think only of himself. Next, he pulls the moon nearer to the earth to impress his girlfriend and the next day misses the TV news reports of tidal waves devastating Japan thanks to the unusual lunar activity. Then he causes a tiny comet to hit earth nearby whilst he is presenting the news – for added drama and to look good for his boss.

Within a day he starts hearing hundreds of voices in his head and realizes that he is hearing individual prayers, but only from Buffalo, as God says he is letting the reporter ease into his new job slowly. Carey has all the prayers converted into emails but soon thinks, 'Stuff this, answering all these prayers is too much like hard work' – and programmes his computer to automatically answer 'yes' to every prayer.

Within days, several thousands of people in the city have won the lottery, but they riot – as the payout is only a few dollars each. Electricity and water supplies are affected by Carey's selfish actions in creating the comet impact. After a week, he realizes that being God is not as easy as he had thought. He truly begins to understand cause and effect at every level and how we are the co-creators of our reality. Before Freeman takes over again as God, he tells Carey, 'No matter how filthy something gets, you can always clean it right up.' And more tellingly: 'If you want to see a miracle, son, *be* the miracle.' We have a long way to go on our path to perfection – but every journey begins with but one step. Try taking one today.

The thousands of people sitting before Sai Baba and other enlightened men and women around the globe generally are there because they want to be in that person's energy field of pure love, or to live in a spiritual community, or to worship that person – or to ask them for help or healing in some way.

Sai Baba and others like him may be amazingly enlightened souls, but as you can see from *Bruce Almighty*, if all prayers were answered immediately not only could the world slip into chaos, but if everything were that easy, how on earth would we grow and learn from our mistakes?

Also, to presume that all ashrams or spiritual centres are full of people who love everyone, never bitch, don't experience jealousy and so on would be a mistake. People are people, and we all contain all parts of the whole, both good and bad, light and dark. Unless of course we become, or are, fully enlightened – and even then we can still choose.

It's unrealistic to think that Sai Baba or anyone else can act as a post box for the prayers of more than 15,000 people every day. Nor can so many desperate people have one-to-one private audiences with one man or woman. And to my mind, if people go to any ashram believing that their guru, swami or whoever is the *one and only* most powerful – God – they need to re-think their perceptions.

I believe there is a handful of beings such as Sai Baba on the planet at this moment, plus 1,000 or so enlightened men and women who are fully integrated masters of the self, with millions at various stages in between.

And that night, as I fell into a deep sleep of complete exhaustion, I had no intention of returning to the ashram the next day. But when I awoke naturally just before 4am, somehow I found myself walking into the dawn for morning prayers – and a huge surprise.

November 14, 2000

As we all began filing out of the temple after prayers to go to breakfast, one of the helpers motioned for me and another lady from our party to follow her. We walked on to the dais, and to my astonishment we were led into a small room in which my host, James, his godson, Charles, and companion, Allison, were already seated.

On the flight to India James had instructed us that if we should be granted a private audience with Sai Baba, then I should not speak. Such is the esteem in which he holds Sai Baba. Silently, a door opened at the back of the tiny room and in walked the avatar. He is around 1.5 metres (about 5 feet 2 inches) tall with a very tiny frame and a shock of frizzy hair that holds more than a hint of grey. He smiled serenely and greeted us warmly.

My mouth went dry and I could feel my heart pounding. He gently asked my host in English what he wanted – and James asked if Baba could help remove the glaucoma that was threatening to take his sight.

Sai Baba slowly looked into my eyes and I drank deeply of the light that emanated from them. He smiled and his palms turned upwards in a gesture of frustration as he mouthed to me, 'But he's 92!' It was a priceless moment and I smiled in return.

Charles kept quiet – this scenario was way out of his territory. Allison did the same. However, such an opportunity I knew might never come again, and at the risk of incurring my host's wrath, I gave Baba a copy of *Divine Intervention*, which he graciously accepted, and I asked if one day I could become a healer again. He told me that I have a wonderful husband who needs my attention and when I asked him, 'But what else should I do?' He simply smiled and said, 'Help the children. There are so many that need help.' Then, as the energy inside the room increased in intensity, from his upturned palms, and being no more than 60 cm or so (around two feet) – from me, Sai Baba manifested two beautiful Indian-style diamond rings. One he gave to James and the other to his godson.

For Allison and I he manifested ash. Typical male, I thought! I realize I should not make light of such an amazing meeting, and I mean no disrespect to Sai Baba or anyone else – but back in 1998 I had almost managed to materialize a ring from my thoughts (matter is organized energy – and what's a thought? It's energy), along with a fair amount of ash. And on my journey I have met people who can turn water into oil, people who can make ash, people who can 'see' into other people's solid bodies, and so on. I don't mean to compare myself with a totally realized, dedicated being like Sai Baba, but I certainly had an amazing taster of what we are all capable of. Sai Baba regularly reminds his devotees, just as Jesus did, 'Everything I do, you can do also.'

If you can begin to more fully appreciate that the universe , God, The Grand Plan, the 'all that is', the Divine Being is – as physicist Amit Goswami states in his book *The Self- Aware Universe* – *'self aware through every one of us'* then you begin to comprehend that we truly are a component part of the whole. We are creators in every sense of the word. But the majority of people on this planet today do not fully realize this.

In Madrid during March 2004, hundreds of people were killed by four terrorist bombs and hundreds more were injured. Fighting started again in Kosovo and the war in Iraq rumbled on. Yet if everyone could know who they truly are, the need to fight and prove that any religion is better or worse than another could be extinguished forever and so much needless suffering and heartache avoided. Hence people like Sai Baba choose to come back in service to mankind in the hope that one day we may all get the message. He asks no one to come and sit at his feet, and has often remarked that hands that work are holier than lips that pray. He is not decrying prayer – merely saying that in many cases actions speak louder than words.

Prayer is a wonderful ritual of intention and thought – and thought is energy. And as scientist Professor Gary Schwartz was to tell me three years later, *matter is organized energy. And what organizes energy? Information and intention.* This is a very important statement. Unless we set an intention it cannot materialize. More about Professor Schwartz's work and how miracles are possible in Chapter 5.

In the meantime, Jacqueline Young witnessed a specific healing 'miracle' whilst working at Sai Baba's ashram with a medical team on a New Year's Day in the late 1990s.

She recalls, 'Traditionally, on New Year's Day something special tends to happen. That year there was a group from South America visiting the ashram whose party included a 32-year-old Spanish man who had been in a wheelchair since birth. He had never taken a step in his life. He and his group were granted an interview with Sai Baba and at the end of it, to the amazement of the crowd, the young man came out walking with very faltering steps supported by two of his friends. Incredibly, he continued to walk the 450 metres (500 yards or so) to the exit gates. The crowds in the audience burst into spontaneous applause at this 'miracle', but some remained sceptical. 'Perhaps he wasn't really a cripple', I heard someone mutter. However, one of the doctors I was with knew a doctor in the group from South America, who told us that this man had actually been a cripple from birth. He had never taken a single step in his life until Baba had apparently said to him, "Get up and walk."

'His doctor had told Baba, "You don't understand, this man has never walked, his legs could not possibly function or support him." But Sai Baba quietly offered the man his hand, and very slowly and feeling extremely apprehensive, the man stood up. With his friends and doctor supporting him, the man then walked 450 metres. As a medical team, we witnessed and verified this story.'

Now was it Sai Baba's energies pulsing into the man that had initiated this 'miracle', or was it the man's belief that he might be able to walk? Or was it a combination of the two?

When I was in a heightened state, I had automatically known when it was appropriate to give healing and when to allow that person to continue with their illness as they had for some reason karmically or subliminally chosen it for a reason; it had been their path. At other times I would release trapped energies that I could see in and around their bodies which were contributing to their illness. There are today documented cases of several women who have X-ray eyes as I once did and I shall return to this subject in depth in Chapter 13.

In hands-on healing, through a healer's intention or via therapies such as electro-crystal therapy, a person can be pulsed with harmonic, frequencies, which over time encourage the body to heal itself. However, if the patient then continues to eat too much junk food, and those that contain pesticides (which emit disharmonic frequencies), stay stressed, don't exercise and so on, they risk multiple frequency imbalances and eventually negative physical symptoms could arise again.

Imagine yourself standing in the middle of a bonfire, and a firefighter is spraying you with a hosepipe trying to put out the flames. But if you go on standing in the flames (by eating a poor diet, being stressed and so on), then how can the firefighter ever finish the job? Healers can only do so much, hence why we need to take more responsibility for our own health on a day-to-day basis.

Roger Coghill, a bio-electromagnetics research scientist based in the UK, says, 'We now know that every single thing on the planet, including humans, emits a unique range of frequencies that are as individual as DNA is to humans. But if, for instance, you are exposed to lots of radiation from mobile phones or electrical equipment, or eat junk foods that emit disharmonic frequencies – or even healthy foods that emit frequencies that are incompatible with your own – then eventually disharmony is created in your energy fields and physical symptoms arise, most commonly experienced initially as food intolerances. Also, if a healer's frequencies are on similar wavelengths to those of their patient, more benefits can often be seen. This is why some healers work for some people and not for others. It's the same with gurus and teachers. Many people say that when they meet their teacher they instinctively know when it's the right one. This can also be a compatibility of frequencies.'

It is essential, Roger says, that we realize that we are in essence a vibrating range of frequencies surrounded by a small amount of matter held together by form-shaping fields. Biophysicist Harry Oldfield, also based in the UK, has spent 30 years researching and photographing energy fields. He says, 'We are basically standing waves of multiple energy fields and currently exist in the third dimension in a very dense set of frequencies that we call matter.' My point here is that what 'matters' is energy and frequencies. It's what we, the whole planet and the universe are made of, and it's how enlightened beings can effect miracles. They truly understand intention and energy and have learned how to play with them.

If you examine the lifestyles of most enlightened people, they tend to eat only pure whole foods; have mostly pure thoughts, practise daily rituals such as prayer, chanting or yoga; and in their presence you should feel only pure love. And eventually, if you do more right things with the right intentions and motives, then you too can hold more pure light and then go out and live your light. You can choose.

Personally I found Sai Baba to be a warm, gentle and loving man. I got the distinct feeling that he is somewhat weary of telling people who they really are and I can only guess at the frustration he may feel day in and day out. But his time here has not been wasted. He has helped millions to 'get it' and they hopefully will go out and teach others to 'get it' too. He has 'been' the miracle just as Morgan Freeman suggested in *Bruce Almighty.* Not many people can say that.

Yet overall, I cannot state that I found my stay in Puttaparthi particularly spiritual. It was more of a huge nudge to remind me to say thank you every day for my life and for all I have, as there are so many who have absolutely nothing and no one.

November 15, 2000

We took our leave of Mrs Menon and her staff at her hotel. They had gone to inordinate lengths to try to please us during our brief stay, and I felt sure that I would never return. But Sai Baba had asked me to help the children and so before I left I agreed to send a small sum to help the orphans at Mrs

Menon's orphanage. It's called the Sunbird Trust – and I still send my tiny contributions every month. Every bit helps.

Stepping back on to the private jet, I left one world and entered another. People often talk about other realms and dimensions and that there might be other worlds out there somewhere. Yet, even though we all inhabit the same planet, many of us live worlds apart from our neighbours. Don't we?

The Synchronicities, a Scientist, America – and Diana Returns

If it is real, it will be revealed.
If it is fake, we'll find the mistake.

MOTTO OF PROFESSOR GARY SCHWARTZ AT
THE HUMAN ENERGY SYSTEMS LABORATORY

The next two years passed in a blur of writing and getting on with life. We moved house, I finished my health book and during 2002 I wrote another book on anti-ageing, which was published in 2003.

Basically I abandoned the spiritual path. Luckily, Spirit had not abandoned me. I should have remembered that once you are on a spiritual path, no matter how much you stray, the spirit realms have a way of creating circumstances that nudge you back on track.

In the spring of 2003, my publisher rang out of the blue to ask me if I would consider writing a new book about my spiritual journey since 1998. At that point my life was really hectic – I was writing for various publications on anti-ageing and health issues, lecturing and doing TV and radio. The last thing I needed was another book to write. Anyway, what would I write about? After all, I had not heard any facts from Diana or anyone else really clearly since 1998. However, I said that I would think about it.

Within two hours of putting the phone down, I received two emails via my website from people who had undergone dramatic spiritual awakenings thanking me for having the courage to tell my story. Weird but nice. Nudge, nudge.

The next day, I had an appointment with my friend Dr Robert Trossell in London for a blood test. As I walked into his office, a well-dressed woman in her 60s gave me a quizzical 'Don't I know you?' look. Robert politely introduced us. Her name was Veronica Keen. Recognition dawned and she beamed, 'I have just read your fascinating story about Princess Diana.' I was flattered and we chatted. It transpired that her husband was the renowned psychic researcher Montague Keen. How interesting. I went in for my blood test.

Two days later I had coffee with a friend from Australia whom I had not seen for almost three years. We had met after she had read my story, as she had gone through a similar experience – except that she had been channelling Michael Hutchence. She was somewhat luckier than me when it came to verifying what she had channelled, as she had met Michael's partner Paula Yates several times, who had confirmed many of the facts that my Australian friend had heard – with a witness present – before Paula's tragic death in September 2000.

When I told her that I was considering writing another spiritual book, she exclaimed, 'Then you must read *The Afterlife Experiments* by a guy called Gary Schwartz from America. It's an absolute *must* for anyone who believes in life after death.' I ordered it the next day – but it would take six weeks to arrive.

The following week I returned to Dr Trossell's office for my blood test results and who should be on her way out but Veronica Keen. We said a brief 'hello'. She was in a rush as she and her husband were travelling to New York to meet a scientist called Gary Schwartz. My mouth fell open. No longer a nudge, this felt more like a sledgehammer.

When Gary Schwartz's book finally arrived, I found that it offered considerable amounts of scientific evidence that human consciousness survives physical death. And this guy is no fringe scientist. Gary Schwartz is a professor of psychology, medicine, neurology, psychiatry and surgery at the University of Arizona. He received his doctorate from Harvard, has served as a Professor at Yale and now, aged about 60, runs the Center for Frontier Medicine in Biofield Science and the Human Energy Systems Laboratory at the University of Arizona based in Tucson. You get my drift. He is a serious, highly accredited scientist. How wonderful, I mused, if I could meet him one day.

A few weeks later I saw Dr Trossell again, and you know who just happened to be in his office? Veronica. I asked her how her meeting went with Professor Schwartz, and what he was like. It transpired that Gary was a great friend of theirs and she asked if I would like his telephone number in the States. Gee, that was easy. Now I *knew* that the universe wanted me to write this book. I had no idea where this journey was taking me, but the synchronicities were just too great to ignore.

For weeks I resisted calling Gary – after all, his books have been bestsellers in the health and spiritual sector, and he rubs shoulders with people like Drs. Andrew Weil and Deepak Chopra. He lectures all over the world. Doubt began to creep in. I sat and meditated and said to Spirit, 'If you really want something to happen here, give me a sign and I'll call him.' A week later I was standing on a beach in the Caribbean and a distinct voice in my head said, 'Call him now' – instantly, I knew who they meant.

Spirits do choose their moments. Quickly I walked back to my room, where I had the number in my diary, and called. Much to my astonishment, Professor Gary Schwartz picked up the phone. He exclaimed, 'You are really lucky to catch me – I had left the house and then had to pop back to collect some papers I had forgotten. I'm almost never at home at this time of the day.'

Trust, I definitely needed to trust Spirit more. Gary was polite but cautious. After all, scientists are only interested in verifiable, repeatable tests that are run under strict scientific conditions. And how would you feel if a total stranger rang you and said, 'Well I had this incredible spiritual awakening, during which I affected electrical equipment, changed TV channels with my mind, became totally telepathic, and a powerful healer oh, and by the way I also had a spiritual "walk in" – when the spirit of Princess Diana and I became as one?' You see what I mean!

He agreed at least to read my book. Within a month, he called and said that if I really had been in contact with Diana, then would I be willing to take part in his Afterlife Experiments under his supervision – and see what transpired. I found myself saying yes. We made a date for Sunday October 19, 2003.

After hanging up I went and bought a map of America, to see where I was going. Tucson is a small city on the edge of the desert in Arizona, about two hours' drive from Phoenix – and about an hour's flight from LA. Persuading my husband to let me go on another 'rainbow-chasing trip', as he calls my spiritual journeys, was no easy task.

Gary had told me that he would arrange for two mediums who had worked with him at the lab to be in Arizona to take part in the tests. I was not allowed to know their names and they were not told who they would be meeting, only that they would be taking part in an experiment. For me this journey felt intensely personal, as it might be my only chance to scientifically verify that I had indeed had contact with the spirit of Diana. I prayed that she would travel with me. By early October, however, doubts crept in once again. What if Diana did not come through? What if nothing happened?

Trust, I just had to trust.

October 17, 2003

Another farewell with Stuart. I hated leaving him and yet a part of me felt that this time something special would happen. At that moment, I had no idea just how special …

The flight to Phoenix was long and tiring. As always I took plenty of vitamin C, plus herbs such as echinacea, golden seal and garlic to help avoid infections, which are so easily transferred in the recycled air. It never ceases to amaze me how much people sneeze and cough on aircrafts without using handkerchiefs. They obviously don't realize that every time we sneeze, millions of bacteria and viruses are spread up to three metres (10 feet) around them. To help reduce any jet lag prior to landing at Phoenix, I placed a powerful magnet on my head for ten minutes, which helps adjust our internal body clock to the local magnetic field. With an eight-hour time change I needed all the help I could get.

After a two-hour wait at Phoenix I connected on to Tucson, by which time it was 4am in the morning back in the UK. A taxi driver was waiting to take me to the Ventana Canyon resort hotel located in the desert, and those final few miles seemed to take forever. But I did notice that most of the houses had no lights on – and my driver told me that Tucson is a designated area of low light emissions, and any night lighting is kept to a minimum to reduce light pollution and enable people to enjoy the night sky. In the UK, scientists are bemoaning the fact that thanks to industrial and vehicle pollution, plus high levels of lighting at night, it's becoming harder to see the night sky at all. But as Morgan Freeman said in the film *Bruce Almighty*, no matter how much mess you make, you can always clean it up. We can choose.

Meanwhile, all I could dream about was getting into bed, and when I finally slipped between the cool cotton sheets, I slept like a log for almost 11 hours. Bliss.

Saturday, October 18 – Tucson, Arizona

The next morning I woke to clear blue skies and a midday temperature of almost 100°F – 38°C. The air in the desert is so dry that emanating from the roof of the poolside bar was cooling steam. My skin felt as though it was shrivelling up like a prune and I ordered plenty of water. Even better, they made fresh watermelon juice – rich in natural carotenes and minerals in a highly absorbable form – which helps nourish the skin from the inside out.

I spent the day enjoying the sunshine and making notes whilst re-reading Gary's books ready for our meeting the next day, which I had marked in my dairy as 'D Day'.

Gary had secretly begun research into the possibility of survival of human consciousness back in 1993 after a colleague, Dr. Linda Russek, a clinical psychologist, had posed the question: Did Gary think it was possible that her father (who had died in 1990) was still alive somewhere? Gary's interest was roused immediately.

He became fascinated by the challenge of trying to validate scientifically that consciousness survives physical death, and secretly he and Linda devised experiments using random 'sitters' who had lost a loved one, along with experienced mediums. In the early days sitters were allowed to answer 'Yes' and 'No' to any questions from the mediums, but as time passed no communication between the medium and the sitter was allowed. Eventually they placed the medium and the sitters, who had never met, in different rooms. And throughout the hundreds of sessions they recorded (and continue to record) the spirits of 'deceased' individuals gave specific information via the mediums to the sitter whom the spirit wished to contact.

Once analysed for accuracy and taking into account any element of pure luck or chance, Gary and his team rated some of the evidence as being one chance in a million, but other information was so detailed that Professor Schwartz rated it as being a one chance in a trillion. As I read through the transcripts of his experiments featured in his book *The Afterlife Experiments*, I remembered how I had heard Diana for months on end as clearly as if we had been sitting in the room together. I whispered to the desert around me, 'Please Diana, be here for me now.' All I could hear were the trees by the pool rustling in the breeze and yet in my heart I felt a warm glow and knew she was there.

I read on. As word leaked into the academic world about their research Gary faced a lot of scepticism and derision. But with the eventual publication of their research in a reputable scientific journal in 2001, the criticism worked in their favour as, for every loophole or criticism that other scientists tried to find with their experiments, Gary and his team tightened up the procedures to eliminate any possibility of duplicity or collusion. They even consulted an expert 'cold reader' – a renowned magician who makes a living by manufacturing made-up evidence for people, purportedly from the spirit world – to help design their experiments to further eliminate any chance of deception. Such was his desire to make the readings totally secure that Gary even took a course in cold reading. Today, their work is considered mainstream and Gary continues his research openly within the University.

As I closed his book, suddenly the air felt cooler – dusk was falling, and it was time to return to my room. I'm not really one for worshipping anything, but that night I got down on my knees and reminded Diana that we had a date for the next day.

Sunday, October 19, 2003

D Day dawned; another crystal-clear, sunny day. After almost five years of wondering if I would ever be able to validate my contact with Diana, here I was, 6,000 miles from home, about to go on a blind date that had seemingly been arranged by the spirit world.

Gary finally arrived at my hotel at lunchtime. We shook hands. With his beard he looked very much the academic, but his jacket and tie seemed rather formal in the 104-degree (40°C) heat. My casual clothes felt somewhat out of place and it reminded me of the phrase *You never get a second chance to make a good first impression.* I hoped that I had not blown it.

Being a Sunday, his offices at the University were closed and we drove off into the desert towards his home, where the mediums would meet us.

Gary soon put me at ease and we had a brief chat after which he placed me in his study prior to the arrival of the first medium. He wanted to take no chances that we could in any way communicate prior to the sitting.

As I sat in his study surrounded by computers, film and recording equipment, my nerves took over. Talk about a few butterflies in my stomach, it felt like Arnold Schwarzenegger was rattling around in my gut.

As the scientist Dr Serena Roney-Dougal had said to me almost four years earlier, time can appear very elastic. If you are with someone you love or doing something you love, time passes very quickly, but if you were to sit on a hot fire then even one minute could seem like an eternity. As I sat waiting, I knew exactly what she meant.

Meanwhile, the medium arrived and I overheard Gary asking her to sit quietly in his drawing room and tune into whoever might be waiting in his study – and to make some preliminary notes and impressions.

After 15 minutes or so the door opened, and Gary came in accompanied by a beautiful dark-haired young woman of around 30 whom he introduced as Allison Dubois. We nodded, as no talking was allowed. He switched on the digital video recorder as well as a back-up digital audio recorder. Allison sat down and began immediately. I took a deep breath.

'Your mother is here. She was small but strong, and yet she had brittle bones. Liked to wear sweaters around her shoulders. She is saying honey and biscuits. Knitting, she liked knitting.'

Well, this was fascinating, and I loved my mum dearly, but it was not why I had come. Yes, my mum had suffered from terrible osteoporosis during the last few years of her life. Yes, she loved sweaters on her shoulders as she felt the cold, and all her life her panacea for every problem was tea and biscuits with plenty of honey. She also loved knitting. One abiding memory I have of her was when I crept downstairs one Christmas morning at 2am to see if Father Christmas had been – only to spy her lovingly sewing up a cardigan that she had knitted for me in secret. She was an angel.

Tears pricked my eyes. This young stranger was so far 100 percent correct.

'Your mother just wants you to acknowledge that she came through to us first.'

I smiled. Lack of patience has always been an issue for me – and Diana had told me that it was for her, too.

The medium continued. 'Mr Brown, there is a psychic connection here with a Mr Brown. I'm seeing a picture of a young woman in a fur hat. Skiing – Switzerland. Oh, now I'm seeing fine boutiques in London and Paris. I'm seeing The Ritz in Paris.'

I held my breath. Gary sat up straighter. And another synchronicity. Just before flying to America a friend had told me to check the website of one Robert Brown, a psychic that Diana had consulted. And Robert Brown and Professor Schwartz have been in touch ... interesting.

Suddenly, Allison flushed bright pink – and said in her Texan drawl: 'Weeeell, I have no idea what's goin' on here, and I hope I'm not wasting this lady's time – but I'm seeing Princess Diana in Paris.'

Gary simply asked her to continue as I could not speak.

'Belgian chocolates, she enjoyed chocolate. Lions, statues, stairs. A mirror face down on a dressing table – could have been an heirloom.'

'Diana' talked through Allison about the importance of 'always being in the right clothes' and 'a diamond that was purchased in Monte Carlo.' Also, that her diary/journal had been stolen; and how her death had been no accident, but that it had been her time to go. 'She has been talking "loudly" into quite a few people's ears since she "died"', Allison continued. 'She is not judged where she is now, and in that respect she has peace.'

'Diana' thanked me for a birthday card and roses I had personally delivered to Kensington Palace near her birthday years earlier and told me to keep her letter. This struck a chord. During the 80s I had been due to meet Diana at a Birthright charity reception, but due to William being rushed into hospital she had had to cancel. And I had sent her wild roses and a card to wish her happy birthday shortly afterwards – hoping that we might meet again one day – which we did a few times. And she had sent me a

THE SYNCHRONICITIES, A SCIENTIST, AMERICA – AND DIANA RETURNS

lovely letter of thanks. This was wonderful personal verification for me.

Allison went on giving me messages from Diana for almost an hour. Towards the end Gary interrupted and asked, 'Please can you tell me what the relationship was between the sitter today and "Diana"? Allison's face softened and the energy in the room became very calm *'It's like they were apart – but together,'* and Allison brought her palms together to try to explain what she was feeling.

'She (Hazel) was brought in after I (Diana) died. Diana is saying that she helped to save Hazel's life. She is sending gratitude for the part she (Hazel) is playing in helping people to understand that we go on after death. It's like she is paying homage to Hazel.'

Tears ran down my face. During that fateful Easter weekend of 1998, as I faced my own physical death, Diana had indeed told me that 'it had been her time to go' – and this phrase is well documented in my book, which was published in December 1999, four years before the meeting with Allison and Gary. Diana had also told me that she had acted like a transformer – she had 'toned down' the divine energy that had almost cooked my brain and body in an effort to help me survive. In effect, she had indeed saved my life. Again, this was documented more than four years earlier.

For a few moments I had left this physical world, but thanks to her Intervention I had returned to live another day.

The reading ended. Finally I was allowed to speak to Allison, but only to say a heartfelt 'Thank you.' Gary assured us both that we could chat later, once the second reading was over. Allison left as Gary let in the second medium. No one was to speak about the sitting.

Patiently I sat waiting for the second medium and I smiled to myself that Diana had not let me down. How could I have doubted that she would? Fifteen minutes passed whilst Gary asked the second medium to 'tune in', and then he brought her in. Gary introduced her as Laurie Campbell. As we were not allowed to speak, we nodded hello.

59

The second reading began.

'Mom's passed – there's a grandmother coming in here. Then I see books, literature, England, spiritual matters and research – meditation, as if this person (Hazel) has something to do with spiritual matters. Travels far and wide and opening to a new reality. Needs to meditate more, which is the key to your (Hazel's) connection to Spirit.'

Talk about spot-on. For the sceptics, keep in mind that we had never met. Laurie had no idea who she was about to meet, and neither did I. However, Gary did tell the mediums that I was coming from overseas, but that could have been anywhere. Yet the first country she mentioned was England.

'Surrounded by farms, family, countryside,' she stated. I live in the countryside next door to farms and for over two years I had hardly meditated at all.

She continued speaking quickly in her Californian drawl. 'And then my feeling is that in mid-direction, all of a sudden, things happened in your life that turned everything upside down – and they took you in a whole other direction. It was unexpected. I can see your taking notes, you're searching, you're trying to find out if things are real. Also they said you made a pact, so I feel some body passed – and a pact was made.'

This made me sit up and take notice. She was certainly on the right track. Over Easter 1998, my life as I knew it had ceased to exist overnight, and I had indeed made a pact with God, that if I could be allowed to survive, I would make time to tell my true story. Again, the very words that Laurie used I had already documented in my manuscript during 1998.

She continued, 'I keep seeing a C and a K ... and I have no idea why but they are showing me Princess Di – something about England.'

Gary and I exchanged looks but said nothing. Laurie, like Allison before her, was worried in case she was on the wrong track. Gary remained impartial and simply asked her to continue.

'Okay – now they are showing me Kensington Palace. I'm seeing clothes

– they were important. Outward presentation was important. They could not give a crap about the inside but on the outside it's so important. Lots of roses, she liked roses. I hope there is some connection here, because if there's none, I'm wasting this lady's time. The carpet was pulled from under her feet by her family. Her good friends became her family. She saw many psychics, but she liked Robert Brown.'

It was incredible that they both independently mentioned Robert Brown. And so the messages went on for almost an hour. They were very specific and detailed. I have seen some good mediums in my time, but Laurie and Allison are both first class. No wonder Gary tests their talents during his research.

And then as before Gary interjected and asked Laurie what was her (Diana's) relationship with me?

'Well it's like a weird thing – but she (Diana) could share with her (Hazel) – without being judged, or that she (Hazel) was open to lending an ear, but she keeps showing me journalist and writings.'

How much more accurate could it get?

'Diana is inviting people to live their potential, don't put off for tomorrow what you can do today. It's like she is taking her (Hazel) through from the beginning to an ending or conclusion ... helping her (Hazel) find pieces that she needs along the way.

'She says she wants to continue bringing hope – wants to help people 'go home' in peace. And she wants, through science, to help get the message through that we all live on. She can see things now from a broader perspective.'

Gary was becoming impatient and pressed Laurie again to clarify what Diana's relationship was to me.

'I feel like she gave this woman a lot of words of encouragement – she (Hazel) was like 'dead to the world' – maybe doctors thought she was dead. Like whatever she went through was like she (Hazel) was hit by a train – she (Diana) makes out that she (Hazel) was like flattened out. But says she is still recovering. And Diana is hoping to guide her ... from the other side.'

After an hour, the second reading came to a close. They had both been amazingly accurate and I defy sceptics to say that any cold reader could have been so precise. They couldn't. *Remember, I was not allowed to speak during the readings.* Both Allison and Laurie had used the same phrases and words that Diana had used to me. They both picked up the roses – Allison even picked up the birthday card which was not mentioned in my previous book, and Diana had written and thanked me. They also both picked up Sarah, Duchess of York, and gave me numerous messages to pass to her. More of this later.

Meanwhile, what a day this had been.

I asked Gary if he, Allison and Laurie would join me for an early supper. He made a few calls, and within the hour we all met as friends on the decking at my hotel overlooking the desert – and a spectacular sunset.

We were like excited children, all speaking at once. Allison and Laurie wanted to know my story, Gary was fascinated that the spirit of Diana had mentioned science … and I wanted to know how these two women had become mediums.

Allison spoke first. It transpired that she is 32, a graduate with a degree in political science and happily married with three young children. Until 2001 she had worked in the State Prosecutor's office in Phoenix, Arizona. As a child of six, she had clearly seen and heard her deceased grandfather in her bedroom just after returning home from his funeral saying, 'He told me to tell my Mother that he was no longer in pain, and so I excitedly knocked on my Mom's door and told her that Grandpa was back and he was okay. Mom was either shocked or horrified and she had no idea what to do or say. And seeing her reaction made me feel bad and so I shut down. Today my Mother feels guilty about this, but back in the 70s you just didn't say you could see and hear dead people, and I was so young.'

Since my interest in spiritual issues was awakened during my late 30s, I have heard hundreds of similar stories. Many like Allison just shut down their valuable gift, as parents often cannot differentiate between a spiritual connection and an active imagination. Such a shame.

At the age of 12 a man had tried to entice Allison into his car – and once again she heard a firm voice saying, 'Take off and run home' which in effect saved her life. And after that incident she decided that when she grew up, she would become a prosecutor and do her best to ensure that such people paid for their crimes. And she did.

During Easter 2000, Allison went through an explosive spiritual awakening. Easter, the traditional time of death and rebirth, is obviously a popular time for spiritual awakenings! She recalled: 'For weeks at work, we had been trying to trace a missing child. Even though I was highly sceptical, as a last resort a few days before Easter I went to see a medium – I desperately wanted to give the parents some kind of closure.

She told me numerous specific facts that she could not possibly have known, which eventually helped us find a body. And while I was with her, she also told me that I had really good psychic abilities of my own – and I was like, *yeah, sure.*

'A few days later when I awoke on the Easter Sunday, there were all these people standing in a circle around our bed. I jumped up and starting shaking and hitting my husband screaming "Joe, can you see all these people?" He looked at me as though I was crazy. To me they looked quite solid and yet they seemed "lighter" than other people, but so distinct – and they were all telling me things. I tried to ignore them, but they were all over the house. My husband was really scared – he was trying to calm me down. Somewhere deep inside I knew that something that had always been inside me had suddenly opened up, and I think going to the medium triggered this awakening. Perhaps, I thought, if I could reach her she could tell me what the hell was happening. I was frightened and so was my husband – and I kept thinking if this doesn't stop I could end up in a mental home.

'Meanwhile, from what my husband had told me over the years about his father and grandfather, I felt that two of these "people" were his relatives. They were telling me how much they missed clam chowder. I began to describe them to my husband – and what they were saying – and he was like, "Oh my God, I must ring mum and check all these facts"' And to our astonishment they were all correct. From that day forward my spirit friends never went away. But I have learned to set boundaries with them, and my daughters are very psychic too, and so very gently I am helping them to retain and refine their gifts.

'Eventually I heard about Gary's research and contacted him, and began working as one of his mediums, as I want everyone to realize through science that life after death is a reality.'

Today, Allison works for many police departments in America as she has the ability to 'see' through the murderer's eyes. She can feel their motives and she usually knows how their victims died. One day she hopes she will be able to see the murders before they are committed and thus save lives. Just like Tom Cruise's film *Minority Report!* Science fiction is here already. Paramount studios in Hollywood are filming Allison's story for a TV series called *Medium*. For more information on her work, log onto www.allisondubois.com.

Laurie's story turned out to be less shocking, but no less fascinating. She is 46, happily married with two children, and lives in Orange County, Irvine, California. She did not realise just how much potential she had as a psychic and a trance medium until she began reading Shirley MacLaine's spiritual books in 1994, saying, 'I was always fascinated by psychics, by people who could hear stuff from people who had passed over – it was all wonderful food for thought. Then I found some books and tapes by Sanaya Roman and Duane Packer – and I tried their Opening to Channel tapes (available from www.orindaben.com). Within a few months, I found that during meditation I would see my guides' faces in my mirror and it went from there. It was not at all frightening, it was as if they were saying, "Keep going, don't give up – it will get easier" – and it did."

Professor Schwartz, who had been listening patiently all afternoon, continued the story.

'In 1997 while I was lecturing in California, a psychiatrist friend told me about Laurie's work as a medium. He knew about my research and suggested we might find it useful to meet. Within a couple of minutes of meeting Laurie, she picked up my mother and of course I presumed Don, my doctor friend, had told her that my mother had died. But Laurie continued on to describe my mother's appearance to a T and then began speaking in a voice that was remarkably similar to my mother's. Don had never met my mother and therefore could not have known so many facts. As a scientist it's my job to be totally sceptical until I can verify evidence, not just once, but over and over again.

'Almost as a casual remark, I asked Laurie if she could receive information from a man named William James. But as Laurie had no formal background in science, I was not surprised when she asked "Who's he?" "A friend of a friend," I replied – omitting to mention that he was a world-famous scientist and philosopher who had died in 1910.

'What happened next was nothing short of incredible. Laurie sat for a few minutes tuning in – and we watched as her face and manner slowly changed completely. For over 15 minutes Laurie, a woman with little scientific knowledge, spoke in a bellowing and highly distinguished tone and delivered a polished lecture on philosophy and soul science. It was fascinating, and became my first lesson in trance mediumship – when an individual spirit overshadows the medium, and for a time, they become as one.

'But the scientist in me demanded more. I immediately called my colleague Dr Linda Russek who had started me on this path, and asked her to listen to this woman, but told Linda not to speak. Laurie picked up the receiver and said, "I'm receiving communication with your father. He wants me to tell you, 'Thank you for the music'".

'Linda had burst into tears on the other end of the phone, and I was totally perplexed why such a statement would have such a profound effect. When I finally saw Linda she told me that as her father lay dying in intensive care, doctors told her he was not aware of his surroundings. Nevertheless, every day for the last two weeks of his life Linda had played special music in his room through a pillow speaker.

'Even I had not known of this. My colleague now had some personal evidence of survival of consciousness, but I wanted proof under scientific conditions and so I invited Laurie to join our research programme.'

If you want to know more about Laurie, log on to www.LaurieCampbell.net

Before we parted, I asked Gary what were the chances of two strangers that I had never met, who had no idea who they were to meet that day, both coming up with similar phrases and information from Princess Diana?

'Firstly,' he replied, 'let me just tell you that in thousands of readings we have done, not once has anyone ever mentioned biscuits and honey together – not once. Moreover, at no time in the history of our mediumship experiments, which began *formally* with Laurie Campbell in 1997, has any medium ever brought up Princess Diana. Therefore, the chances of them both picking up Diana and your connection to her so accurately are extraordinarily improbable.' Gary stressed that he uses the word 'extraordinary' very carefully; he follows scientist Carl Sagan's motto, 'extraordinary claims require extraordinary evidence.'

A million questions buzzed in my head. It was just as well that over the next day or so Gary had agreed to spend several hours explaining the science behind his theories and research. I could hardly wait.

I was grinning from ear to ear as I finally fell into bed. Perhaps I should just watch TV for a few minutes to wind down. And who was on the first Channel I clicked to? The Duchess of York.

Nudge, nudge.

The Scientist Explains

One cannot know what is the content of another station or channel without tuning to it.

EMERITUS PROFESSOR WILLIAM A TILLER

Monday, October 20, 2003 – Tucson, Arizona

Another beautiful clear day dawned in the desert, and as I sat preparing a list of questions for Gary, who was joining me for breakfast, a newsflash appeared on my TV showing a picture of Princess Diana. Quickly, I turned up the sound. Apparently a British tabloid paper had published a letter that Diana had supposedly written to her butler, Paul Burrell, stating that 'someone' had been planning an accident for Diana.

Another synchronicity, I thought, as only 18 hours earlier Allison Dubois had told me that Diana's death had been no accident.

And yet as I watched the news reports I thought, If Mr Burrell has had such a letter for six years, why didn't he hand it over to the police years ago? And then I found myself saying, 'Why don't you people just let her rest in peace? It seems so ludicrous to keep dragging this stuff up – after all, it's not going to bring Diana back, is it?'

But who am I to comment – here I was taking part in the experiments, hoping Diana would come through. I'm not letting her rest, am I? I switched off the television and just stared at the blank screen, mumbling to myself, wondering what Diana would have made of it all.

Almost instantaneously, the energy in my room became highly charged and I heard the following words in my head. (Before you judge, I am *not* claiming that this was Diana – I'm just telling you what I heard and felt.)

'It's so ridiculous (said with a fair amount of frustration) – they need to understand that before and during the split, I became somewhat paranoid. If anyone is involved in a very stressful situation, you can begin to imagine all sorts of things – and the way you view a situation or person can be horrendous one day and different the next. I was going through a stressful period. The way I saw things then is not the way I see them now.'

Weeks later it was divulged that the name in that letter was Charles – and even now as I type, I hear, 'It had nothing to do with him.' Me, I have no idea.

The Professor arrived. And as we sat overlooking the swimming pool tucking into eggs and bacon (not fried, of course!) I switched on my recorder and dived straight in to ask, 'As a scientist, do you now believe that life after death is a fact – does consciousness survive physical death?'

Gary smiled. 'It's not important what I believe; it's important what I know as a scientist. And, what I know from all the data from our laboratory – using many mediums and multiple sitters under more and more stringent conditions – is that there is a very real phenomenon. Secondly, I know as a fact that when you examine the enormous amount of data in totality, not just our results – but also data from Professor Archie Roy and Tricia Robertson in Scotland, Dr Emily Kelly at the University of Virginia and others, the simplest explanation is that survival of consciousness is by far and away the best explanation. Having said that, I would then say that even though I know it's true, I still have a hard time believing it.'

'Why?' came my obvious query.

'Because I was raised to believe that life after death came in a similar category to the Easter Bunny and the Tooth Fairy. And as a youngster, and throughout my early academic life, I was told that even thinking that human consciousness survives physical death was ridiculous. My colleagues would say that it's only religious, wacky people that have such ideas – and they kept telling me that the mind is inside the brain. These people have big grants and bigger titles – and when you are constantly being bombarded with "facts" from such authorities, on a whole host of topics and theories, you eventually conclude that it's hard to believe that all these people could be wrong.'

I knew just how he felt. How many times have I heard people say that it's wicked to talk to the 'dead' – but millions of people talk to Mohammed, Jesus and Buddha and so on in their prayers every day – and those guys have been 'dead' for quite a while. And many religious fanatics take every word and story in *their* bible, prayer codes or whatever as being the literal, one and only truth – even though huge amounts of historical evidence often shows otherwise. It's how each man or woman through the ages has *interpreted* the information that has laid the foundations for so many of our misguided beliefs and actions today. After all, some of our New Testament was written 600 years or more after Jesus died. Let's face it, even today if you read ten newspaper reports of an incident, quite often you get several different views or sets of facts. Anyway, could you write with 100 percent accuracy what someone said or did – or *meant* – in 1405? Neither could I.

So where, I asked Gary, does science feel that the mind is, if it's not in the brain?

'In my early academic life I studied electrical engineering and carried out numerous experiments with television sets. It's important to remember that the brain is a mass of physical cells in which a lot of electrical activity takes place. So try to imagine for a moment that your brain is something like the inside of a highly complex TV. My experiments on the TVs were similar in principle to those that neurosurgeons carry out on brains. And they have concluded that the mind is inside the brain.

'But at the end of my experiment I did not come to the conclusion that the TV signals (which carry all the information) were emanating from inside the television set. Neuroscientists can tell you what is happening physically within the brain, but they cannot tell you the location of consciousness – which you could compare to the huge amounts of information contained in the TV signals, which are transmitted to the set via a host of frequencies. A TV set is both a receiver and a transmitter; so is a human brain.

'And consciousness, or the "incoming information" could be inside the head or outside. To test this theory, if you put a television set inside a shielded chamber you block the signal coming into that set and it won't work. But if you put a medium inside a shielded chamber, this does not prevent them from receiving specific, verifiable information which they transmit to us and the sitter. Of course experiments are ongoing, but our research and that of others indicates, as great scientists such as Sir John Eccles and Professor William James predicted long ago, *that the human brain is a receiver and a transmitter of energy and information from outside our physical bodies*. The brain is merely a tool through which consciousness or the universal mind works.'

This is the way I had always understood that mediumship, telepathy, remote healing and channelling worked – but it's still magical to hear it from a renowned scientist.

'So how big,' I asked, 'is this universal mind?'

'It's bigger than the entire universe. It's infinite. And it's everywhere.'

This statement made me recall that when I was in a heightened state back in 1998 I had felt as though I was on line to the 'all that is'; that if I needed to access any information on any subject then it was instantly available to me. I had felt as though I could do or know *anything* – and I will discuss this more in later chapters.

Gary laughed. 'You had access to infinite potential.'

'Okay,' I continued, 'so how is it possible to materialize physical objects when you are in an enlightened state?

'Firstly, the idea that thought can generate matter is something that most people think is impossible and the majority of people have never witnessed it. Secondly, many demonstrations of such phenomena are trickery. But for now, let's make believe that we have a Sai Baba in our laboratory. To start with, you rule out any possibility for cheating, and this person can still produce objects or whatever – from thin air – repeatedly. In theory it is possible, but I need you to bear with me while I give you a quick science lesson.'

Inwardly I groaned as I had never had a physics or chemistry lesson at school, and find science difficult to understand, but fascinating. If you are in a similar position, please stay with me – as this information is absolutely crucial to understanding how miracles and other dimensions are possible.

I asked Gary to talk to me as if I were about ten years old, in the hope that I would be able to truly understand how so many of the phenomena that I and others have experienced are possible.

'The question,' he began, 'is, what is the relationship between matter and energy? There are currently three world views. The first is that matter is primary, the material world is primary and that what we call energy is a side effect of matter. An example: you have the sun, which is the material object, and the sun emits energy. That's theory number one.

'The second world view arrived with Einstein – which was that neither energy nor matter were primary. He said they were two sides of the same coin, that energy can be converted into matter and visa versa.

'But with quantum physics, the new and third world view is that what's primary is energy. And that what we call "matter" is a special kind of energy – it's *organized* energy. And before I tell you how energy can become matter, there's another fact you need to understand.' I sighed ...

'All material things in the universe, including us, are ultimately made from atoms, which in turn are made from subatomic particles – and atoms are pieces of matter. For instance, one type of atom could be hydrogen and another atom, oxygen. They come together and make water.

'Molecules are made of atoms – cells are made of molecules that are made of atoms – organs are made of cells, which are made of molecules, which are composed of atoms. In simple terms, the atom is the fundamental unit of organized matter – and in the birth of the universe, one of the first atoms to be born out of energy was hydrogen. In physics, we explain that as the temperature of the early universe cooled down and the frequencies within it slowed down, then energy congealed into subatomic particles and ultimately atoms. But what you *really* need to get your head around is that when atoms congeal into matter, that matter is still almost entirely empty space.'

Time for a coffee. I'm not a great fan of caffeine, but I needed help here to keep my brain sharper. But believe me, what was to come was worth waiting for. As I poured the coffee I couldn't help saying, 'Well, this coffee table and the chair I'm sitting on feel quite solid to me.'

Now it was his turn to sigh. 'Jesus,' he frowned. 'Didn't you learn anything at school?' I smiled.

'Okay, let's go back. Imagine there is an atom in front of you – and atoms are extremely tiny and can only be seen with the most sensitive microscopes. But for now, let's say we have a hydrogen atom – and pretend that this atom is the size of the Empire State Building. Okay? Now, in the centre of every atom is a nucleus – which is where most of the mass (matter) is. How big do you think the nucleus is in comparison to the atom – which we are imagining is the size of this enormous building?'

I had absolutely no idea.

'The nucleus is only the size of a grain of sand. The atom, which is mainly empty space is the size of the Empire State Building and the nucleus of that one atom is the size of a grain of sand. Now that grain of sand constitutes almost the entire weight of that building, but it still means that what you think of as solid matter is more than 99.99 percent empty space.

'So, matter equals organized energy and organized energy is mainly empty space. *Therefore, the trick to creating matter is to organize the energy.* And what organizes energy? The mind. Mind and consciousness come first. In fact Max Planck, the father of quantum physics, said, "I regard consciousness as fundamental. I regard matter as a derivative of consciousness."'

'So,' I mused, 'I managed to almost materialize a ring because my mind was very focused?'

'Absolutely, and you did it with a very pure heart. You were not trying to harm anyone and you knew 100 percent that you had the inherent (instinctive) potential to create an object. And remember, matter is organized energy, and what organizes energy? Information. Mind and intention form patterns, which form matter.

'But it's also important to realize that materialization is not transforming nothing into something. What materialization is doing is taking energy and organizing it into a form that is sufficiently concentrated or dense, so that it can be experienced in our three-dimensional world via our physical senses. Think of glass, which is solid but we can see through it. So just because you cannot see something doesn't mean to say it's not there.'

'Well,' I moved on, 'when Allison Dubois saw all those dead people physically standing around her bed and she communicated with them, she had not materialized them. How is it possible to see a dead person?'

'How do we see stars?' Gary smiled.

'Through their light' – even I know that.

He needed to digress again.

'Right. A star might have been dead for millions of years, but we continue to see its light. I invite your readers to really think about this, to look at the sky and remember that the light you see from these long-dead stars carries information. What you are seeing is, in effect, its history, right here, right now. And when you look up at the stars, their light, their information enters your pupils – so you have huge amounts of information penetrating this one tiny part of you all the time.

'If you can truly get your mind around the fact that every atom – the fundamental unit of organized matter in the universe – has been here since the universe began. They just keep being recycled. What goes around comes around, evolves around and stays around in circles. It's all about vortexes. You could theoretically have atoms inside you that might have once made up Gandhi, Henry VIII or your auntie Nellie.

'Meanwhile, Diana or anyone else who had 'died' physically no longer has any primary mass in the physical sense – but their unique energy field, which carries every minute detail or information about that person, is still out there, in the great, infinite consciousness within the "vacuum" of space. Again, I remind you that just because you cannot see something doesn't mean it's not there.

'And our research and that of others indicates that millions of people have far more than the five accepted senses of sight, taste, hearing, touch and smell. Mediums and people like them are extra sensitive ... they see more, hear more, feel more and so on – than the rest of us.'

Many months later in London, biophysicist Harry Oldfield was able to show me this concept on his specialist scanner. He showed me the energy field of a phantom limb. The person's arm had been amputated, but the energy field where the arm had been was still there in a clearly defined shape. He even took an energy-field picture of a 'ghost' in a mortuary – which can be 'seen' as resembling a human figure, on his scanners. This is possible because the ghost's energy field is composed of organized light that is either too dim to be seen by most of us and/or vibrates at a higher frequency than most of us can see with our physical eyes. You can read more about this in Chapters 8 and 13.

Mediums, psychics and clairvoyants such as Allison, Laurie and many thousands of others are sufficiently sensitive that they can 'see' more spectrums of light (which are frequencies), than the majority of us. They can also hear a greater range of frequencies. They see 'dead' people just as the energy field can be seen in the phantom limb – except more clearly. How? Because the human brain has access to infinite potential and abilities. Most people just don't know that yet, nor how to access them.

But we are learning fast.

And in 1998 when I was in that heightened state I knew that the ultimate 'I' had emanated from the beginning of time and that every cell in my body contained all parts of the whole, as if some kind of nano chip is inside every cell and it contains everything. 'So does that mean,' I asked Gary, feeling somewhat apprehensive at my deduction, 'that every cell is God?'

'In the deepest sense of course it does, and what God is, is an expanding and evolving consciousness that is self-aware through us. Most people think of God as a dead white, black, Chinese or any other size or shape male! You need to really think about this. *If God, or what I prefer to call the Guiding Organizing Designer, is the fundamental guiding, organizing, designing process in the universe, with the potential to create all organized energy, then God exists in everything, including atoms and even sub atomic particles.*'

'Anyway,' he asked impatiently, keeping me on my toes, 'what are cells made of?'

'Atoms,' I answered quickly – as he was on a roll.

'Right. And I know it's hard for people to even begin to comprehend what I'm saying here. But think of the atomic bombs that were dropped in Japan in 1945. Small bombs, split atoms – which resulted in a devastatingly huge explosion of energy. It was a relatively small object that contained enormous power.'

Gary's voice softened. 'Try to think of it this way – the all is in the small, no matter how small it is. Everything, all information, is within it.'

I had to take a break to think about all this. If every atom contains all parts of the whole, then every single thing on the planet – be it a rose, the coffee table, my cup, my food, even my mother-in-law – is made of what we call 'God.' Gary could see that I was struggling with the enormity of what he was telling me, and yet back in 1998 when people had asked me, 'Who are you?' I had simply said, 'I am.'

'But I don't think of a coffee table as having consciousness,' I replied.

'The table,' Gary explained, 'does not have consciousness as you or I do, as there are many levels of consciousness. Also, the table does not have eyes to convert protons of light into a visual experience, but it does have "awareness" of the organized energy with which it can resonate. Remember, as Max Planck said, "I regard consciousness as fundamental."'

Imagine the global implications if we could all comprehend what quantum physics is now telling us – religion as we know it could be transformed. The way we view our world would be shattered forever. To know that we all contain God, and that *everything* has this infinite potential and knowledge inside itself that just keeps being recycled. But surely if everyone realized and experienced this ultimate knowing all at once, there would be complete chaos?

'And then some,' chuckled the Professor. 'After all, you had access to infinite potential. You could materialize the ring and the ash because you were in a hyper-coherent state – you absolutely knew with every fibre of your being that it was possible – and so you created your reality instantly. But you also had trouble integrating all the knowledge and potential you had access to. Now if we all became enlightened in one day – without the right training and understanding – you would have people just like in your film *Bruce Almighty* – where everyone is experimenting with what they could do and create, and we would slip into total and utter chaos.'

I had to laugh. It made me recall how I felt as though I was the light – in fact at one point I partially began to dematerialize as all I wanted to do was merge with, and become, light. In meditations we are always being invited to bring in more light. So I asked Gary how would it have been possible for me to become light.

He took a deep breath.

'In theory, if somehow you were able to make your atoms vibrate faster than the speed of light then you would no longer be visible. But most atoms never travel at the speed of light because their mass would become infinitely heavy. However, our thoughts may travel at the speed of light or even faster.

Only things that are mass-less can travel at the speed of light and this includes "dead" people.

'And again, being a sceptic, I would say you may believe this happened – but we have no verifiable evidence. If you want a more logical explanation, you should think more along the lines of asking, "How can a material object become invisible to light?" And the answer is that it would need to become less dense so that light could pass through it.'

Ah–ha. I have interviewed people who have watched in groups as enlightened masters disappeared in front of them. And when I had interviewed a young man in London who had become enlightened, I remembered staring at him, watching incredulously as gradually he had turned into light. I *know* it's possible. I had felt myself merging and becoming one with the 'all that is' and my physical body had begun to disappear. I had become light.

'Maybe somehow you did,' Gary remarked. 'In the meantime, when it comes to ghosts there is great confusion. Remember, the human body is only a minuscule percentage of matter and mostly empty space. A "ghost", which is a ball of energy, has no mass and can therefore walk through what we experience as everyday three-dimensional matter – they are totally unobstructed; when Allison Dubois went through her spiritual emergency on that Easter Sunday, much to her husband's astonishment, her husband's "deceased" grandfather walked straight through her.

'Also, if a living person were able to "disappear" at will it doesn't mean that the matter has been dissolved or lost its mass, but its mass may have been distributed to the point that light can pass through it, thus making it invisible in this dimension. But again, if everyone had the ability to become "unobstructed" and thus invisible, think of the chaos it would cause. Irresponsible people could steal anything, murder someone, eavesdrop and so on. You may have experienced such a phenomenon, but fully enlightened people usually have pure intention, they understand karma and cause and effect. With such powers you would need to have a huge sense of wisdom and responsibility. And thank goodness you could only do these things to yourself, you could not for instance think, "I would like this traffic warden to disappear" – and have it happen. Such a prospect would be outrageous.'

Not to me and thousands of frustrated motorists, it wouldn't. But I got his point. By this time we had been talking for hours and Gary needed to go. We were due to reconvene the next morning for just two more hours.

That night I found it almost impossible to sleep as dozens more questions buzzed in my head. I realized that for every question I asked Gary, once I had listened to my recordings I would have 100 more. But he is a busy man. And of course, if I tried to ask him every theoretical question there ever was or could be – we would need a lifetime to get through them all.

Tuesday, October 21, 2003

That morning as I got in the lift to join Gary for another breakfast, I suddenly remembered that I needed some bottled water for our meeting. I joined two ladies in the lift and, don't ask me how, but we started talking about how much the hotel charged for bottled water. 'Oh,' said one, 'we are flying out this morning and we have five huge bottles that we're leaving behind – would you like them?' During my lifetime I have been in an awful lot of hotel lifts and such an incident has never happened to me before.

I laughed out loud at the synchronicity. Whatever was happening, it was somehow speeding up. It reminded me that Gary had mentioned vortexes. The enormous energy field around me in 1998 had felt like a huge tornado all around and above me. And when I wanted something to happen, whatever I wished seemed to be drawn into my vortex, my energy field, and thus arrived – in many cases instantly. And in the moment that scientist Dr Serena Roney-Dougal had desperately tried to ground me by saying, 'You are only Hazel, say this,' and as I had said those words it was like a gigantic genie was suddenly sucked back into its container – my body!

Gary returned. We tucked into our eggs and got back to work.

'So, where is Diana now?' I began. 'And how can people reach her or others they would like to contact?'

'Diana can be anywhere she likes. Think of it this way. If you were standing in the middle of a huge field, and on the wind you distinctly heard someone call your name, what would you do?'

'I would turn around.'

'You would pay attention. And that's what our experiments indicate. If you have a deep connection with a departed person, they come when you call them – when you make the intention. And where there is a common purpose or intimate bond, the spirit is also keen to pass on messages. When we did the tests with Allison and Laurie, you had a strong intention that Diana should come through. And she heard you.'

Hearing that touched me to the core. Then Gary turned the tables on me by asking, 'What does she want from you, anyway?'

My mouth and mind seemed to go into automatic as I said, 'She wants to help prove that life after death is a fact – and she would like justice through truth ...'

'Interesting,' smiled Gary. 'We shall have to see what we can do!'

'Okay,' I continued. 'We have talked a lot about divine light, and so many people are confused as to what this light is. Healers talk of a light passing through them, out from their hands and into a patient. In meditations we are told to bring in light. What is this light? Is there a scientific explanation for it?'

'That question is an amazing synchronicity,' he smiled.

'Why?' I asked.

'Because we have just finished analysing data from experiments we conducted in 2002. We invited an experienced healer, Rosalyn Bruyere, to come to our lab for five days to teach a group of 26 doctors and nurses how to give healing.

'Firstly, you need to understand that cosmic rays are super high-frequency gamma rays – which are the highest frequency that we can measure. We measured levels of frequencies being absorbed and emitted by these people before and after the five days. And we found that after the training, the subjects were absorbing more gamma cosmic rays, but emitting more X-rays, which vibrate at a lower frequency than the cosmic rays. In other words the human body seemed to be acting like a transformer, stepping down the cosmic ray frequencies into X-ray frequencies before pulsing them into another person. So we now have good evidence that we have the capacity – through intention – to absorb super high-frequency cosmic rays which could be what the Chinese call *chi*, the Indians call *prana*, and so on. We can absorb them through the breath, through our pores and through intention. In these ways, the participants became more absorbent of the highest frequencies.'

This was music to my ears. Diana had told me during 1998 that she had saved my life, which Allison had verified the day before during our experiment. In some way Diana had acted as a transformer, toning down the divine energy that was pulsing through me. I had indeed felt as though I was going to explode with the huge amount of energy spinning inside and around me.

'Yes,' agreed Gary. 'If you had received a massive influx of pure cosmic rays, your physical body would have just burned up – and so I can now speculate, based upon scientific observations, that this could indeed have happened to you.'

Great.

'So what about my eyes, which kept changing colour?'

'Not only have I witnessed this in other people, but I have experienced it personally.'

More music ... this was becoming a symphony!

'In our research we know that all things both reflect and absorb light. Plants emit light, but they also absorb various frequencies from full-spectrum light which they then convert into matter; that's how plants grow. The eye also receives light and emits light. For the iris to change colour, it must change its chemistry so that it absorbs and reflects different patterns of frequencies, which can then be perceived as different colours. So yes, the phenomenum is explainable.'

'Well then,' I continued, becoming bolder in my questions, 'during my experience, for many weeks it seemed as though I was not being allowed to eat (and I *love* food) and my weight dropped to under seven stone. I was definitely less dense, and some friends would say, "Hazel, you are so pale, you look as though you are transparent!" Diana had told me that I needed to be purer in body (less toxic) so that I could hold more pure energy. Months later I met a woman from Australia called Jasmuheen who has caused enormous controversy by stating that basically – apart from water and the odd hot chocolate, interspersed with rare small meals – she lives on pure divine light. I had felt that the "all that is" that I was on line to, or in synchronicity with, contained everything that I needed. And yet I still lost loads of weight very quickly by not eating.'

A paradox indeed.

'Indeed,' smiled my new best friend. 'I met a fellow scientist some years ago, who is very thin – save for some water, a little tea and a few calories, she eats virtually nothing. It has been known for thousands of years that monks in Tibet and China, who are very spiritually advanced, can do this as well.'

'I need to repeat something here,' Gary impressed upon me. 'What is organized energy? It has pattern, form and frequency – which means it's information. Matter is informed energy – and what *matters* is the information. And if you could learn to live on the *information*, it is like living on *matter*, because what is matter? Matter is organized energy. What's organized energy? It's information. So if you know how to *digest* the information, you are getting the *essence* of the matter.

'And what is the soul of matter? Information. What is the spirit of matter? Energy. This is how in research, a scientist can pulse you with the unique frequency of say magnesium, and levels of magnesium will rise in the body. But you have not physically swallowed anything. It's like star trek medicine – and it's here now. But – and it's a big but – you have to be willing to receive the divine light, you have to seek it out and then integrate it into the physical body. And this takes time.'

This was great stuff. I had interviewed Jasmuheen when she was in the UK and she had been totally discredited by orthodox doctors, scientists and the press. A woman who had heard about Jasmuheen had pitched a tent on a lonely hillside and tried to live on light without food. She had subsequently died of starvation. To live on light, you need to be spiritually advanced. To avoid tragic consequences, you need helpers on hand who know what they are doing.

Remember, right now we are at a transitional stage in our evolution. If I were to make a guess, I would say that around six million or so people (0.1 percent of six billion on the planet) are now opening up to what is possible, to our true potential. A tiny, tiny handful of people are able to live on light. Spiritually, we have a long way to go. But how do you scale a mountain? Inch by inch …

'Okay,' I asked, 'What about sound therapy, when researchers have sung certain tonal notes when people were, say, bleeding after accidents, and the bleeding stopped whilst the tone was being sung?'

'Because,' Gary replied, 'sound is organised energy – or frequency – which is ultimately information. Sound is vibration – vibration is information.'

Well, we had got this far without Gary losing his cool, and so I went for the big one: 'During Easter 1998 when there was this huge storm over me and I had said over and over "I am the weather" – and then for several weeks I always seemed to be where a storm was – could my energy field have triggered that storm, or was it just the weather?' After all, I have received several letters from people who say they are somehow affecting the weather.

He took a deep breath.

'As a scientist I would say there are several explanations. Number one is that you just happened to have your kundalini (energy) experience at the same time that there was a storm – and the weather just added more energy to the energy within you.

'The second explanation is that you and the storm were connected – that your energy was "feeding" the storm and the storm was feeding you. Like a microphone, an amplifier and a speaker, you might have been in a huge feedback loop. In other words, imagine you have a microphone, you plug it into an amplifier and now point the microphone towards the speaker – and what happens? You get feedback as the sound is amplified. And if you go on and on doing this and don't turn the microphone away, it can amplify to the point of literally blowing the speakers. So, I can theorize that you and the storm were in some way interacting like a speaker and a microphone.

'The third possibility, which is really extreme, is that you were creating the storm as your thoughts (energy and information) were in such chaos.

'In truth, I don't know. We didn't know each other then. Perhaps if we could have tested you in that moment I would know for sure …'

My allotted time was running out. I quickly asked Gary, 'Can we travel in time?'

'It depends what you mean by time travel,' he said patiently. 'If you mean can we perceive the past, the answer is "Yes". If you mean can we take our physical bodies back in time, I believe the answer is "No", because you are in the present. I told you earlier that some of the atoms formed shortly after the beginning of the big bang are in this room. Atoms have been here since that moment and are just being recycled, re-circulated. So, in a sense, the past is in this room with us and I believe time travel is accessing the recycled information (energy) within the atoms that are in the here-and-now. The past is like a video that is playing in the present – but you would need to access the specific "tape" that you want to see. For example, when remote viewers, who are highly sensitive people, are given co-ordinates for any location on the planet, they "travel" there in their minds. The mind can be anywhere. And some of them will "see" a specific location as it looked in the past. Their information has been verified as being highly accurate. What I believe happens is that they are "reading" the information of the past via atoms that are here in the present.'

'So,' I surmised, 'if energy can neither be created nor destroyed, everything that ever happened or will ever happen is already here?'

'Yes, either historically or as potential. It's important to realize that the past, the present and the potential future are all present in the moment.'

It was time for Gary to leave.

I needed to come to one big final conclusion here, if only for myself.

Gary was tired. He is used to teaching people who understand all this stuff and we both needed some fresh air.

'Okay Hazel, let me say this before I go. We don't have the energy of the whole of God, but we have access to some of it. We do not have all the information of God, but we have access to some of it. All the information and all the potential exists everywhere. Potential cannot be seen, it is everything and no-thing.'

Then he turned the tables again.

'So, now you have chosen freely to come here. But tell me, why are you doing what you are doing? You have a good husband who can afford to keep you – and yet here you are in Tucson – searching. So, why have you come?'

I blustered. This was not at all what I had expected. 'Er, well,' I blurted. 'Of course I had an incredible experience that almost cost me my life. I felt like I had reached the top of the mountain and now I'm at base camp again. But in my heart I feel like I want to prove that the whole thing was real – in science – and to somehow help others to climb the mountain again and to know that they are not crazy. And in doing so, maybe re-climb it myself.'

'And why do you want to take people up the mountain?'

Meekly I whispered, 'So that they can realize their potential.'

Gary gave me a whoop and a big bear hug.

'*Right. You have got it.* And because potential is invisible, most people think it's not there. The whole universe is just one big quantum soup of potential and in this realm all possibilities already exist. This is why some of the greatest inventions in history have been discovered by two or more people at the same time – although living countries apart. They were very focused on wanting a specific outcome or answer, and by tuning into the realms of pure potential – or lets call it an infinite collective database, which is what all our thoughts are, they found an answer.

'All people need to do (and it's a big "all") is to set an intention, use any gifts that you were born with and get focused by sending out accurate information that can then be converted into organized energy - matter.

'Finally, know that you have all the time in the world. Because we are all recycled energy, if you don't do it in this lifetime, you will have plenty more lifetimes to try again.'

What a lovely, lovely man. And if you would like to know more about his amazing work, I strongly suggest you read his two fascinating books *The Living Energy Universe* (Hampton Roads Publishing) and *The Afterlife Experiments* (Atria Books).

That night, I was on an adrenalin rush from everything that Gary had shared with me. I needed to burn off the adrenalin if I was ever going to get any sleep. As the sun set, I walked over to the hotel gym and switched on the TV. Why was I even surprised when Larry King announced that his live guest that night was Sarah, Duchess of York?

And what did almost all the callers want to talk about? Diana, of course.

Choices and Other Realms

All that lives must die, passing through nature to eternity.
WILLIAM SHAKESPEARE

Wednesday October 22, 2004 – The Chopra Center, Carlsbad, near San Diego, California

It was time to leave Tucson. And as the taxi sped towards the airport I thought that no matter what might happen in the coming days, my experiences with Gary, Allison and Laurie had definitely been worth the journey.

But where to go from here? Before I had flown to the States, I had spent some considerable time trying to contact Professor Stanislav Grof and his wife, Christina, who are the world's leading authorities on spiritual emergency, in the hope that I could meet them in San Francisco around October 25. Eventually I obtained their email address and fired off a letter. But no reply had arrived and my laptop now had technical problems which prevented me receiving emails, so I couldn't keep checking for a response.

Also on my wish list for interviews was Dr Deepak Chopra, based near San Diego, and I had called his centre numerous times from the UK in the hope of making an appointment – with no joy. He is apparently inundated with such requests.

By the time the 22nd dawned I was, for almost the first time in my life, living in the moment. I could either take the flight to San Francisco in the hope that an email would come in, or I could take a chance on Dr Chopra and fly to San Diego. I could choose.

Because the weather forecast was fantastic – clear skies and 26°C (80°F) – I chose San Diego. In one sense, it was a mistake. The Chopra Center is a converted colonial house set in the midst of the 162-hectare (400-acre) La Costa Spa and Golf Resort. The centre is really sweet, but you cannot stay there – you have to check into one of the resort rooms. To my disappointment my room was furnished with heavy mahogany-type fittings, and I found it rather depressing. To add to my disappointment, my secretary back in the UK had left a message saying that Professor Grof had offered to see me that very afternoon in San Francisco. She had left the same message in Tucson – but it had not reached me in time. I could have cried, as when I called the airport the last flight to San Francisco had already taken off.

Again, I should have trusted more and taken more notice of the messages the universe had given me. After all, I had called, faxed and emailed the Chopra Center several times requesting an interview and they had not responded. How many times had I said to myself that if doors don't open easily, then listen to the messages and try other doors? If only. How many times in life do we say, *If only I had done this, if only I had done that* – how different life would be? If only Dodi and Diana had stayed at the Ritz, but they didn't. We can't go back – we can only go forward.

As I unpacked, another synchronicity occurred when I found a card from my husband which read, 'Grant me the serenity to accept the things I cannot change, the courage to change the things I can, and the wisdom to know the difference.' This famous yogic saying brought a philosophical smile. Anyway, my situation was far from desperate. The sun was shining, the pool beckoned, my bathroom was huge and I booked some crystal bowl sound therapy at The Chopra Center for the next day. Who knows what might happen. The good news was that in his message Professor Grof had included his home telephone number – so with a bit of luck, I could arrange a telephone interview.

Being a person who always travels with far more than I need, I had packed several research books, in the hope that I might find odd moments to skim through them. And in that moment, I had all afternoon – which was indeed perfect! I began with *Journey of Souls* by Dr Michael Newton (Llewellyn Publishing), which makes riveting reading.

Three years earlier at a book fair in Chicago I had met Michael, a master hypnotherapist who holds a doctorate in counselling psychology. He gave a fascinating lecture on lives between physical lives, based upon more than 20 years' clinical experience of hundreds of patients during hypnotherapy. He told us that during his early days he had been a complete sceptic regarding life after death, and when patients asked if he could help them to discover what their previous lives might have been he had resisted any such procedure, believing it would serve no useful purpose in his patients' treatment.

However, one day, a patient with severe chronic back pain had reported under deep hypnosis that he felt he had been stabbed in the back in a previous life during World War One. And when the treatment ended, much to Dr Newton's amazement the patient was completely free from pain. Michael went on to devise his own method of helping people to truly understand that we do live on, and to help them comprehend why they have chosen this lifetime. Today, he has a worldwide reputation in the field of clinical soul memory research.

As I read on, what interested me was how much of his research correlates with the conclusions I had come to as a result of my experience. For instance, he often mentions how, after leaving the physical body, each individual soul is automatically drawn to its correct tonal frequency or dimension. This is what I suggest in Chapter 2 when talking about enlightened masters (see page 29). Their specific blueprint for each incarnation depends upon the dimension or frequency from which they have come. And when enlightened masters physically die and leave this dimension, their souls return to their specific dimension or frequency just as we all do.

Also, everyone passing over (unless they are highly evolved souls and know exactly where they are going) is met either by their guides or by a loved relative, *even if that loved one has already reincarnated.* A part of them remains on other frequencies, whilst another facet of their unique energy reincarnates. Again, think back to Chapter 2, in which I say that when you become enlightened, all vibrational aspects of the ultimate you can finally come together; you become whole or 'holy'.

Reading more of Michael's book, I laughed when he says how he has lost count of the number of his patients who say, 'I know I am an old soul.' In fact he has found from all his research that most souls on the planet today are quite new. He believes there is only a handful (he suggests 1 percent) of really highly evolved old souls, which he terms as being at level five. At level four, he suggests 9 percent, level three 17 percent, level two 31 percent and level one 42 percent. Of course there are hundreds of levels, but nevertheless his figures illustrate just how few old souls are currently on the planet. They also help me to more fully appreciate that in trying to raise global human consciousness we still have a very long way to go. But make no mistake – we will get there one day.

This made me think about the Mayan calendar which predicts that the world will end in 2012. But maybe the Mayans were predicting the end of the world as we currently know it. Perhaps by 2012 there will be many more enlightened beings – and their prediction actually symbolizes a huge shift in our reality and consciousness.

Many people may ask, 'Well, if everything that has or will ever be here is already here, then where do all the new souls come from?' Good question. Remember that Gary Schwartz said how the universal mind (what we call God) is infinite; it's everywhere, and keeps recycling. Then, keep in mind that as approximately 353,000 babies are born every day whilst 154,000 people die daily (in 2003) – the need for incoming souls has increased, and so the ratio of new souls to old or more evolved souls has become unbalanced. To my mind, a useful tool for correcting this imbalance would be birth control. I'm not inviting a religious debate here; I'm just stating a simple fact.

Michael also reports that his patients when regressed are often quite casual about when they choose to enter the newly forming physical body. As unique souls on the threshold of entering new incarnations, some arrive earlier, but most seem to leave it until the last few weeks of pregnancy. They choose. And if things don't work out, they go back and start all over again.

If you find it hard to believe that an infinite number of souls is an impossibility, firstly consider that every snowflake that has ever fallen on this planet has its own unique crystalline pattern. It's a scientific fact that no two snowflakes are the same, nor ever will be. Each individual soul that incarnates is also unique – and emits its own unique range of signature frequencies. Therefore, when you think about how many new babies need souls every day, which are drawn from an infinite (whole) consciousness, in this context it would make sense to surmise that some of these unique energies may be new to being in a physical body in this dimension. This is why new, young souls need direction and loving discipline – they need to understand some rules, so that they can grow and evolve. Unfortunately, you only have to watch the news every day to know that too many souls are not learning or understanding the 'bigger picture'. Why? Because they learn from example and from what they are taught by those who should know better – who were also taught by example. And so the cycle goes on.

Consequently, the violence, bigotry, escalating health problems and so on continue. Yet, if you were to be in the presence of truly enlightened beings, you would literally feel pure love emanating from them. These people have been reincarnating for thousands of lifetimes and they know instinctively what's right and what's wrong at every level. I use these words loosely in this context, as when you are in a state of 'perfection' or 'bliss' you do not judge right or wrong – *you just are.*

And so in one lifetime a soul may choose to learn how to conquer jealousy, ego or impatience, for instance. Yet these traits could take several or hundreds of lifetimes to conquer. The ultimate trait to conquer is fear.

Interestingly, Michael also reports that some souls may decide for a time to merge with rocks, '… *to experience the essence of density, trees for serenity, water for a flowing cohesiveness, butterflies for freedom and beauty, whales for power and immensity,'* and so on. He also writes that souls can even integrate into a specific feeling, such as compassion, to sharpen their sensitivity.

Such statements from a renowned researcher help to expand our comprehension of what a soul is. We tend to think of human or animal souls as a 'thing', or an object that is only in living things. But how often do we think of a rock as having consciousness or a soul?

Medical trials have shown that sitting at the base of a tree and simply tuning into the energy or 'soul' of that tree every day can, in most cases, help to lower high blood pressure as effectively as prescription drugs. Everything is vibration and energy, which contains a drop of the whole. Michael also discusses the fascinating process a soul goes through to choose its parents – how it is allowed to view some of its possible futures before it incarnates. Michael shares one amazing story of a young woman who says she chose to come back and have a dreadful accident in her early teens so that she would be crippled, which would enable her to concentrate on studying music – which she could not do in a previous life. This story will please those who believe that *every* aspect of our lives is our own individual choice.

However, then he tells the story of a young woman who in a previous life was killed by an Indian raid on a wagon train. She is heartbroken in spirit as she watches her husband try to save her, and she is angry that her brief life has been shockingly cut short. But the arrow kills her. And along comes her spirit guide, who helps with her transition into the realms of spirit, and waits with her until after her funeral – when she finally moves on into the reality of another dimension. Practically everyone who has researched the realms of spirit state that most people like to 'see' their own funerals, as it gives them closure on that life experience. This reminded me of how Diana had told me that she had waited around with her father until after her funeral before moving on. And I have received many letters from people who say that they saw visions of Diana quite clearly whilst they were queuing to sign the books of remembrance.

Other spirits, however, immediately move away into other dimensions with their guides as they cannot wait to 'go home'. Michael's research also makes it clear that yes, we choose to come, but that some lifetimes do not quite work out as expected; and that certain souls are not so keen to return, but realize that their next reincarnation is necessary for their souls or soul group's growth.

At this point some of you may ask, 'Why would a soul come in and choose to be beaten, starved or to live on the streets?' Think on multiple levels. Perhaps in another life they abused or hurt a certain person, and that they chose to return to work out their karma. Cause and effect. Others choose certain parents for a whole range of reasons. It might be location or status, and sometimes they return to the same family. However, bad life experiences may be a result of their community or country circumstances changing quickly. Remember, shit happens.

A soul agrees an overall purpose with its guides and helpers, but the future is a series of potential possibilities that can change depending upon our own and other's choices and actions. Thanks to free will there is plenty of scope for various scenarios in many of the details of your life, but the original blueprint remains. And if for some reason you make a few choices that culminate in your physical death, then if it's right for you, you can come back and try again.

For example, imagine that you love being a nurse. You have always wanted to be a nurse and take care of people and this was the main reason you chose to come back. You complete your training and then decide to go and work for an aid agency, which eventually posts you to Iraq. They could have posted you anywhere but you go to Iraq and are killed in an air raid. You were doing what you love – working on your blueprint – but you get interrupted. So then you can go back 'home', have lengthy discussions with your guides in other dimensions and, at some point, return to another physical body of your choice to continue your purpose. Thinking along multi-dimensional lines, you may also have chosen to die this way for a specific reason for your soul's growth, or maybe you were just in the wrong place at the wrong time. That's free will.

But then I ask you to consider what *could* have happened if you had been on line to the 'all that is', the universal mind, the collective database – where all realities and possibilities already exist. Maybe because you had meditated or opened up in some way to this ultimate mind, and you had asked whether working in Iraq was a good move for you, your guides and helpers may have said, 'Not a great idea.' And subsequently if this information had felt correct to you, then you could have chosen what to do next, based upon all information available to you, from this world and others.

During 1998 I used to hear my mother as clearly as if she were sitting next to me. She would say that from the perspective of her dimension she could see a little more of what's around the corner for us if we keep going in the direction that we are going in – *in that moment*. But if we change our minds or actions, then we can change our probable futures. And the higher you go in the spirit realms, the more a soul can see, hear, sense and understand. But she always made it clear that any decisions I were to make should be 100 percent my own.

If Diana and Dodi could have done this, could or would they still be here today? I don't believe so. Diana had told me that if they had not died in that underpass, she would have died shortly afterwards. It had ultimately been her and Dodi's soul choice to go when they were young in order to help raise consciousness.

Diana had also said that certain major events, such as her death, had been set in stone – and maybe they are. But then again, if the universe is one big quantum soup of pure potential, maybe certain events that we had *not* expected or chosen only become our reality if we continue doing the same things but continue to expect different results. Think about it. Everything truly is a paradox.

As I sat thinking about myriad possible realities, I thought about my choosing to come to The Chopra Center at Carlsbad. In that moment, it was from my small perspective the 'wrong' choice – but it was still okay. Perhaps my situation could have been more productive had I gone to San Francisco. Nevertheless, I was still on my pathway researching higher consciousness. Choice. Free will.

You may then ask, 'What about the death of a baby or child, who has hardly had a chance to learn or grow?' On one level I believe that that soul may have chosen to come in to teach the parents a specific lesson. Or, that the soul may have needed to be here for only a very short time to fulfil what it needed to experience and then move on to another stage.

On another level, the mother may suffer some kind of sudden accident or illness, or eat a poor diet or be addicted to drugs – and her child therefore suffers. I believe that not everything is perfect in this dimension. I reiterate that it is as it is, because of all our thoughts, words and actions. In this way, life and an incoming soul has the *potential* to be perfect if we do more perfect things.

Pondering multiple realities was really thirsty work – I needed a cup of tea plus a piece of apple pie to help keep my brain ticking, and some water, too, as it was very warm. The pie would fulfil my need for a treat and the fluids would keep me hydrated. It felt like a sensible trade-off. For supper I would enjoy one of Dr Chopra's healthy-eating choices from my room service menu – and then go for a walk. Balance, I would aim for balance.

As my teeth sank into the pie, I considered that, as we do have considerable free will, how much the spirit realms can affect what happens in our day-to-day lives. That's a very big question. If I tried to answer every reality on this one, we would be here for a very long time (and I write on this subject in more depth in Chapter 8). But on an everyday level, I would say that Spirit are ready, willing and able to help guide you – but firstly you need to acknowledge their existence, by asking for their help in your prayers.

Then you may want to consider to what extent you want their help or intervention. Believe it or not, there are some people who won't leave the house in the morning unless they consult their spirit guides, whilst others intuit their way through the day asking their guides, 'Should I do this, or should I do that?' I would say that these people don't really want or appreciate the luxury of free will, as they are sure not doing anything that *they* want – they have handed total responsibility over to someone else.

The only problem is that for now we are still living in a physical world. Picture a man sitting on the roof of his house whilst flood waters rise around him. And when an army helicopter hovers overhead to rescue him, he shouts to the pilot 'No thanks, I'm waiting for the Lord to save me.' Then another man comes along in a dingy and offers to give him a lift, but the man repeats, 'I'm waiting for the Lord to save me.' And so he drowns. Once in spirit he meets St Peter and asks, 'Where was the Lord when I really needed him?'

The secret as always when working with the spirit realms is to find a balance. And if you consult a psychic who says, 'I have your dearly departed Auntie Mary here and she wants to warn you that you are going to have an unwanted pregnancy – if you keep doing what you are doing with that young man Simon!' then at this point you can choose. If the information is correct, you can use precautions or continue on the same path and potentially conceive. But you *can* choose.

If a psychic tells you that you will be spending a lot of your life in America, Russia or anywhere else, just think about what *you* really want before setting up circumstances in your life that can make someone else's predictions come true. Don't force things to happen; allow them to unfold. Psychics can usually only tell you what has the potential to happen in your life based upon your situation on the day of the reading. But if you make different choices and decide upon another path, other possible futures open up to you.

Therefore if you want help or guidance from other dimensions, you can tune into whichever realm feels comfortable to you – angels, elves, guides, relatives who have passed over, or who or whatever is sacred to you. Just sit quietly for a few minutes each day and allow your mind to be still. Then ask. Don't be desperate about what you want; ask as though you are asking for something from someone who loves you very much. And think about your motives and intention, and also ask to remember what your soul purpose was for incarnating in this lifetime.

In the film *Bruce Almighty*, the first thing that most people tend to wish for is lots of money. But remember that whatever you wish for, you are not just an individual 'you' or 'I' – there are other aspects or facets of the whole of you that exist in other dimensions. So when you wish for something, ask, be very specific and trust that if this wish or purpose is for the good of all the aspects of 'you' – then it can happen.

Think about what I have said about enlightened beings, masters of the self – that when they become totally integrated, any desired aspects (from the whole of pure potential) can be manifested through that person if they so request it. In that state, manifesting whatever you wish for is *potentially* possible, but fully enlightened beings usually only ask for things that are good for the 'whole' and not necessarily for themselves.

For instance, remember Mother Teresa, who wanted to raise lots of money to help the sick and the dying. People fell over themselves to write cheques for her charity, and in this way thousands of people died with dignity, were fed and so on. The money was used for the greater good.

But as most of us are not fully enlightened, integrated masters of the self, to get what we want or need we need to work on our intention, motives, thoughts and actions before realizing our dreams. And most importantly, when your dreams and desires are in sync with the other parts of 'you' (the whole) then synchronicities start to happen on a daily or even hourly basis, which indicate that your dreams are on their way.

And things don't always happen in quite the way you think they might. You might wish for £10,000 and a week later break your leg at work – and the money comes from an insurer after months of court battles and time off work. Please be careful what you wish for.

When I was in an extremely heightened state, talking to the spirit world and other worlds was literally like child's play. At that point I was hearing the spirit of Diana, what she had to say, and I experienced multiple physical effects that I could attribute to her unique energy field overlaying mine. And there is no doubt in my mind that Spirit can have a huge impact on our lives.

However, I now realize that my experience became a crisis because I did not listen to or act upon all the messages I had received during the months prior to what happened in Harrods. I was like the man in the boat – I took no notice of the signals and signposts. In the end it took a sledgehammer spiritual awakening to really get my attention.

As I have said, I believe that most relatives who have passed on can see a little more around the corner than we can, and in that respect you could treat any advice from them exactly the same as if they were still here. You can choose to listen or not.

During the last six years, I have met some very credible people who report having fantastic experiences with Spirit. One young woman, a medium who later became a good friend, told me how a few years earlier she had been driving late at night and had lost control of her car. As she had sped towards an oncoming lorry, she heard a voice telling her, 'close your eyes and trust'. A loud buzzing noise filled her car as she braced herself for the impact, closed her eyes and prayed. Yet after a few seconds she realized that the noise had stopped and no impact had occurred. She opened her eyes to find herself many miles further down the road – which was empty. She was fine.

Gary Schwartz has heard similar stories from highly credible sources, but again he reiterated that the woman in the car had no physical proof. However, he didn't say such an occurrence was impossible ... and that's great news. There are thousands of documented incidents in which Spirit have offered verifiable details, such as telephone numbers – and you can read one such astonishing case in Chapter 8. A couple of years earlier, when I had interviewed Dr Deepak Chopra, he had told me that when he had needed the telephone number of an old friend which had been mislaid, he had sat and meditated – and a number popped into his head. He dialled it and found his old friend. This sounds incredible, but remember that *all* information that ever was or will be is already out there in the infinite potential of what Dr Chopra terms 'the infinite collective database'. He compares this 'mind' to the internet. You log on, you search for what you want and up come many choices. Sometimes it's accurate information and sometimes it's not. You learn how to receive that information and then if you are wise, also to differentiate between what is correct and what is not – and so make informed choices. It's the same with any information from Spirit.

In the meantime, the smell of smoke brought me back into the moment. And as I stood and looked to the hills of San Diego I could see huge clouds of smoke. It was time to return to my room and watch the news.

Apparently a host of bush fires had broken out above and around San Diego – and they were beginning to burn out of control. I decided to stay just one more day, have my treatment and then head off to Hollywood, just a two-hour car ride away.

October 23, 2003 – Carlsbad

After a wonderful breakfast overlooking the immaculate golf course, I walked over to the Chopra Center for my treatment. My therapist was delightful; her eyes were full of light and joy. She introduced me to other therapists at the centre, and you could not help but notice that all their eyes were like laser beams of light. It was like being with friendly aliens!

After my crystal bowl treatment, which helped to tune my chakra energy centres, I was invited to join the daily meditation class. As we sat in silence I invited lots more cosmic rays into my body so that I could beam too.

Later on, I was introduced to Dr David Simon, medical director of the Chopra Center and Dr Chopra's partner, a lovely, peaceful man who trained as a medical doctor specializing in neurology, but who has also studied anthropology, shamanism and the ancient healing method of ayurvedic medicine. He has an encyclopaedic knowledge of all types of healing and encourages orthodox medical practitioners to work alongside alternative doctors and practitioners to help address the root cause of illness – whether it be mental, physical, psychological – or a combination of factors.

I briefly told Dr Simon about my experience and asked if they see many people who are going through similar situations and how they would help such a person. He told me, 'Firstly it's important to help the patient understand what is happening to them. Realizing that these experiences are unique in every individual, but that we have seen similar patterns of behaviour before, helps to ground them and reduce any fear they may be experiencing. Then we talk to them at length to make sure they are having a spiritual experience and not a paranoid, psychotic one – in which case we can recommend them to a specialist.

'They may not be eating, which of course quickly shows up physically. They may not be able to sleep and usually talk of being connected to the 'all that is'. We help to ground them by encouraging them to eat the right foods, plus giving them massage with grounding oils such as sesame, and so on.

'And what,' I asked, 'would be the single most important step I could take to return to that heightened state?'

'Meditate daily. When you still the mind, it has the opposite effect to stress on the body and mind. So when you meditate, your body's rhythms settle down. Blood pressure comes down, the heart rate is reduced, stress hormones return to normal levels, and the brain becomes more organized

— *more coherent.* The longer people meditate, the more common it becomes for the same physical patterns that are experienced during meditation to show up in the waking state. Generally, someone who meditates regularly becomes healthier and looks younger for longer. It's this practice that ultimately transforms people from human beings to spiritual beings.'

It wasn't exactly what I wanted to hear. Somewhere deep within, I suppose I was still hoping to experience a single magic bullet as I had in 1998 — but so many people had said that if I wanted to return to that heightened state I would have to work at it.

If you would like more details of The Chopra Center, log on to www.chopra.com

Friday, October 24, 2003

The next morning I felt quite sad to be leaving, just as I was getting into the spirit of the place. But the fires were now spreading, and I could hardly comprehend that some were being started by arsonists. San Diego was fast becoming a disaster zone and we could see miles of smoke. Why can't some people understand the knock-on effect of their actions?

As my cab turned towards the freeway and Los Angeles I thought about what Dr Simon had said about meditation and coherence. Professor Schwartz had used the phrase super coherent. And in that moment I had no idea just how important this word would one day become to my quest — as it offered me the ultimate answers to the secret of enlightenment.

Meanwhile, Professor Grof had offered me a telephone interview — so it was back to one step at a time.

The Growing Phenomenon of Spiritual Emergency

Self-importance is man's greatest enemy.
CARLOS CASTANEDA

Saturday, October 25, 2003 — Avenue of the Stars, Beverly Hills

Four years ago I heard about a young woman who at the height of a spiritual emergency was imperiously suggesting that people would want to part in the street to let her pass, or to kneel and worship at her feet. Without meaning to appear flippant, she would have felt right at home in Los Angeles. There is no shortage of people in LA who are so full of themselves that if their maid has a day off, they need therapy. After two days in Beverly Hills, even I was beginning to question what 'normal' behaviour really means. Tantrums, extremely tall stories, acting like a 'prince' or 'princess', gigantic egos, plus a need to be adored and in demand are normal traits in this town.

Sadly, the young woman experiencing spiritual emergency was eventually committed to an institution, as neither her parents nor her doctor could understand what was happening. In vain, I suggested that they read Professor Stanislav and Christina Grof's book *Spiritual Emergency*, as I knew it would help explain their daughter's strange behaviour. A friend had told me about this book at the height of my experience. After several weeks I had located a copy, and it really helped to keep me sane. Today, if I am contacted by anyone who believes they are going through a spiritual crisis, I am somewhat more forceful – as now I understand considerably more than I did then. But in the circumstances I had done my best, and that's all anyone can do.

As I sat looking over Century City from my hotel balcony, I felt sad not to be meeting the Grofs in person, but it was great that finally I was to interview Professor Grof on the phone. Before calling, I read their more recent book on spiritual emergency, *The Stormy Search for Self* (Tarcher/Putnam), which is an absolute must for anyone wanting to understand this complex subject in greater depth.

Professor Grof, now 72, has spent a lifetime trying to change the way many psychiatric patients are diagnosed and treated. Originally, he trained as a medical doctor in Prague during the early 1950s, and then went on to study psychiatry, which became his passion. He was taught that most 'mental illness' was some kind of pathological process – the symptom of a disease for which there was no obvious cure. Today, he knows differently.

Whilst beginning his research during 1956 at the Charles University School of Medicine in Prague, the clinical department he worked in was sent an experimental substance from Sandoz pharmaceuticals in Switzerland which the drug company hoped would become a useful tool for the study of biochemical processes in psychosis, including schizophrenia, and an effective treatment for emotional and psychosomatic disorders. They asked a number of major psychiatric research centres to report feedback on its positive potential, as well as side effects. That parcel was to radically alter the course of the young Dr Grof's life – as it contained something called LSD.

Little did anyone realize back then the part that LSD would play in our evolving understanding of the virtually limitless potential of human consciousness. Dr Grof volunteered as a guinea pig for the new drug.

He recalls: 'With the first experiment, I experienced a fantastic display of colourful visions and felt an amazing array of emotions with an intensity I did not know was possible. My brain waves were measured during the experience, and I was also exposed to strong lights to accelerate any effects.

'The cumulative effect was that I was "hit" by a radiance that seemed comparable to the epicentre of an atomic explosion. My non-physical consciousness was catapulted out of my body and I lost sight of my research assistant, then our lab, and then the planet. It was an incredible moment that was to change my outlook on psychiatry, on life, the universe and our place in it.

'And when we began administering the LSD to patients, many reported similar experiences to mine. Whilst some "saw" themselves in other lifetimes, others reported that it felt like dying and being reborn, and feelings of a oneness with nature were commonplace. Initially I thought that these states of being were the pharmacological effects of LSD or similar substances. It took me many years to understand the deeper truth – namely that they represent a normal potential of the human psyche.'

By the mid-1960s, Dr Grof had moved to America to become the chief of Psychiatric Research at the Maryland Psychiatric Research Center and then Professor of Psychiatry at the world-famous Johns Hopkins University School of Medicine in Baltimore, Maryland.

He told me, 'Time and again I would see patients with symptoms similar to those we had seen in more than 4,000 LSD experiments. But most of these people had not taken any psychedelic substances. Their experiences emerged in the middle of everyday life without any noticeable trigger.

Many of them were indistinguishable from those described in various mystical traditions and the spiritual philosophies of the East. And it slowly dawned on me and some of my colleagues that human potential to transcend our three-dimensional world of experience is not a product of unknown pathological processes affecting the brain, but everyone's birthright. Psychedelic substances simply catalyse this innate potential. The problem is persuading the psychiatric establishment to accept this reality.'

He spent the next 40 years researching higher states of consciousness and working with many people who would traditionally be diagnosed as psychotic, until he concluded that a large percentage of them were going through crises of spiritual awakening, which – if properly understood and supported – were actually conducive to healing, positive personality transformation and consciousness evolution. Professor Grof and his wife, Christina, coined for these states the term 'spiritual emergency'. It is a play on words that reflects their ambiguity – alarming intensity – but also the potential to 'emerge' to a higher level of functioning.

Professor Grof told me, 'When we allowed theses experiences to run their course, the therapeutic results were far greater than any results we could have achieved with years of therapy or drugs. Unfortunately, most orthodox doctors and psychiatric units have never heard of spiritual emergency – and instead of allowing and supporting the patient to move through the experience – which can often get temporarily worse before it gets better – for the most part they work on suppressing symptoms by long-term medication, which can have a negative and destructive impact on people's lives – lead to impoverishment of personality and serious side effects.'

He is not kidding. For anyone who has not undergone such an experience, understanding the consequences of how spiritual awakenings have the potential to either heal – or to destroy a person's life is hard to imagine. As he spoke, I recalled the harrowing two hours spent with my husband and our doctor in the spring of 1998, when I had used every ounce of energy and focus I possessed to persuade them that I did not need a psychiatrist – because I realized what the consequences might be.

In October 2003, before travelling to the States, I received a heartfelt letter from a woman in France who had enjoyed reading *Divine Intervention*. My intuition told me to call and find out more – and Julie James's story truly brought home the reality of what can happen when a spiritual breakthrough is misunderstood. Courageously, she agreed to tell me her story for this book in the hope of helping others.

'I was born in Nottingham, the second of four children. For as long as I can remember I loved nature, I had a pure joy for life, adored rescuing animals and I suppose you would say I was spiritual even then. My father, who was a compulsive gambler, adored me, which made my mother obsessively jealous, and the anger she felt towards my father became totally focused on me.

'I was very bright, and when I passed my Eleven Plus exam my father was thrilled, but my mother's aggressiveness increased a hundredfold. She told me that any studying was a waste of time and refused to let me do any homework. Eventually I buried my school books in the garden out of sight. Her refusal to allow me to continue my studies at the age of 16 came as no surprise, and she instructed me to get a respectable job. An unfulfilling position with an insurance company was all I could find – and the only way I felt that I could escape my mother's continual abuse was to get married, which I did during my late teens. Shortly afterwards we moved to Germany and then Holland.

'My first baby was born in 1969 after a seven-month pregnancy – and he died, as did the second. To say I was depressed is an understatement, and two weeks after losing my second baby I had my first "psychotic" episode.

'I began to view the world around me as a very drab place, where everyone was struggling to own more "stuff" – and I felt that God was speaking to me, telling me there was a better way. I heard many different voices. My husband was very fearful and of course he called our doctor. Initially the doctor said I was physically and mentally exhausted, and he prescribed high doses of the tranquillizer valium so that I could sleep and sleep. With the drugs, the voices stopped.

'Then in 1973 I was on the escalator in a department store and suddenly I felt this huge energy surging through me. My eyes became large and luminous and I was filled with seemingly limitless amounts of energy. I began talking very rapidly, my body temperature fluctuated wildly, I began affecting electrical equipment and my head was jammed by all sorts of voices. I felt as though I was being given information that could help make the world a better place, and that my sharing it with people would make them happy too. But I was wrong.

'My husband became more and more frightened and negative and eventually persuaded our doctor to have me committed. They came with a straitjacket and bundled me into an ambulance and I was taken to a mental home.

'Deep within myself I knew that I wasn't mad; yes I was frightened, as I knew my behaviour was abnormal and I needed help to sort things out, but I did not need to be forcibly strapped down in an ambulance and treated like a murderer. Naively, I thought the doctors at the clinic would understand. They didn't.

'I was incarcerated with dozens of people who were clinically insane. If you complained, you were put in solitary and they did awful things to us. It was made worse because I could not speak Dutch very well. Also, in the early days I thought I could live on air, and therefore refused to eat, which led to my being force-fed – which was appalling.

'Inside I was screaming in outrage, but you quickly learned to keep complaints to yourself, or it was more solitary. It's hard to describe the depths of my despair and utter isolation. By 1985, I had been in and out of several institutions and was labelled psychotic, which to our friends meant "mad".

'When I was finally discharged in the early 1990s, I had become totally addicted to the drugs they had given me for almost 20 years. Deep humiliation and shame engulfed me. You have this label of having been diagnosed as "psychotic" and I was utterly terrified it might happen again. And yet somewhere deep within the core of my being I tried to keep some self-esteem, and throughout all my experiences I marvelled at what the human mind is capable of.

'Meanwhile, when I tried to re-integrate back into society most of our friends suddenly became unavailable. People would avoid me, as they were absolutely terrified of "catching" what I had or being associated with a mentally ill person.'

When I had heard Julie's story, I kept pinching myself at how fortunate I had been to have good friends like Dr John Briffa who had stayed with me over Easter 1998 and had saved my life. For my husband and our doctor, who allowed me to stay at home in the hope that I would "get over" whatever was happening.

Julie has lost 20 years of her life and today, at 58, although she still suffers the physical side effects from her ordeals in the institutions, she is trying to rebuild her life, which she now terms reclusive. She has weaned herself off all the drugs and if she 'hears' anything today or has insights, she keeps them to herself. Thankfully, she is not bitter. Most tellingly, when her psychiatrist moved to another town a few years ago, his parting words to Julie were, 'Your case makes me realize that we know so little about psychosis, and today I think you are more sane than most people!'

What makes Julie's story even more heartbreaking is that similar events are happening the world over to thousands of people every day.

In fact, it was Christina Grof's spiritual emergency that brought her and Stan together. Back in 1964 Christina, a yoga enthusiast, graduated from college and soon after married a high-school teacher. In their book *The Stormy Search for Self* she tells movingly of her spiritual crisis, which began four years later during the delivery of her first child. Christina recalls: 'As the medical team encouraged me to push ... push ... push ... suddenly I felt an abrupt snap somewhere inside of me, as powerful and unfamiliar energies were released and began streaming through my body. I started to shake uncontrollably. Enormous electrical tremors coursed from my toes up my legs and spine to the top of my head. Brilliant mosaics of white light exploded in my head and instead of continuing the breathing methods I had been taught in preparation for giving birth, strange involuntary breathing rhythms took over. I was both excited and terrified – yet these phenomena were nothing like what I had been told to expect.

'Two shots of morphine stopped this process and I began to feel foolish. Very quickly, I pulled myself together.'

Two years later with the birth of her second child, Christina had a similar but more forceful experience which again was shut down by powerful prescription drugs. She presumed that what was happening was surely a sign of illness.

One day in 1974, a friend suggested they should attend a yoga retreat with revered spiritual teacher and head of the Siddha Yoga lineage, Swami Muktananda. During one of the meditations the swami slapped her on the forehead several times, and suddenly all the repressed emotions she had held in for so long exploded. The kundalini energy, known as the 'coiled serpent', which lies dormant in the base of the spine area, was suddenly released. The doorways from this world to others were flung open.

She recalls: 'I felt as though I had been plugged into a high-voltage socket as I started to shake uncontrollably. I wept as I felt myself being re-born; I experienced death; I plunged into pain and ecstasy, strength and gentleness, love and fear. I knew I could no longer control what was happening – the genie was out of the bottle.'

Christina's life began to fall apart, just as mine had during 1998. Her spiritual awakening triggered severe panic attacks, and eventually her marriage collapsed under the strain. In May 1975 she went through a near-death experience during a car crash, which further intensified many phenomena, and she began to conclude that she was going insane and would need to be sent to an institution.

Then a miracle happened. One day she was inspired to call an old college friend and poured out her confusion to him. He suggested she should read a book by a Dr Stanislav Grof – which she did – and was amazed at the similarities between her experiences to those reported from his many LSD experiments. But Christina had never taken LSD.

She travelled to California to consult Dr Grof. He assured her that she was not 'insane' in the accepted sense of the word, and that in the East these types of experiences were called Holy Madness. He gently explained that although the process can be difficult and traumatic, she should stay with the process and move through it. Also, that the drugs she had been given had suppressed her symptoms, thus delaying what he assured her would eventually be a hugely healing and transitional experience.

By October 1975 they had begun a relationship, and Stan continued to help Christina. She writes movingly of her many visions, of the electrical tremors and the excruciating pain behind her eyes.

Like Julie James, Christina also became addicted – in her case, to alcohol. Her incredible experience (which makes what I went through seem like a walk in the park) lasted 12 years. And she firmly believes that without Stan's help her story could have turned out like Julie's.

Today, Christina works with her husband. Together they have helped many hundreds of people come through spiritual emergency and a huge variety of mental health problems.

At this point I was interested to hear what Professor Grof has found as being the main triggers or causes for such profound experiences. In Christina's case it was linked to her giving birth, but I had simply been shopping in Harrods when my whole body had felt as though it was being ripped apart.

He told me, 'The situations that we have found are most commonly linked to intense kundalini awakenings are intense meditation, intervention by an advanced spiritual teacher or specific exercises of kundalini yoga. On occasion this can happen during childbirth and during intense lovemaking. It may also be triggered by extreme physical or emotional stress, shock or trauma – or it can happen at anytime, anywhere, in the midst of everyday life without an obvious trigger.'

As he said this, I thought back to how stressed I had felt that day in Harrods. Stuart and I were gearing up to finish the building of our new home and on that fateful April day I was running late for a site meeting. During the previous weeks I had been working tremendous hours with insufficient rest. Two days earlier I had almost been mugged, but managed to escape, but the shock had affected me deeply. It was also two days before Easter – the traditional time in the West for death and rebirth.

And as I remembered the hundreds of sensations I had felt in the days, weeks and months following my experience, I had asked Professor Grof to share what he has found are common symptoms and phenomena that typically affect a person undergoing a spiritual emergency.

'Well,' he began, 'as there are many types of spiritual crisis and every awakening is unique to each individual, the hugely varying symptoms depend on which form of 'spiritual emergency' they are experiencing. For instance, with the awakening of kundalini, most people feel extreme temperature changes as the physical body tries to cope with the huge influx of spiritual energies which can stream up their spine and throughout their nervous systems. There is often shaking or spasms and the person may feel they are no longer in control of their movements. Their psyche can be flooded by powerful emotions and knowledge – and the patient may begin speaking in tongues.

'Additionally,' he continued, 'intense orgasmic feelings can also accompany these types of kundalini awakenings. Symptoms could also include laughing or crying hysterically, or the person begins reciting rare poems, chants or prayers, which were previously unknown to them. Hearing choirs singing, seeing visions, demons, mythical characters or animals, angels or saints are also common. Some women also report a sacred "marriage" or union with God. Others might have tremendous and blissful feelings of total and unlimited connection to everything and everyone. Whereas another person may have a profound crisis of psychic opening, in which they may not experience the energy phenomena. In such cases dominant symptoms could be telepathy, precognition, clairvoyance, clairaudience, out-of-body experiences, telekinesis (moving objects without a physical connection) and so on.

'Another fairly common type of spiritual emergency is the shamanic initiatory crisis, similar to spontaneous visionary states that begin the career of many shamans. Here the focus is on a profound experience of death and re-birth, visits to the underworld, and journey to the supernal (heavenly or divine) realms. Sometimes this can be associated with a biological crisis – a near-death experience during a severe disease, accident, or operation – and, at other times, it is symbolic. These patients also report contact with animals, real or archetypal animal spirits or "power animals". This experience can result in healing of various emotional and psychosomatic disorders, or even somatic (physical) diseases.

'In many types of awakening a common theme is also one of paradox. Being nothing and everything at the same time. Great knowing but not fully understanding. An experience that combines terror and ecstatic rapture, or light with darkness. Insights concerning the relativity of good and evil. Questioning – and receiving multiple answers. Everything can become a paradox.'

My favourite phrase …

It was fascinating to hear his list, and as he spoke I felt that I must have experienced an intense kundalini and psychic opening at the same time. Most amazingly, Grof told me that many people might think that these types of experiences will mirror their cultural beliefs, but in some cases he has found the opposite to be true. He cited the case of former Harvard psychology professor Richard Alpert, who was brought up in the Jewish tradition in America. But when he underwent his own awakening in the 1960s, he began 'seeing' visions of Eastern deities. These visions eventually led him to Neem Karoli Baba, a Himalayan guru, and Alpert began practising Hinduism and other Eastern belief systems.

'This is because,' says Grof, 'when the psyche opens to the collective unconscious, the symbolism people experience does not necessarily have to come from their own culture, it can be drawn from the entire cultural heritage of humanity. As C G Jung, the famous Swiss psychiatrist, has shown, this can be cultures of which these people have absolutely no previous intellectual knowledge.'

Professor Alpert has spent almost 40 years researching and teaching the nature of human consciousness and, since 1967, he has become a world-famous 'New Age' teacher – known as Ram Dass, the name given to him by his guru.

As I chatted with Professor Grof, I realized that for the average person and some doctors, some of these symptoms may seem mind-boggling.

'Yes,' he agreed. 'For a person not familiar with the archetypal realms, the patient may appear delusional. And, whilst their doctors and relatives think the experience has no basis in reality, the person may feel that their everyday life is like a dream and that their new reality is far more real. This is a perspective that is well known from the spiritual philosophies of the East and other mystical traditions.'

'So how,' I asked, 'should doctors and psychiatrists approach a patient with these types of symptoms?'

'Firstly the person in crisis should receive a thorough medical examination to eliminate the possibility that the problem has an organic basis – in other words, to eliminate any physical condition that could influence mental functioning, such as brain infections, tumours, intoxications, circulatory problems, degenerative diseases, drug abuse, lack of essential brain nutrients, hormone imbalances and so on.

'Secondly, the patient's experience would involve elements that can be induced in normal persons by relatively simple means, such as the holotropic breathwork that my wife Christina and I have developed, meditation techniques and shamanic rituals. This includes reliving memories from childhood and infancy, death/rebirth experiences, past-life memories, archetypal visions, experiences of unity with other people, with nature, or with God. Mainstream psychiatrists see these experiences as products of unknown pathological processes afflicting the brain, but in the extended cartography (map of the mind) that I have outlined in my books, these are all normal manifestations of the human psyche.

'Thirdly, during a spiritual crisis, patients are usually aware of the fact that what is happening to them is predominantly an internal process which is not being caused by events in the outside world. Outside events may have triggered the experience, but from then on it is a confrontation with one's own psyche, a journey into the deep, normally hidden, recesses of one's own unconscious. The persons in spiritual crisis may be very bewildered and confused by the enormity of strange experiences – but they are usually very coherent and articulate in reporting their experience. And they are willing to receive and act upon advice and help.'

As he spoke I thought about the huge kaleidoscope of feelings and events I had experienced during that Easter weekend. I was hugely confused by what was going on, but remain forever grateful to Dr John Briffa, who moved in with us during that weekend and who realized I was not "psychotic" in the accepted sense of the word, in that I was totally coherent and very detailed as to what I was experiencing and did not change my story minute by minute. At that time, John had no idea what was going on, but he felt that as I was aware of the day and time, and knew who was with me – and as long as I was not threatening to harm myself or others, that it was okay to allow my experience to unfold and 'wait and see' if I would come through it. Others, like Julie, are not so lucky.

Grof agrees. 'If the person is going through an intense and rapid awakening and they try to harm themselves or others, feel invulnerable because they confuse spiritual immortality with physical immortality, or think they can fly and so on – supportive 24-hour care is necessary. They need to be in a place of safety until such feelings pass. The current medical approach would be suppressive medication and hospitalization, but what is needed are 24-hour care centres with trained personnel, who can help support and reassure the patient.'

'And so,' I asked, 'what might be typical symptoms of a psychotic episode as compared with spiritual emergency?'

'What is important to realize is that "psychosis" is not a medical diagnosis, except in those cases that have an organic basis, as I mentioned earlier. For the rest of the conditions diagnosed as "psychoses", we have no specific laboratory findings, suggesting that they are diseases in the same sense as, for example, diabetes or anemia. We call them "endogenous psychoses", which is a very transparent cover for our ignorance; it is a meaningless term, which translates as "generated from within". Since there is no medical diagnosis of psychosis, it is difficult to offer criteria for differentiating "psychosis" from "spiritual emergency". What we can do instead is to describe, which aspects of the patients' experiences suggest that they are not good candidates for an alternative treatment – psychotherapeutic support rather than psychopharmacological suppression.

'Some of these criteria would be: these patients usually believe that everything that is happening to them is someone else's fault, is caused from outside, has nothing to do with them; in technical terms, they are using the mechanism of projection. They might say, "My neighbours are trying to kill me, they are pumping poisonous gas into my house through a pipeline. They have placed bugging devices and little TV cameras throughout my house. I have no privacy anywhere, my life is being threatened. This is part of a big mafia plot," and so forth. This type of patient would not recognize that their experiences have something to do with their own psyche. As a result they would not be interested in any help, other than in dealing with their "dangerous" neighbour or perceived enemy. And these types of patients would not be good candidates for our alternative approach.'

The longer we chatted, the more I realized that we all have so much to learn. Obviously in this book, there is not space to discuss every aspect of the mind and spiritual awakenings – but before ending our call I was keen to know what would be his main recommendations to help relatives and friends who are trying to cope with people going through intense spiritual awakenings.

'The most important thing,' he began, 'is to determine whether the individual in crisis is capable of coping with the situation in his or her own domestic setting, or whether they need professional help and institutional support. For those individuals who are able to deal with spiritual crisis on their own, understanding and help from friends is very important. We have found that inviting them to our breathwork workshops is extremely useful. In this way, they can learn a lot about non-ordinary states of consciousness by a personal experience, as well as by assisting others (we work in pairs). They can then apply this knowledge in helping their friends or relatives in crisis.

'There are other things that are good to know. For example, when people are in emotional crisis, the brain burns a lot of fuel and the resulting hypoglycemia tends to facilitate further emergence of material from the unconscious. A heavier diet and particularly fast sugars (such as honey and bananas) can help calm down the symptoms and ground the person.'

These words made me smile and I thought back to the first night of my experience when my brain had felt as though it was literally cooking. I had called my dear friend Bob Jacobs, a homeopath, who had told me to eat sugar. At that moment I would have done almost anything to cool my brain – and I had stood in our kitchen at midnight eating ginger cake as if my life depended on it. As a health writer I knew that refined sugar is not a healthy food, but like Professor Grof, I found that when the feelings became intense and overwhelming, sugar really helps. It's the only time that I viewed a jam sandwich on gooey white bread as a life saver!

As the days had become weeks, I gradually realized that I needed to control my blood sugar, which helped reduce the phenomena that were happening all around me. I began eating even more earthy foods such as porridge, soups, potatoes, stews and root vegetables – plus protein – as when the body is under tremendous stress it needs more protein. Again, when you are in this heightened state, you might 'feel' the energies from a dead animal or fish, and may automatically become vegetarian. In which case, try to eat more eggs, cheese, tofu, beans, live yoghurt or whey protein. Your body and brain need plenty of nutrients. Food will literally help keep you 'down here' instead of 'up there'. It helps you to walk the tightrope between this world and others …

If all else fails and you cannot face food, try to force yourself to eat soups, fresh fruit smoothies, plenty of water, plus calming herbal teas such as chamomile with honey, and take a high-strength multi-vitamin and mineral along with an omega 3 and 6 essential fats formula.

Rest is also vital, so that your body and brain can begin to sort out and integrate what is happening. If you don't get sufficient rest and peace and quiet, the intensity of the experience can increase even more, which greatly stresses the physical body. You have already had a major breakthrough, and you don't want to blow any more fuses — such as your heart. Take it easy. You may also be pumping lots more adrenalin, so take some regular exercise to burn it up. Find a balance.

The Professor reminded me that the majority of phenomena are outside most people's control during the experience, and that the person should not experiment on their own or consciously play with the energies until they become more grounded and learn how to integrate so much new knowledge. Most importantly, Grof stressed that when people connect to other realms, the ego can become exaggerated and you can have an inflated sense of your own divinity and feel God-like. He continued, saying, 'You may not realize that many other people are also having these experiences, and this is when troubles can arise in everyday life.'

He made me laugh when he added, 'At such times people can feel that they are at the centre of events that have a global or a cosmic relevance. Their psyche can become a fantastic battlefield where the forces of good and evil are engaged in combat that seems critical to the future of the world. This would not be a good time to call the White House and tell them that you are a new world saviour. Some women at this time also believe they are giving birth to a divine child, while men may see themselves as reborn into the role of a saviour. It is the task of the therapist to accept this process and validate it for the clients, but keep reminding them that this is an inner transformation process and discourage them from acting it out in the external world.'

As he said this, I thought about a young Indian man I had spoken to at length during 2000 who, during his spiritual crisis, had become totally convinced that he was the one and only most powerful God – to the point that he felt indestructible. He had told me on the phone that if he travelled to India, Sai Baba would want to worship at his feet and I remember thinking, 'I don't think so.'

Unfortunately, his ego became so inflated that he begged his family to shoot or stab him, as he felt that he had total control over his physical body. In discovering the eternal God within himself, he had forgotten for that moment that he is part of God, from his perspective, in a physical body. And he had not integrated or balanced the energies. Ultimately, he was imprisoned and his mental condition deteriorated. It's so sad – just as Julie James during her experience began sharing all her insights with everyone and ended up being committed to an institution. It is far better to write down what happens – because inevitably you can forget huge amounts of what you discover, but at the time you presume you will always know these things. I made many of these mistakes myself.

Meanwhile, Grof reiterated that a spiritual crisis can have huge potential for healing, but it can also have many pitfalls in the context of everyday life. For instance, a person may also feel such total gratitude and benevolence that they give away all their money.

This is why I shall be forever grateful to my friends and family for their endless support and patience. They stopped me from doing some of the more crazy things that I became convinced were essential to the planet's survival. I didn't call the White House – but I almost called Downing Street. What a mistake that would have been! Also, when I phoned Sarah Duchess of York and arranged a meeting during June 1998, I believed that I absolutely knew it all – and our meeting could have gone very pear-shaped as a result. In any event, Sarah was patient and supportive and she eventually agreed to go on the record in *Divine Intervention* to say that she believed me and what I had been able to tell her. But if I had called Earl Spencer or tried to force myself on to him … I shudder and also laugh to think what might have happened!

On a more serious note, consider the intruder who broke into George Harrison's house in the 1990s and almost fatally injured the ex-Beatle. He told anyone who would listen that God had told him to do this. Remember, as UK-based parapsychologist Dr Serena Roney-Dougal had told me during 1998, the underlying personality of the person does not necessarily change whilst they are going through the experience. It's only much later that they might 'see the light' – if at all. She had said that their experience and its outcome could greatly depend on their life's circumstances, their beliefs, their diet, health, upbringing and so on.

Before I said goodbye to Professor Grof, he related the true story of a mafia Don who several years ago was shot, and for a time was physically 'dead'. But when he was resuscitated by the medical team he told his family that he was appalled at his old life. How could he have done such terrible things? He had literally 'seen the light' and from that moment he determined to contribute more positively to the world.

By this point you may now be thinking, 'I don't want to go through a near-death experience or a spiritual emergency to "see any light". What's the point?'

It's an obvious question. The point is that my personal experience showed me a fraction of our potential capabilities – and as far as I am concerned they are limitless. Reading about it and *experiencing* such knowledge – as Stan and Christina Grof know – are worlds apart. And if you would like to know more about their work, log on to www.holotropic.com or contact Grof Transpersonal Training in California on (001) 415 383 8779.

Meanwhile, in our psychiatric homes and on our streets are people who are going through their awakening. There is great ignorance. Even today, some six years after my experience, I have friends who say with patronizing grins on their faces, 'When you were *ill*, Hazel ...' still presuming that I had fallen off some precipice of what they considered to be "normal" behaviour. Such people need to understand who we are, what we are capable of, and the many roads we can travel to access this knowledge.

And I and many others believe that right now we are in a period of acceleration and mass transition. Christina Grof's experience happened as she gave birth to her physical child. But on a larger scale humanity is birthing a new consciousness, a new reality. This birth can be easy, or it can be difficult. We can choose. And if we are prepared to have a greater understanding of the human mind – then when our genie appears our potential capabilities to change our world for the better will accelerate at an incredible rate. The secret, meanwhile, is learning how to live between worlds during the transition.

Some days I think about how different my life would have been had I not gone through my awakening, as the gifts and insights it brought were priceless. And, after all she went through, even Julie James agrees, saying, 'Today I have a clearer "knowing" about the world and the universe, plus gifts that others don't yet know they have.'

A lovely lady.

Meanwhile, back in LA, it was time to end my telephone interview with Professor Grof, who had given me over two hours of his valuable time. As I sat saying goodbye at the desk in my room, outside the sun was shining – and Hollywood beckoned.

Sunday, October 26, 2003

I only had a couple of days left before flying home and I wanted to check out Rodeo Drive. Shopping is very grounding indeed ...

It was slightly surreal as I shopped in the 35°C (95°F) sunshine; a thick pall of smoke wafted eerily across the city and in places blotted out the sunshine. It was coming from the huge fires that had begun in San Diego a few days earlier and that had spread for miles, and were now burning out of control in the hills outside the city. Fourteen people had died and 1500 homes were lost. The TV news was heartbreaking. I watched as people fled with nothing other than what they wore or could carry as their homes were engulfed by the inferno. The fire fighters were working until they collapsed from heat exhaustion – while arsonists set new fires. If ever there was a time that we could all do with 'seeing the light' surely, I mused, now is as good a time as ever.

That afternoon as I searched intently in a bookstore for a guide on Californian wines for my husband, I knocked over a sign board. As it fell, a pile of books came with it. I turned bright scarlet and an assistant rushed over to help extricate me from the mess. To my astonishment, the title of the books scattered before me was *A Royal Duty*, by Princess Diana's ex-butler, Paul Burrell.

This may sound implausible, but I truthfully had no idea he had written a book. That night as I devoured its contents, I burst out laughing when I read that Diana had once thought of buying a house in Beverly Hills! It was as though she was saying, 'Keep going … you are where you need to be.'

Monday, October 27, 2003

On my final full day in LA, I drove to the world-famous Mulholland Drive to meet with film director Peter Hunt. So many synchronicities had brought me here. Many months earlier, before this book had even been suggested, I had interviewed Jane Iredale for my 'Stay Younger Longer' column in the *Daily Mail* newspaper. Her natural mineral cosmetics are used by many Hollywood stars. Weeks later, she sent me some wonderful samples – and to thank her, I had sent my books. Much to my amazement, she read *Divine Intervention* and sent me an email saying if I was ever in Hollywood I must meet a friend of hers. I had thanked her, but explained that I had no plans to return. But I had kept her number – just in case.

And here I was about to meet her friend – a real, honest-to-God Hollywood director, whose niece Helen Hunt is an Oscar-winning actress. And when we started chatting, the next synchronicity totally blew my mind. *The previous week*, one of Peter's daughters had dialled 911 – and reported that her room was full of dead people. Initially, the police presumed that there had been a dreadful murder and turned out in force. But when they arrived no bodies were to be found, and because Peter had read my book prior to our meeting, he and his wife quickly realized that their daughter was in fact seeing the spirit world.

To me this 'coincidence' was totally incredible. It felt as though I was in some kind of vortex, like a tornado, that sucks in all related incidents, people and experiences that one needs to align with one's intention and purpose – and whirls them down into your reality.

Peter and I discussed the possibility of making a film of my story. In that moment neither of us knew what the future might bring – but at least he was interested and believed in my story. We knew it had potential – and we determined to organize our energy to bring it into our reality. Thoughts, focused intention and actions, create our reality!

Tuesday, October 28, 2003

The next afternoon in the lounge at the airport, as I attempted to navigate a complex tea and coffee machine I said 'Hi' to an English chap waiting patiently behind me. We started chatting. And when he told me that his job is the head of Walt Disney pictures in the UK, I dropped my tea!

Enough, I thought. I had experienced sufficient excitement for one day – and it was time to sleep.

Heaven only knew what more was to come …

Things That Go Bump in the Night

... absent in body, but present in spirit ...
1 CORINTHIANS 5:3

When you are desperate to sleep, what is the one thing that eludes you? You are right ... the ability to surrender can be an elusive companion at times. By flying to America, I had surrendered to whatever the spirit world was preparing for me, but at the end of the day it had been my individual choice to go. And as I walked around the humming aircraft and looked at the sea of faces in various stages of sleep, I was envious of their ability to switch off in such cramped surroundings. There are indeed many gifts that no amount of money can buy.

To help me idle away another hour, I picked up an American newspaper. The case of Terri Schiavo caught my eye. This young woman had suffered heart failure in 1990 during her twenties after taking drugs for an eating disorder that have left her in a vegetative state in a hospice, being kept alive by machines and drugs. Her husband, Michael, has been fighting in the courts for over seven years to allow his wife the right to die with dignity, but her family is contesting the case. Whilst I had been in the States this story had featured on virtually every news bulletin – and even chat-show host Larry King devoted an entire show to the ethical issues involved.

When I had seen the pictures of Terri, I had honestly thought that had she been my sister, mother or daughter I would have allowed her to move on naturally, to be free from the prison her physical body has become. After all, renowned scientists such as Professor Schwartz are at last speaking out – stating that life after death exists, that we reincarnate, that we are recycled energy.

Yes, we need to respect all life, but I firmly believe that there are occasions where our obsession with keeping the physical body alive at all costs is misguided. On one hand people are being blown up on the whim of fanatics, and on the other are poor souls like Terri Schiavo. Yet again, there is an imbalance.

Every physical life is precious and should be treated with respect and, as much as possible, given the best treatment available – but at times there comes a point when, for whatever reason, physical surrender occurs and the body dies.

On a physical level, Diana did not want to die in that tunnel. She was young, vibrant and beautiful, and she had so much to live for. I believe that at a soul level, she had chosen to die young to help raise human consciousness – but I also truly believe that in the majority of cases most violent or sudden deaths are definitely not 'chosen' prior to incarnating.

Thinking along these lines, I recalled my conversation with an Irish medium, Christine Holohan, whom I had interviewed after being introduced by my old friend in synchronicity Veronica Keen.

Christine's is an incredible story. She has been psychic since childhood, but had learned through lessons at her local spiritualist church to tune into the spirit world more effectively via meditation. By her twenties, she had become an adept medium.

On Saturday, February 12, 1983 Christine was 29 and living in Ruislip, Middlesex, in the UK. She began to have a very uneasy feeling and started ringing around her relatives to make sure that everyone was okay. They were fine. And as the weekend progressed, Christine began to hear messages from a young woman who said that she had just been murdered.

Christine takes up her story.

'Initially the young woman's story was not clear, as her spirit was very upset and stressed. I told whoever she was to calm down, which would enable me to hear her more clearly. By the Sunday she was giving me really detailed facts. Then, on the Monday as I waited to pay at the till in my local store, I heard two women talking about the shocking murder of a local young woman called Jacqui Poole, which had happened on Friday 11th. But the spirit had said her name was Jacqui Hunt. As I sat to meditate that afternoon, I asked the spirit, "Are you this same Jacqui that was murdered on Friday?"

'"Yes," came the reply, "but my name used to be Poole."'

Christine had offered to help. As the police receive all manner of crank calls, Christine asked Jacqui to give really specific data as she did not want to waste valuable police time. Jacqui proceeded to tell Christine how she was killed, and that the killer's nickname was Porkie. She described his tattoos, gave the date of his birth and said that he had worked with cars; also, that he had come for her jewellery knowing that she carried it everywhere, but that he had left two rings that he could not prise off her finger in his haste. Additionally, Jacqui even told Christine that she had left a prescription for menstrual cramps in a specific place, and that she had been growing her nails and had scratched her murderer. The spirit even described how she had left the coffee cups on her draining board on that fateful day.

It's important to keep in mind that Christine had *never* met Jacqui. In psychic circles, such a case is known as a 'drop in' communicator. Jacqui was obviously trawling the area until she found a sensitive that she could approach – just as Diana has on many occasions since her physical death.

Christine eventually plucked up courage to phone the police when she heard Jacqui instruct her to 'Please call the police now' – just as Spirit had advised me when to call Gary Schwartz back in August 2003. And when she was put through, she was told that Tony Batters, the detective handling the murder, had just walked in. Surprise, surprise!

Once the police realized that Christine was in possession of intimate details about the case unknown to anyone else but themselves, they took her very seriously. She even provided the police with facts about their prime suspect of which they only became aware when they checked their databases.

Jacqui kept telling Christine to tell the police that when they found this man they should hang on to any of his personal belongings and check them against the evidence from under her fingernails. Unfortunately, in 1983 the police did not use DNA testing. But when they traced Porkie, who had claimed to be a friend of the deceased, they kept one of his sweaters along with samples from under his fingernails in cold storage for 18 years.

In 2001, thanks to DNA testing, the man known as Porkie – later named as Tony Ruark – was re-arrested, tried and convicted for Jacqui Poole's murder. He is now serving a life sentence.

Christine recalled that the spirit of Jacqui continued to visit her now and again over the years until after Ruark was arrested, but thankfully she then moved on. And Christine is now writing her own book, *Justice From Beyond the Grave*.

And when I had asked Christine, 'In all your years as a medium, whenever you have communicated with someone who has died suddenly or has met a violent death, have they ever said that their death was meant to be, that it was their time to go?'

'*Not once,*' was her emphatic reply. Interesting.

Meanwhile, the mystery surrounding Diana's death goes on, and I hope that one day, through good mediums like Laurie Campbell, Allison Dubois and Christine, that certain facts communicated by people who have passed over, including Diana, could be independently verified. Watch this space.

Tuesday, October 28, 2003 – London

After landing at Heathrow, as I hurried through the terminal, the newspaper headlines caught my eye. 'What a traitor,' they proclaimed, featuring pictures of Paul Burrell, Diana's former butler, castigating him for telling his story and thus 'betraying' Diana.

After the Princess's death, Paul had told the world that he would never tell his story. But I learned from my experience that you should never, ever, say never. Anyway, he had made that statement when his life had been going well. Mr Burrell was being fêted by the rich and famous, writing newspaper columns and books on style and etiquette. He was also working with the Princess's Trust.

Diana had 'told' me back in 1998 that Paul was 'Heading in the wrong direction, he was on the wrong track, which he would regret' – and because I had not at that time received Professor Grof's sage advice of *not* acting on all the insights and information one receives when going through an intense awakening, I had written to Mr Burrell. Silly me.

I invite you, for a moment, to place yourself in Mr Burrell's shoes. Imagine that your boss, the most famous and adored woman in the world, has died tragically; and your sense of loss almost destroys you, as you totally adored that person with every fibre of your being. During the following months, you receive hundreds, if not thousands, of letters about your ex-boss, plus dozens – or hundreds – of letters similar to mine, from mediums claiming contact with Diana. As I have said, you can listen to any messages that are purportedly from the spirit world, and you can choose whether to act upon them or not. That's free will. In the end you have to go with what you feel is right for you, and that's what he did. Much to my amazement though, he replied, saying that he felt his life was going on the right track, and he had thanked me for writing.

Now, I don't know Mr Burrell and I have never met him, so I do not judge him. Do you? He has to pay his bills like most people – and after his arrest most of the doors that had opened for him were slammed shut overnight.

When he was accused of stealing some of Diana's possessions, I thought of the dozens of outfits, plus handbags and objects, that over the years I have given to friends, to my housekeepers or secretary as gifts. So when I read his version of what he went through, you wonder why his case ever came to trial. I believe that there was a lot more to the case than we, the public, were ever told. And to me it seemed ludicrous that if Burrell had personal letters for the princes, why did he not just hand them over to Diana's sons – to whom it seems he had access – immediately after her death? Whatever the truth may be, I thoroughly enjoyed his book and felt that Diana would have loved it, too. As I sat reading I could not hear Diana myself, but I had received unique messages from her via Laurie and Allison that in my opinion could have only come from the spirit of Diana.

In the meantime, I needed to get back to my research. As I sat the next day mulling over where to turn next in my quest, I realized that no matter how many scientists you meet, and how much knowledge they share with you, there are always hundreds more questions to ask.

Later that week, I came across a fascinating interview I had done five years earlier with parapsychologist Dr Serena Roney-Dougal. Serena is a highly accredited and published scientist who has done important work, not only on spiritual emergency and related phenomena, but also on healing, life after death, precognition, and reincarnation, the power of the mind, plus ghosts – and things that go bump in the night.

I wondered if she might see me again. After all, back in 1998 she had helped to save my life. When I had seen her that June at the height of my awakening, I was struggling to remain physical as I had an increasing desire to merge with the 'all that is' and thus dissolve into pure consciousness. Eventually I had contacted Serena, whom I had met when I was working at *The Sunday Times*, in the desperate hope that she could offer me some answers. When we had met, she had listened with compassion whilst I related my story. And as I felt myself becoming lighter and lighter Serena had acted quickly, placing her hands firmly on my shoulders, whilst looking deeply into my eyes and stating with great authority:

'You are only Hazel, you are only Hazel. Say this.'

Like a robot I had whispered, 'I am only Hazel.'

And because my thoughts were creating my reality instantly – and I had believed her 100 percent – what did I become? Of course – only Hazel. In grounding me so effectively, Serena had saved my physical body from total burn-out and death. For several months afterwards I had remained psychic and could still hear Spirit, but a great percentage of the other phenomena ceased.

November 10, 2003 – Bristol, England

Again, the universe was assisting my quest, as when I called Serena, she told me that she had just one day left that she could spare for a meeting, before leaving for India on a research project. Perfect.

We greeted each other as old friends and as her schedule was tight, I plunged straight in. 'If,' I began, 'we are all part of some huge melting pot of consciousness, then how is it possible for mediums and psychics to receive specific – and at times verifiable – messages from either loved ones or total strangers who have passed over?'

'From all the research into mediums, ghosts and near-death experiences,' Serena explained, 'it appears that some newly arriving souls in the spirit world do not for some time either have access to, or merge with, the whole. During this period of up to 30–50 years the individual personality ego can remain in what you might call a waiting, or transition area, until such time that the soul is ready to move on and merge into the greater pool of consciousness. And in most cases mediums tend to contact souls of those who have died recently.'

'But,' I chipped in, 'what about mediums who claim to be receiving information from, say, Henry VIII, Joan of Arc or Jesus who have been dead for a long time, as numerous mediums often claim contact with such individual souls?'

Serena gave an ironic smile. 'The problem with the psychic world is that, as in any other sector of life, you occasionally have to deal with rather inflated egos. People can claim all kinds of contact with guides, or individual spirits – but as scientists, we need verifiable evidence.

'Also, there are cases in which psychics claim a direct contact with the unique soul of, say, Beethoven or Chopin, and these mediums channel similar music to that written by the individual composer. In this case, I would say that the person is bringing through the *spirit* of Beethoven's or Chopin's music – as when you question mediums in these cases, they rarely know anything about the composer's childhood, for instance, or intimate, little-known details of that person's life. It's mainly the music they bring through. The UK-based medium Rosemary Brown, who passed away in 2001, brought through the spirit of Beethoven and Chopin, and experts agreed that the music she channelled was very good.

'However, it does not quite have the unique genius of the individual composer; therefore in this instance I would say the medium has accessed the spirit of the music rather than the unique soul or personality of Beethoven or Chopin. Once the ego personality, the unique essence or soul that was Beethoven or whoever, merges with the whole, then what is channelled is Beethoven – but fuzzier. Like when you put on your TV and if a particular channel is not correctly tuned in there can be quite a lot of static on the screen, and yet you can still watch and hear the programme. But it's not crystal clear.

'Therefore, once the individual has left the waiting, or transition area or dimension, and merged with the whole pool of consciousness (which some people refer to as the akashic records) what the medium is tuning into is an aspect or facet of the whole.'

At this point, I was confused. 'Just a minute, Serena,' I interjected, 'are you saying that the akashic records are the same thing as the whole pool of consciousness?'

'In a sense. The akashic records are the information aspect of the whole.

When you talk about the whole or what Deepak Chopra and Professor Schwartz refer to as the collective database, or however people refer to it, you need to remember that as the whole manifests through to our see-and-touch reality, it goes through various levels of manifestation, one of which is the information level – which is a non-physical aspect of the whole. Therefore, when people channel specific information from a soul that has merged with the whole, what the channel is tuning into is the akashic record rather than the individual soul.'

Fascinating.

'Also,' she continued, 'you can tune into the spirit of a place. For instance, people see Roman soldiers marching up the Fosse Way, but they are not seeing the actual personalities of the soldiers that are still there. This is more like an energy video clip that keeps getting re-run. What you are connecting to here would be the spirit of Rome. The Romans left a huge energetic imprint that we can still experience. Or you can also tune into the collective spirit of science, or medicine and so on.'

As Serena said this, I thought about the ghost of Catherine Howard, Henry VIII's fifth wife, who was executed in February 1542, which has reportedly been seen hundreds of times in the haunted gallery at Hampton Court. Visitors have often reported screams and apparitions... surely, I asked Serena, this is an individual soul that has refused to move on?

'There are literally hundreds of realties in this and other realms. In this particular instance the 'ghost' of Catherine Howard, as far as I know, has never walked up to one of these visitors and said, "Hi, I'm Catherine Howard, how are you today?" There is no personal interaction. What you have here is not necessarily a trapped individual soul, but again a re-run of the traumatic energy which has remained in the energy field of Hampton Court.'

Okay then, I thought, what about ghosts that affect physical phenomena? There are thousands of documented cases where a specific ghost causes objects to be thrown around.

On this subject, Serena said, 'This is a classic case of what we would normally call a haunting, where a person dies physically but for whatever reason the energy remains. Unless they are helped to move on by specialist mediums, they can theoretically hang around as an 'energy ball' for a very long time. In this case the soul or spirit may contact anyone in their vicinity by making their presence known by moving objects, and so on. Mind and psychic energy can definitely affect physical matter. It can open and close doors, it can sound footprints, it can throw pots and pans around, it can do anything.'

Professor William Tiller, based at Stanford University in America, has spent 30 years researching the structure of matter and in his book *Science and Human Transformation* (Pavior Books) he explains how the spirit's individual emotional strength and intention can trigger such phenomena in our physical world. You can read the science behind this phenomenon in Chapter 14.

'The cases that involve teenagers, however,' added Serena, 'are normally known as poltergeist cases and there are many similarities between them and hauntings. However, hauntings normally last years if not decades, whilst poltergeist cases tend to last weeks or months. Also, hauntings are place-centred, whilst poltergeists focus on a particular person.'

As she said this I quickly asked her where people could turn for help in such cases.

'There are many trained priests, especially within the non-denominational Spiritualist Church; also, a trusted body like the Society for Psychical Research in London can put them in touch with an appropriate person.'

'In the meantime,' Serena continued, 'we need to keep in mind that just because someone is dead in the physical sense, they do not suddenly turn into saints overnight. If they were angry in life, then they tend to take their anger out on whoever is around. Ghosts can be just like us, moody and irritable, or benevolent and happy. It depends on what they were like in life, and the circumstances of their death. Again, multiple possibilities abound, but generally once a medium is called in and they can ascertain why the particular spirit has not moved on to the spirit realms, usually through negotiation the individual soul can be persuaded to move on.'

Listening to Serena I pictured the millions of 'energy balls' floating around the universe that most of us just can't see. Perhaps it's just as well; imagine the chaos if all dimensions merged into one. It would be like the film *The Sixth Sense* with Bruce Willis – most of us would not know who was real in the physical sense and who was not!

Then I asked Serena about the roomful of people that medium Allison Dubois, back in Arizona, had seen as being fairly solid individuals – they had spoken to her and turned out to be her husband's deceased relatives.

'But,' Serena explained, 'if Allison had placed a lighted cigarette on their 'bodies', no burns would have appeared. If you had tried to cut them with a knife they would not have bled. You state that Alison said that these 'people' had seemed slightly lighter and less dense that the rest of us, which is obvious as they no longer have a physical body. What appears is usually known as the etheric, astral or energy body. Yes, it can look solid – but fuzzier. We have heard of cases in such materializations where people shake hands with the 'ghosts' and have lengthy chats. It sounds incredible, but it can and does happen.'

Over several cups of herbal tea and copious amounts of delicious sandwiches, we also discussed spiritual possession, which is now termed as a 'walk in'.

'Before we scare everyone to death,' Serena began, 'possession as most people think of it – as in horror movies – is virtually unknown, and any type of spiritual possession is extremely rare. And it depends upon a person's culture; some people would consider that certain symptoms were linked to a spiritual possession, whereas in the West we might diagnose the same or similar symptoms as psychosis.

'But yes, I have seen cases of demonic possession, in which the person has been taken over by the spirit of evil. But possession does not have to be evil. For instance, when you claimed contact and possession by Princess Diana, would you say your experience was in any way evil?'

'Absolutely not!' I exclaimed.

'Every case is unique, and people often ask me, "Why has this happened to my daughter?" or their father, friend or whoever. As Stan Grof says, sometimes there may be an obvious trigger such as extreme stress, but where there is no apparent trigger or cause then I would say, why not them? It's like asking why one person develops meningitis and yet others don't. We don't always know why it happens, but we acknowledge that it does. And if people or their relatives believe that they may be possessed rather than psychotic, then they should contact specially trained members of the clergy such as Michael Perry, Dean of Durham Cathedral, and his experienced team.'

Serena also went on to explain that a few spirits, especially those who have met a violent or sudden death, can on occasion 'bounce' back into a new physical body. 'This is especially common in the cases of children who remember intimate details of their past lives. Such cases are more common in the East where there is a cultural belief in reincarnation, and let's say as an approximation this occurs in around one child in every million in the East, and in the UK and Western countries it is more like one in every ten million. It is a very rare occurrence. Such children are usually reborn within two years of their previous death and they tend to return to the local vicinity where they died, or even to the same family.'

As Serena said this, I recalled a fascinating interview with Ian Stevenson, Professor of Psychiatry at the University of Virginia Medical School in Charlottesville, America, who has documented over 2,000 cases of children who recall intimate details of previous lives. When we had last spoken I had asked him to recall the most amazing case he has come across. He had told me:

'In Thailand, I examined a child aged seven who had a small birth mark on the back of his head and a larger one above his left eye. Around the age of three he had begun playing at being a school teacher and had told his family that he had been murdered in his previous life. His illiterate parents ignored what they considered to be his childish imagination. However, when the child persisted, his grandmother eventually took him to the town over 18 miles away (30 kilometres or so) where her grandson, by then aged six, said he had lived.'

Professor Stevenson had interviewed the widow and family of the deceased teacher and the police pathologist who examined the body. The teacher had been shot through the head and the pathologist stated that the child's birth marks were in the same positions, and were the same sizes as the bullet's entry and exit wounds. The young child also spoke to his children from his previous life and after hearing him they began to call him 'father'. Stevenson was satisfied that neither family knew of the other's existence prior to this visit. His book *Where Re-Incarnation and Biology Intersect* (Praeger) documents many other fascinating cases.

'On the other hand, when it comes to individual souls bouncing back,' Serena reminded me, 'there are also enlightened souls like the Dalai Lama who, when departing from their physical body after death, are sufficiently spiritually advanced to hold their individual consciousness here on earth, so that they can be conceived again almost immediately, *whilst retaining all their memories.*'

This of course also answers the question as to why certain enlightened beings are born already knowing who they are and why they are here. 'And talking about living and dying consciously,' I interrupted again, 'what about inviting in the perfect spirit when one conceives?'

'Ah well, I can only talk about my own experience,' smiled Serena somewhat coyly. 'When I conceived my youngest daughter, my partner and I decided to conceive consciously. Whilst in a heightened state of expanded awareness during lovemaking, we invited our daughter in. And I became conscious of a light coming down, getting smaller and brighter and implanting itself in my womb.'

I was keen to hear Serena's opinion about when an individual soul enters the body.

'Different cultures believe different things. For some it can be the moment of conception as it was with me, for others the spirit can enter at any time until just prior to the birth.'

This made me think about all the times that I have heard parents say, 'I have no idea why we have had such a child – we seem to have nothing in common. They are not like us at all in personality.' Perhaps what we need to consider, I mused, is that unless we consciously choose a soul; we may get a soul that we did not bargain for.

'That's not quite correct,' Serena laughed. 'Think about it this way. When a baby is born, it typically has very little, let's say, hand–eye co-ordination. But day by day the baby grows and passes through various stages of natural development in the physical body. And if they are taught by loving parents, who set rules and boundaries, then in most cases that child grows up in a balanced and healthy way.

'But every physical body has a soul – the body is the temple of the soul. And within us all is the potential for joy, sorrow, good, evil, laughter, anger, compassion and so on. And for the most part how that soul develops greatly depends on how it is brought up, its life circumstances and so on, which interact with the unique soul and personality. So many people say, "Oh, this happened in that person's life because it's their karma," or "they chose this or that before they were born." Indeed there are to an extent multiple choices, but there is no way that people should say that if a child ends up with dysentery living on the streets of Brazil that the child chose to suffer from dysentery. Such statements are an "old age" concept. You cannot blame someone for the fact that their culture is bankrupt or their government's dishonest. My understanding of karma is the holographic concept, that every thought, word and action reverberates throughout the whole universe. Every thing is totally interconnected so what you do affects everything and you are likewise affected by everything.

'Unfortunately, the majority of humanity is still in nappies in spiritual terms; but little by little, our intuitive side is being prised open. In some cases people are having spiritual emergencies and some end up in mental homes because too much happens too fast; whilst others read spiritual books, meditate, chant or whatever and wake up more slowly. All we can do is encourage people to open up to this side of themselves, to live more at a soul level, so that they can truly understand what we are all capable of, and to come from a space of working together for the higher good.'

I couldn't have said it better myself. However, I was keen to return to the subject of every atom and cell containing all parts of the whole – as the majority of people find this quite difficult to comprehend.

As we chatted I kept harping on about how omnipotent I had felt back in 1998, like I had been the one and only, all-singing and dancing God.

Serena smiled. 'Okay, think of it this way.' She turned her chair around to look out of the two hotel windows in our meeting room and she invited me to do the same.

'Now,' she instructed, 'tell me what you can see from your window over there.'

'Well, the hotel skips, bags of rubbish – a wall, and so on.'

And what can *you see*? I enquired, rather tongue in cheek.

'A couple of trees, the road and a few people walking by.'

I was struggling to get her point.

'When you were in that state, you were "God", but in a very fuzzy way; you were "God" from *your* perspective. But you were not properly tuned in and you could not hold and integrate the pure signal, therefore you thought you knew it all, but you didn't.'

I sighed wistfully, recalling the magical moments back in 1998 when I had seen and understood the 'whole' clearly, when I had felt omnipotent, awesome, benevolent, all-knowing – but also totally humble. Serena gently brought me back into the moment.

'Think of the free hologram cards that you can find in various breakfast cereals. In order to see the whole picture you need to angle the card perfectly to the light.

'Every human being is like a hologram of the whole. For a time, you became more aware of being part of the whole, but from *your perspective from your angle.* The individual soul, which is part of the whole and contains all parts of the whole within it, has limitless potential depending on all its life's circumstances and some of the choices that were made before incarnating. You became the whole from the perspective of Hazel – this is a crucial point for anyone to consider who is going through a spiritual crisis, or even to a monk in a monastery. There is a seed of God in us all – but like all seeds it needs water, light, air, nourishment and plenty of TLC. And this is what the world needs to become whole again.

Serena really is a smashing lady. She doesn't mince her words, but her heart is definitely in the right place. And you will read more of her wisdom in Chapter 15.

Meanwhile, during that week I had received an email from a girlfriend in Australia telling me about her spiritual teacher – who she said had spent the last 15 years being taught by 800-year-old living saints in the Himalayas. I was highly sceptical, and in that moment I had dismissed her email as another 'Of course he has'-type message.

But, the universe was yet again weaving its incredible magic and in that moment I could not see the bigger picture that was due to unfold.

I was in for some amazing surprises.

The Melting Pot

The definition of madness is to keep doing what you have always done — and expect different results.

PATRICK HOLFORD

Saturday, November 22, 2003

The England team won the Rugby World Cup in Australia ... and the country went wild. I have never watched a rugby match in my life, but even I found myself glued to the TV during the final moments. The deafening cheers that went up in that stadium as thousands of fans including young Prince Harry celebrated were echoed in millions of homes, pubs and clubs around the globe. For several days afterwards there was a carnival atmosphere that reminded me of how our thoughts and emotions can affect our lives. The euphoria shared by so many fans was infectious – it felt as though we had all caught a dose of positive thinking. It had worked for a time, but as the winter set in and with so much negative news all around, the magic quietly evaporated. Also, in the run-up to Christmas I had completely forgotten about the email from my friend in Australia telling me about her spiritual teacher. Little did I know then what grand plans were being put into place ...

As the world celebrated Christmas, supposedly the traditional time of peace and goodwill to all men, suicide bombers went about their gruesome work in Israel and Lebanon. This carnage was dwarfed by mother nature on December 26 when she displayed her awesome power with an earthquake in Iran in which more than 25,000 souls perished. As I watched the horrors unfold on TV from the warm comfort of my home, I thought about how often people say, 'Welcome to the real world.' While watching the tragedies happening around the globe, I thought about the huge number of 'real worlds' on this planet alone. Millions are starving, whilst millions more are developing diabetes and heart disease – common factors in over eating. Some are as rich as Croesus, whilst others live on a few paltry seeds and grass, or they starve. And so on. The real world is what we all make it and it's where you are in this present moment.

The New Year dawned with cool sunshine in the UK – whilst my daughter was experiencing 35°C (95°F) – in Australia, and trying to cope with bush fires. Same planet, but worlds apart, yet both in the 'real' world.

In my real world, a newspaper feature on mental health caught my eye. 'Killings by the mentally disturbed increasing' proclaimed the headline. It went on to say that because numerous homes, hospitals and hostels for the mentally ill are closing, many confused, disturbed and sometimes volatile or dangerous people, a handful of whom may end up murdering someone, are finding their way back on to the streets.

As a health writer, almost six years earlier I had written about how dangerous and violent criminals in American prisons underwent positive behavioural changes, when they were given a healthier diet supplemented with extra vitamins, minerals and essential fats. I had also written about hyperactive children and teenagers who became calmer and easier to live with when artificial additives such as aspartame, plus excessive sugar and colourings were removed from their diet.

My friend the nutritionist and psychologist Patrick Holford, and many of his learned colleagues from the medical world, have long held the view that 'a significant proportion of mentally unwell people do not actually need prescription drugs – because the primary cause of their problem is not a lack of drugs, but most often a chemical imbalance brought on by years of inadequate nutrition and exposure to pollution, stress and environmental toxins.' And I wholeheartedly agree. But after reading the newspaper article, I was wondering how many mentally ill people might also be going through some kind of spiritual emergency. To answer this question, Dr Serena Roney-Dougal had suggested I should travel to Southampton to meet Isabel Clarke, a clinical psychologist who works in the National Health Service in the Department of Psychiatry at Royal South Hants Hospital, as Isabel has a specific interest in spiritual emergency. A rare lady indeed.

January 24, 2004 – Southampton, England

In preparation for my meeting with Isabel, Serena had sent me a fascinating magazine called *Network: The Scientific and Medical Network Review* – containing a feature by Isabel entitled *Psychosis and Spirituality – Finding a Language*. It began:

'Psychosis and spirituality both inhabit the space where reason breaks down and mystery takes over. For me as a psychotherapist working with people with varying psychoses, this encounter poses questions such as, "Why is religious/spiritual preoccupation and subject matter so prominent in psychosis?" and "How come they both share a sense of portentousness and supernatural power, and where does this sense come from?"'

Where indeed, I wondered. She then discusses how, over the years working in psychiatric rehabilitation, the accepted parameters of conditions such as psychoses and schizophrenia had begun to blur. A lady after my own heart.

And as I delved further into the magazine I came across the story of a woman who had gone through her own unique kundalini awakening, and I thought that anyone going through a profound spiritual experience would find many useful contacts via this network. Find details on www.scimednet.org

An hour or so later, and a little wiser, I stepped off the train to be met by Isabel, and in her car we instantly struck up a rapport and chatted easily about her work. Her husband, Chris, greeted us with great enthusiasm and it's obvious that they both enjoy their work hugely. Until recently Chris Clarke was Professor of Applied Mathematics, Physics and Astrophysics at Southampton University, but these days he is using his considerable IQ to help fellow academics understand the science of spiritual phenomena. Both he and Isabel are keen to encourage their colleagues to change the labelling classifications of mental illness. It was an honour to meet two such like-minded individuals.

Over an incredibly healthy lunch of organic soup made with warming lentils and fresh organic vegetables, I asked Isabel how she defines a spiritual emergency.

'Like Professor Grof, I'm not keen on labels as such – and you have already listed many of the symptoms in Chapter 7. What interests Chris and me is encountering people who cross into what we term the 'transliminal' – they are crossing a threshold that separates them from their normal everyday life into a far greater reality. Words and labels at such a point cease to be particularly precise, and as you and Stan have already explained, for some people this "crossing over" can cause terror, whilst for others it's blissful, with myriad symptoms and experiences in between. And so my job is to try and negotiate a balance with the patient, so that they can cope. When it's appropriate, I teach them to control this "gateway", or threshold, into other realities, so that firstly they can tell the difference between this reality and others; secondly, I offer them the tools for coping in the present in this world, and thirdly, to move between the two and not to get completely lost in the other state, as then they would find living in the here and now almost impossible.

'I have to use a language that the individual can relate to and understand. This approach fits reasonably well within the framework of Cognitive Behavioural Therapy, which is the recommended therapy for psychosis in the NHS. This therapy helps people to make sense of their experiences and stresses working together, which gives the patient a feeling of being more in control of their healing process. The difference between myself and most of my colleagues is that I use the spiritual dimension to assist in the 'sense-making' process. In the meantime, I would never recommend that anyone tries to manage these kinds of situations on their own. You need friends or a community to help keep you grounded and to help stabilize you, otherwise the potential dangers are enormous. Also, at such times, people are very vulnerable and this is when they can easily become involved with cultish-type activities.'

As she was speaking, I truly wished that I could have met her back in 1998, when my realities had definitely begun to blur.

'By the time someone is referred to me,' she continued, 'they are usually on some kind of medication. I would like people to be given more choice about this, but I'm afraid the current situation will remain for some time. However, as the client-led recovery approach is gradually adopted, the outlook should gradually improve.'

I wondered had Isabel witnessed phenomena such as levitation, telepathy or manifesting objects in her patients?

'Many of them report phenomena such as telepathy and telekinesis (moving objects from a distance) – but I quickly work on bringing them down to earth, or the drugs shut down such experiences – so the phenomena stop when they are with me, so no, I have never personally witnessed any.'

What a shame. Three days earlier I had received an email out of the blue from a young woman in southwestern Gujarat in India who had read *Divine Intervention*; she was asking for my help as she had begun to levitate and see frightening images in her bedroom. Initially I had been wary of becoming involved, as some people in the East who may not have received an impartial education, or no education at all, tend to believe customs and phenomena from within their culture, or what they are told by people who they presume know more than they do. In fact Dr Serena Roney-Dougal had told me back in November that in her 25 years as a parapsychologist she had never once seen anyone from a Hindu, Moslem, Buddhist or Shamanic culture with stigmata. The cases she had witnessed were either devout Christians or people who had grown up in a Christian culture in which the cross is a common symbol. But she is now hearing of more Western people who are, for instance, making ash as I did, because they have been exposed to Indian cultures. In other words, because I had *known* that Sai Baba and others could materialize ash, I *knew* that I could do it, too.

However, this young woman, Jatinder, was studying for a degree in sociology, archaeology and English, and she was not particularly attached to any specific religion. She was still searching. Out of curiosity I telephoned Jatinder, who told me her experience had begun three years earlier (she is at the time of writing 22). She had woken up one night to find herself floating five feet above her bed. Her scream of incredulous surprise and fright caused her to fall back on the bed. There was, she believed, no obvious trigger for this phenomenon to happen. Within days, she had become very psychic and began predicting the near future for her classmates.

During the first year Jatinder had great fun with her newly discovered talents, especially when she found that she could 'travel' out of her body and visit other cities, which she would then describe in intimate detail to her amazed friends. But when she started to see 'dead' people, like in the film *The Sixth Sense*, she suddenly became very afraid. And surprise, surprise − what happened? Of course, her fear attracted some rather negative spirits, especially at night. Like attracts like. At this point, she finally confided to her parents, who took her for numerous medical tests at the best hospitals, and all the doctors were perplexed.

These days she sleeps with her bedroom light on, and in this way she manages to keep out most of her nocturnal visitors. We chatted at length, and it soon became obvious that Jatinder is a highly intelligent and balanced individual. And as many of the occurrences she described had in some ways mirrored my own, I advised her to sit quietly for about 20 minutes each day and visualize herself as being enclosed in a balloon shape filled with pure white light. Also, to imagine that this balloon was mirrored on the outside and that it was made of solid metal. In other words any nasty visitors would 'hit' her mirrored balloon and be reflected back from whence they came. She promised to try this exercise and recently I was relieved to hear from her that this simple technique has greatly reduced the negative incidents. Less fear, less negative incidents. The science as to how levitation is possible and why the visualization works can be found in Chapter 14.

Having received letters from people of all ages going through varying types of spiritual emergency, including a 13-year-old girl, I asked Isabel if there is a common age for her patients undergoing spiritual experiences.

'Because I work in a rehabilitation unit, I don't treat young children,' she replied, 'but it's well documented that children tend to have more open minds and they can generally move backwards and forwards in between these realities far more easily than adults.

'The patient's age may depend on what has triggered the emergency. For instance, drug-related cases tend to be in their teens or twenties; some are younger, whilst others are in their thirties onwards. But this type of crossing over can happen at any age. We see men and women of all ages going through what you might term spiritual emergency.'

I continued, 'Then, would you say this type of experience is becoming more common?'

'Yes I do … why? Because today many family traditions are being abandoned and what we are seeing is greater fragmentation in our cultures. Whilst some religions offer people a better sense of community and support – and by the way, if you study the world's major religions, in essence they all recognize this sort of reality in some form – unfortunately, with so much fragmentation, we are seeing more cases of rigid black-and-white beliefs that do not help individuals to navigate this territory. In fact, like Stan Grof, Serena Roney-Dougal and many others, I firmly believe that diagnosis is

Above left: This is me on the private jet on my way to see
Sai Baba in Puttaparthi in November 2000.

Above right: Sai Baba the Avatar, in India, who is surrounded by controversy.

Above: This is the main street of Puttaparthi, leading to Sai Baba's ashram.
Hardly Fifth Avenue!

Top: Sunday 19th October 2003 with professor Gary Schwartz (on my left), and mediums Allison Dubois (on my immediate right) and Laurie Campbell, plus Allison's husband Joe, after a long, hot day taking part in Gary's Afterlife Experiments in Tuscon, Arizona.

Above left: His Holiness Satguru Shree Shivkrupanandji, a fascinating spiritual teacher whom I interviewed in April 2004.

Above right: This image appeared on Harry Oldfield's scanner during research into energy fields present in mortuaries. I can clearly make out a male-looking figure who appears to have long hair and a beard. Like many spiritual people, I believe that spirits come to 'help' people when they first pass over, and Harry speculates that this might be such a spirit – hence why Harry named this 'figure' Angelos.

Picture reproduced by kind permission of Oldfield Systems Ltd.

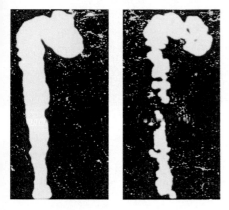

A scan shown in black and white clearly denotes a fully active kundalini energy tracking up the spine on the left and how the kundalini energy 'calms down' (right) after Harry treated the patient, who was in the midst of a spiritual crisis, with calming frequencies.
Pictures reproduced by kind permission of Oldfield Systems Ltd.

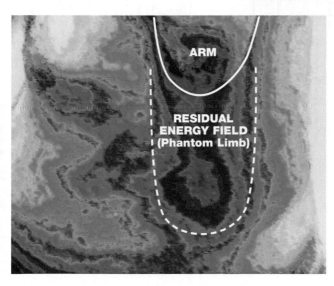

ARM

RESIDUAL
ENERGY FIELD
(Phantom Limb)

Above: Harry showed me this picture of severe pain (shown as bright pink) tracking down my leg from my spine, which did not manifest until a month after the scan was taken. He 'saw' the pain before it manifested physically, which to me was incredible.

This amazing scan of the left side of the body shows the end of a severed physical arm, but also a defined energy field in the shape of an arm where the arm had once been, thus helping to explain the phantom limb phenomenon.

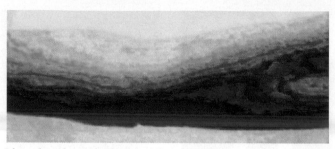

For years I have heard people decrying that the meridian energy channels are in our imagination. Well, here they are. This is a PIP scan of my right arm taken in July 2004 – the energy channels are the blue, yellow, green and red lines.

Picture with kind permission of Oldfield Systems Ltd.

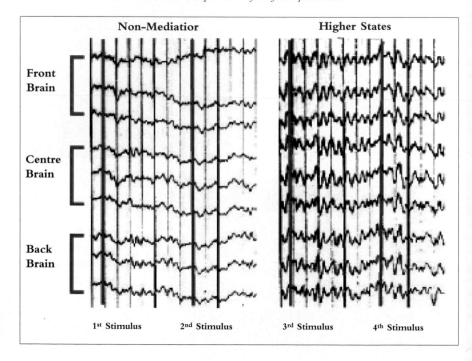

The left-hand tracings show brainwaves of a 'non-meditator' during a reaction-time test. The red lines are the points at which stimulus in the form of numbers were shown to the person. The brain is completely focused on the task, which results in low-voltage EEG (electroencephalograph) readings. The right-hand tracings show the brainwaves of an enlightened person. Notice the high coherence of the EEG, in other words the activity of different parts of the brain are working together. This unified level of brain activity allows the individual to access and become as one with the full field of universal intelligence that is underlying all of life.

Reproduced by kind permission of Travis et al, Consciousness and Cognition, 13:401–420, 2004.

misleading here and the entire concept of schizophrenia, for instance, is highly dubious.'

When Isabel mentioned schizophrenia I thought about the Hollywood film *A Beautiful Mind*, starring Russell Crowe, who brilliantly portrays the life of John Nash Jr, the Nobel Prize-winning academic who at the age of 31 began experiencing what Dr Nash terms 'dream-like' delusional states. He began 'seeing' and 'hearing' people who did not exist in this dimension and was diagnosed as being schizophrenic. Serena had told me that when people are in spiritual emergency situations they are in essence experiencing vivid dreaming whilst they are awake, and Stan Grof had said, 'while their doctors and relatives think the experience has no basis in reality, the person may feel that their everyday life is like a dream and that their new reality is far more real.' During my experience I had definitely felt that my 'dreams' were becoming part of my reality and at times I had found it difficult to distinguish one from the other. And so did John Nash, who had spent several months in various hospitals in America, always, as he is at pains to point out, on an involuntary basis, and always attempting a legal argument for his release.

Sitting with Isabel, discussing 'crossing thresholds', I could not help but come to the conclusion that John Nash and thousands of people around the world today (and for eons before us) were and are in many cases passing through a spiritual-type awakening that becomes unbalanced.

Consider for a moment the story of St Joan of Arc. She was obsessively religious and often attended confession three times a day. At the age of 13, with all her teenage hormones gearing up, she began seeing visions of Archangel Michael, and later saw and heard St Catherine and St Margaret. Whilst she was winning battles, Joan of Arc was a celebrity; but when she started losing them she was executed for heresy at just 19 years of age. How different history might have been, I wonder, if Joan could have read and understood books such as these and eaten more porridge!

It helps to think on multiple levels at this point. On one level you could suggest that schizophrenia runs in families – and to an extent it does, especially in genius-level families. But you should also consider that fluctuating blood sugar levels, mainly due to eating far too much refined foods and sugary foods and drinks, can also trigger similar symptoms. Your brain chemistry can become highly imbalanced, and taking more Omega 3 and 6 essential fats found in fish oils, hemp seeds and linseeds and so on, plus vitamins A, B complex, C and E, and minerals like zinc and magnesium can help re-balance the brain. Extreme food intolerances and negative stress can also trigger unusual mental symptoms. On Patrick Holford's great website www.mentalhealthproject.com there is a large amount of information on mental illness, depression and schizophrenia that may match your or a loved one's symptoms, along with numerous ideas on how to cope with them more naturally. Believe me I'm not trying to stop anyone seeing a doctor, but at least go to your doctor armed with this information, and you may be able to point him or her in a more appropriate direction.

As I sat discussing my concepts with Isabel, I asked for her professional opinion.

'I agree that instead of instantly labelling a person as suffering from this or that, we need to look at their whole health, their stress levels, their lifestyle and circumstances and so on. And this is what we try to do at our clinic.

'Of course there are some people who definitely do not fit into what you might term a spiritual emergency situation, and such people need appropriate help. However, a lot of cases in which spirituality is involved unfortunately still end up in hospitals, as at this moment they seem to be the only resource available.'

Thank goodness there now seems to be a light on the horizon. Isabel told me that mental health services in England are slowly adopting a client-led recovery approach which should offer the patients more choice. She also told me that the concept of spiritual psychosis has been recognized by the official American guide to diagnosis in psychiatry, which is called the

DSM4. Isabel reiterated that she is not keen on labelling or diagnosing, but she is now working with professionals who want the individual's experience to be taken seriously, and she hopes that in the years to come many cases can have far happier endings.

This was great news, especially after listening to Julie James's horrendous story in Chapter 7. Thinking of the number of hypochondriacs I have met during my years as a health writer, I asked Isabel if some patients became very attached to their experiences.

'Absolutely. If it's a blissful-type awakening then obviously the person does not want it to go away; if it's fearful, they definitely want it to stop. For some of those in between, it brings them attention. But whatever is happening, we always work towards helping these people find a balance so that they can return to a "normal" everyday life.'

This statement reminded me of a girlfriend who has now been going through her spiritual awakening for over five years. And every month or so she rings to tell me the whereabouts of her kundalini, or that she is definitely working with the energy of the Indian goddess Shiva, that Jesus has told her (and only her) the answers to many profound questions and that she is one of the most enlightened people alive on the planet today. Yeah, yeah, yeah. In between these insights, she manages to run a fairly successful business and look after her family. On numerous occasions I have tried to tell her that some of her experiences are also happening to others. But will she listen? No. As I have said before, you can lead a horse to water but you cannot make them drink. She is what I term a spiritual emergency bore. Back in late 1998 I became one, too. Walking in Hyde Park with my healer friend Kelvin Heard, excitedly sharing my latest insight, prediction or what I believed Princess Diana had said, he turned to me and sighed, 'Hazel, it's time to let all this go. You have had the experience, and now it's time to move on.' A very wise statement – and yet like a teenager who 'knows' everything, I found in the long term that my outcome has been more positive because I allowed the experience to run its natural course.

Before leaving Chris and Isabel, I asked if they had come across anyone who had gone through an unusual spiritual awakening who might agree to an interview. They suggested Janice Hartley from the Wirral, near Liverpool, who bravely agreed to share her story here. In the meantime, if you would like to know more about Professor Chris Clarke's thought-provoking work, log on to www.scispirit.com or for Isabel, look at www.scispirit.com/Psychosis_Spirituality/

In the autumn of 1998, 40-year-old Janice Hartley was working full-time in the IT industry in Liverpool – a normal busy mum with two young children who were 7 and 11.

Her world fell apart when her husband, who was only 43, suffered a severe stroke which left him paralysed. Janice takes up her story.

'It was like a bolt out of the blue. One day you have what you consider to be a good, steady life and the next your world is turned upside down. 'Obviously, as the weeks passed, the situation became a major stress for us all, as I was trying to keep up with my job and take care of my children and visit my husband, who was understandably very depressed at the enormity of his disabilities.

'The physiotherapy people at the hospital insisted that I should learn how to work with my husband on myriad necessary exercises, so that he would improve sufficiently to enable him to come home for Christmas.

'In preparation for his coming home, several medical people arrived at our home, moving beds and furniture and measuring everywhere ready for the wheelchair. I know they were only doing their job, but to me they seemed like invaders, and their intrusions wound me up even more. Every day the pressure built until I felt as though I couldn't carry on.

'In late January 1999, all our repressed emotions exploded, and my husband and I had a terrible row – it was appalling. We both said hurtful things – and something inside me snapped. Overnight, I began to see the world as a very negative place, and in the heat of the moment I demanded a divorce. My sanity was at breaking point. The hospital reluctantly agreed to take my husband back to give me a break as we were no longer speaking to each other.

'Four days later I walked to a headland on the Wirral where there is an island, Tilbury Island, between us and the Welsh coast. As I looked across at the grey stormy islet, I felt it was where I needed to be, it was where I might find some peace. The tide was out, and without any thought for my safety, I just walked out across the sandbanks. Whether I lived or died no longer held any fear for me, nothing mattered, and everything began to have this surreal dream-like quality to it. And in those moments I experienced this incredible sense of freedom; any attachment to *anything* had gone. When I reached the island, all these sea birds were circling above my head and I suddenly realized I knew the names of each type of breed – which I had never previously known.'

I interrupt Janice's story at this point to remind you that stress is definitely a huge trigger for spiritual emergency. If Janice had been less fit, at this moment she could have suffered a heart attack – any physical fuse could have blown. What I experienced in Harrods, Janice experienced on Tilbury Island – this can happen anywhere. I have even met a man on a plane whose kundalini had blown in a Chinese restaurant! At that moment of total freedom I believe Janice's kundalini energy had exploded, just as mine had, and that she had access to the 'all that is'. Her brain chemistry would have been greatly altered not only by the prolonged stress, but also by the huge release of spiritual energy. As Isabel might have put it, Janice had 'crossed over a threshold' into another reality.

Back to Janice's story.

'As I made my way home, it was as though I was seeing things through new eyes for the first time. When I saw an old man with his dog it was as though I was feeling the love inside me that he felt for his dog. As the days passed, I was continually woken up at night with these incredible insights and I no longer wanted to eat. At one point I became extremely cold and frightened and things started to become very negative. I went through an out-of-body experience in which I felt this hugely negative presence, and I thought I was going totally mad.'

This was almost exactly what had happened to me; the initial euphoria, then desperately trying to sort things out from this reality and the new ones at the same time. Because you are creating your own reality, your thoughts at this moment can greatly affect what happens next. This was definitely the case for Janice, who went on:

'I had been brought up in the church, and thought that perhaps God was in some way punishing me. I remembered all this stuff from school – that God punishes people if they do wrong, and I wondered if He was coming for my soul. When it reached a point at which I could not sleep at all, in total despair I dialled 999. I was taken to a psychiatric unit, and they gave me some drugs that have now been banned.

'Until that moment, like most people in our society I had always felt some prejudice towards people who were mentally ill, but I slowly began to understand that mental illness is more about life's circumstances. One extremely powerful insight that came to me in the hospital like a bolt of electricity is that there is little real mental illness; the doctors have got it wrong. It was a powerful realization to find that most of the people in that hospital were like me, and I came to have an empathy with them all. In fact I met several people who had been diagnosed as schizophrenics and medicated for 20 years – and to my mind these are crimes against humanity.

'After a week I was allowed home, but received no counselling or support. To try to help myself I began studying psychology in an effort to understand what had happened to me, and at a conference I met Isabel Clarke, who talked about a whole new approach to mental health, which made absolute sense of my experience. Slowly but surely I rebuilt my life. I began to sort myself out, and to understand that most of the negative stuff was coming up from my subconscious, and it was all old wounds that I needed to heal.

'And how has it changed me? Well, I am definitely more intuitive and more sensitive, and I have far more patience then I did before, and I now know that in some way we are indeed all ultimately linked. Today I do voluntary work within the Hearing Voices Network, who try to help people from all walks of life who are going through their own unique experiences. I am no longer ashamed to say that I suffered from psychosis – in fact I am proud of it – in the hope that other people can come through their own crisis and learn from it. Thankfully, my husband and I weathered our own crisis and today we are very much back together, and he has regained much of his health.'

What a magical, cheerful and positive lady. For anyone experiencing voices or visions and would like more help the Hearing Voices Network can be found on www.hearing-voices.org

Meanwhile, during February I escaped with my husband to Cape Town to discover another reality and another real world. Upon returning home, my Reiki healer friend Debbie Heron had sent another email from Australia, telling me that her spiritual teacher, who is considered to be an enlightened master, was coming to England in April – and would I like to meet him? Would I ever.

10   The Enlightened Masters

*All this talk and turmoil and noise and movement
and desire is outside of the veil – within the veil is silence
and calm and rest.*

BAYAZID AL-BISTAMI

April 22 – Cheltenham, England

As I sat on the high-speed intercity train, making my way from London
to Cheltenham to meet my friend's spiritual teacher, I wondered how we
might all determine if a man or woman is truly an enlightened being.
Wouldn't it make life easier for us mere mortals if they had various
certificates stating,

'We/I hereby certify this person is enlightened to level 1, level 2 or
level 10?'

But they don't.

And yet there has to be a way of *knowing* that a person is who or what
they – or more likely their followers – claim them to be. In fact, most truly
enlightened beings don't go around saying 'Hi, I'm enlightened,' they just
live their light and their love. And if a scientist were to try to measure pure
unconditional love, how would they do that? This is an area in which we
can begin walking on quicksand, as there are indeed many false prophets.

When I asked Dr Serena Roney-Dougal how she judges whether a person is fully enlightened, she asked me what I meant by 'enlightened'. Don't you just love people who answer a question with another question?

I had summarized my interpretation by saying that a fully enlightened master of the self has limitless potential — in that they can choose which 'miracles' to effect, from altering the weather or appearing in different locations from where they are physically, to having the ability to control their heartbeat and blood pressure; they are telepathic, super psychic, can effect miracles of physical healing, manifest physical objects, and so on.

Firstly, Serena had recommended that I stop using the words 'master of the self', as such a term she stated suggests hierarchy, authority and autocracy.

I understood perfectly what she had meant. I had seen so many people worshipping Sai Baba, Mother Meera and other enlightened people. The problem is that some worship the physical body of their guru rather than the energy or consciousness that flows through that person. They still think of God as being 'out there', which creates separation.

'Great teachers, or whatever you choose to call them,' Serena had continued, 'have gone beyond the physical animal level of being — they are operating from a soul level of being, in that they can go beyond thought and then go on developing even further. They have done years of training — this is not just someone who has had a kundalini-type awakening in Harrods and thinks they are enlightened. Anyway, there are hugely varying degrees of enlightenment.

'Such men and woman have total mastery over their physical bodies but can also function on an everyday level. Therefore, when you meet a person that you believe to be enlightened, look at their lifestyle, look at how they live their lives, what they eat and what spiritual practices they do. Are they honest with you? Do they have a big ego? And, most importantly, how do you feel when you are in their presence?'

When I had posed the same question to Dr David Simon at the Chopra Center in California, he had told me that during his experiences with a fully enlightened person he had no sense of drama, anguish or anxiety – more a sense of joy, lightness and even playfulness.

Keeping all their advice in mind, as I watched the rolling countryside flash by I brought myself back into the moment by studying the information about the holy man I was about to meet. His name is His Holiness Satguru Shree Shivkrupanandji Swami – which is quite a mouthful in any language. *Swami* means 'a master of the self,' and *gu-ru* means 'from dark to light', so a guru is someone who removes darkness and brings light. And remember, light carries information.

On the website dedicated to his work (www.shivkrupanandji.org) I had found a short biography, which reads like a fantastic spiritual fairytale. There are also some amazing pictures taken with an ordinary camera that clearly show considerable amounts of white light emanating from his chakras.

Born into a Hindu family in India in 1954, from a very early age Swamiji displayed an unusual curiosity about the existence of God. Until his late twenties he lived a normal family life, completed a Masters degree in Business Studies and then worked for a large commercial company.

One day he was sent to the north of India, but when he finally arrived there was a 10-day bank strike which prevented him from doing his work. And so, on the spur of the moment he decided to fulfil a long-held desire to see Kathmandu. On his first morning, during a visit to a local temple, he was approached by an elderly gentleman who greeted the young businessman by name and told him that he had been expecting him for three days. Swamiji was stunned as he had only decided to come to Nepal on a whim because of the bank strike …

The elderly man invited the inquisitive youth on a journey lasting several days. Eventually, they came to a tiny village, in which he was asked to sit on a large stone outside a cave – and wait.

At sunset, another elderly man appeared from the cave. Swamiji was in awe of what was happening, but intuitively he knew that this aged man with piercing blue eyes was a true holy man, and therefore knelt before him. The old man introduced himself as Shivbaba, and told his newly arrived guest that he had been waiting for him for almost 40 years – long before Swamiji had even been born! This made me think again of my concept that certain events are indeed 'set in stone'.

Within the cave Shivbaba gave his guest some water that he had vibrated with his energy – which took Swamiji into a trance lasting three days. At this point, I wistfully thought how great it would be to go into a trance for just 15 minutes.

Meanwhile, when the young man finally awoke, Shivbaba told him that he had passed all his knowledge and power to Swamiji, and had therefore completed his mission. The next day Shivbaba, aged 96, 'died'.

Meanwhile, the banks returned to work after their strike and so did the young man. He returned to Calcutta, got married and had three children – two boys and a girl. Years later, seemingly out of the blue, another holy man arrived at their home to tell the young father that it was now time for him to begin his true purpose. With his wife's permission, Swamiji left his family to travel with the holy man far into the Himalayas.

For the next 15 years, Swamiji lived an austere life in some of the world's harshest environments … and one day, I thought, I would love to hear what happened in detail during those years – but for now I just had to prepare my questions.

The short version of those years is that he was taught by various gurus, monks, siddhas, rishis and yogic masters who each taught him what they knew, and then passed him on to another guru, each working with even higher vibrations, until finally he sat with the high gurus, yogic masters and living saints – who communicate *only* by vibration.

When he had completed his training, he was given his current name, which represents the universal consciousness which flows through his body; *shiva* means 'supreme consciousness'; *krupa*, 'blessing'; and *ananda*, 'bliss', which reads 'supreme consciousness (God) blessing us with divine bliss'.

At this point, Swamiji was asked by his gurus to retrace his journey back into the world, to share his knowledge and light with those who were ready to listen. His individual mission is to assist in the awakening or attuning of the kundalini energy via meditation, to help accelerate people's spiritual awakening process in a safe way. And today in India between 10,000 and 100,000 people at a time come to receive his blessings.

What a story. I had heard of great masters who have lived for several hundred years in the same physical body – and I was about to meet one of their pupils. When I began this book, in my wildest dreams I had not conceived that I might be granted a one-on-one interview with a living enlightened being. Not only that, but one who happened to be in Cheltenham! *Divine Intervention* for sure …

Yes, I had spoken to Sai Baba in India, but very briefly. Yes, I had met and talked for an hour or so to Swami Satchidananda in America, but he passed away in 2002. Suddenly the full reality of what my friend Debbie in Australia had meant when she had said, 'Do you realize what an honour it is to be invited to meet with him one on one?' finally hit me. In the moment she had said this I had been very flippant, but now I wasn't. Everything to do with this book was unfolding in the most incredible sequence. Suddenly I felt very humble indeed.

As my head began to throb in anticipation, I knew that I needed grounding. A bowl of brown rice, tofu and vegetables would have been great – but on a train such food is hardly on the menu. I would have to make do with a coffee and biscuit, which was all the buffet service had left. Yet again, I made a note to write to the train operators and suggest some healthy snacks they might like to offer their customers. Never give up, as Winston Churchill used to say.

I alighted into a beautiful spring day and was met by a devotee of Swamiji called Emma, who works for the Ministry of Defence. Very grounding. Her flat was light and airy, and following introductions to Swamiji's charming and gentle interpreter, Srila, and her engineer husband, tea and more biscuits followed. As I swallowed yet another digestive biscuit,

I mentally thought about the salad I would enjoy when I got home. Balance, I reminded myself, it's all about balance.

The four of us chatted like old friends, and after ten minutes Srila suggested we should sit quietly before Swamiji joined us. The next few moments seemed to last for hours, but after about 15 minutes in walked the Holy man. He was wearing a bright orange full-length robe, just as Sai Baba had when we met in November 2000. Physically Swamiji is also tiny – maybe 1.5 metres (five feet two inches or so) – his receding hair and beard are long and grey and initially I thought he looked somewhat older than his 50 years. Until he smiled – when his face changed completely, resembling that of a small, cheeky child; it was like watching the sun come out. I tried to recall a Bible quote from Jesus – something like, 'Be as a child if you want to enter the kingdom of heaven.' It was a smile of pure innocence.

Once he had made himself comfortable on the sofa opposite me, Swamiji became more formal as he focused intently upon me with his large dark eyes. Instantly I knew that he was completely telepathic. I mentally brought myself totally into the moment and concentrated on the questions I had written during my journey. Just as well, otherwise I might have started jibbering, just like a star-struck fan upon meeting someone like George Clooney. I was in spiritual Hollywood.

I returned his gaze without blinking and began, 'At what moment did you consider yourself to be a fully enlightened being?'

Srila looked apprehensive, but she interpreted. Swamiji began answering in Hindu before she could finish.

'Swamiji,' she smiled, 'is asking what you mean by enlightened?' Maybe he is related to Serena, I thought, but then checked myself. My personal interpretation was duly translated.

'Oh,' said Srila and Swamiji almost in unison, 'we call that liberated or self-realized.'

Through Srila, the holy man told me that he had finally accepted that he had become fully liberated during August 1999, when a vision of Sai Baba of Shirdi (who 'died' in 1918), asked the Swamiji to awaken the kundalini energy of one of his (Sai Baba's) devotees. Swamiji did this willingly – and at that moment accepted that he had been chosen by many 'dead' and living saints and gurus to completely surrender to the ultimate source that they all represent. Thus he began his mission as one of them.

This was interesting as Sai Baba in India has stated that he is the reincarnation of Sai Baba of Shirdi. Yet when I had met Sai Baba – who obviously does great work and is revered by millions – his specific energies did not ring my bell. The energy of the man sitting before me did. A different teacher emitting a different range of frequencies I presumed. With this in mind I asked 'Could one guru such as yourself be right for everyone?'

'No,' he smiled humbly. 'One guru cannot resonate with all people, as all people are resonating on their own unique range of frequencies. You need to find a guru whom you feel comfortable with, whom you can totally surrender to at a soul level, and then you can stop searching and start learning and experiencing. You have read many books, but knowledge without experience and wisdom is not necessarily helpful. My knowing comes from the inside, and from all my experiences.'

As I stared into his eyes and absorbed the light emanating from them, all thoughts began slipping gently from my mind. This, I knew, was the effect of being in his powerful energy field, which is one of pure unconditional love and total detachment. Rather than any kind of physical adoration, it was more a feeling of being 'at home'.

He spoke again without the need for a question.

'I have no existence or name of my own, so think of me as a flowing river – and if people want what **I** offer, then they need to draw water and drink of **My** energy, **My** consciousness.'

Here, when he says '**My**' and '**I**', he is speaking as a fully God-realized being; there is no longer any separation – as Jesus said, 'My father and I are one'. Great saints have known and understood for thousands of years that there is ultimately no separation. The fifteenth-century Christian mystic

Catherine Adorna of Genoa once said, 'My being is God, not by simple participation, but by a true transformation of my being.' The fourteenth-century Kabbalist Moses de León said, 'God in the complete unfolding of His Being, bliss and love, in which He becomes capable of being perceived by the reasons of the heart ... *is called You.*' Meister Eckhart, the thirteenth-century Dominican monk, wrote: 'In this breaking through I receive that God and I are one. Then I am what I was, and then I neither diminish nor increase, for I am then an immovable cause that moves all things.'

To help ground our interview, I returned to basics by asking the holy man in front of me if he needs to eat physical food.

'Of course I do,' he laughed. 'If I wanted to fast for months, I could do this. Last year I meditated for a whole month and went without food or drink, but eventually my disciples begged me to eat, which helps me to remain physically in this dimension.'

Thinking about Serena's advice and noticing his large tummy, I asked, 'Are you careful about what you eat?'

'Many yogis,' he smiled indulgently, 'have large abdomens. When a baby is in the womb it receives nourishment through the cord attached to its navel, and yogic masters store a lot of life-force energy, or pure nourishment, in this area.'

Swamiji is a strict vegetarian, and he says that it's not so much what people eat but the amount of food they eat that triggers many modern illnesses. Of course this is true, but he obviously hasn't had much experience of our Western diets, laden with fat, salt, sugar, pesticides, antibiotic residues, additives and colourings. Almost 60 percent of people in the West are now obese, thanks to the amount of junk food that people put in their mouths – plus lack of exercise. We can take more responsibility and we can choose.

He also reminded me that we need to be able to absorb any life-force energy from our diet, but because so many people are stressed and rushed, and through eating excessive refined foods devoid of life-giving nutrients, usually too quickly, we are experiencing an epidemic of digestive problems which often prevent or greatly reduce the body's ability to absorb any life-force energy from food.

'People today are so busy running after something,' he said, 'they eventually tend to forget what they are running after. Many have forgotten happiness. By surrendering to a guru, and by doing your own spiritual practices, you can slowly and safely find happiness within yourself once again. And if you can be happy now, then when you have more of what you think you want, then you can become even happier.'

Umm. I wasn't sure about this one. After all, if we start worshipping a guru then surely that encourages people to worship outside themselves, rather than expanding the God within?

Swamiji answered instantly, again before Srila could finish her translation.

'*Surrender* is *not* the same as worship. Gurus are teachers. For instance, if you want to learn to swim or play a piano, it's easier if you have a teacher to whom you can talk and learn from. I encourage everyone to connect with the energy of a living guru that people feel in their hearts is right for them. Then you can learn, and in turn teach others to swim or play a piano. But if you can already swim really well, or play piano to the highest standard, then you may chose not to have a teacher. This is your choice.'

And so, considering the millions of people who still pray to Mohammed, Jesus, Buddha, or whoever is sacred to them, I wondered if Swamiji considered a living guru as being 'better', or more effective, than a 'dead' one?

'Many people still pray to gurus who have left their physical bodies, but a 'dead' guru is not as easy to connect to as a living guru. Therefore, if a person, for instance, prays earnestly at the shrine of their 'dead' saint, teacher or guru, then they are usually directed to a living guru. I work with 100,000 souls, some living and some not. Remember that the knowledge and energy of a 'dead' guru or teacher needs living gurus to work through. And the more pure souls who work through me and others like me, the more my and their energy increases. It is the knowledge that is transferred ... we are simply vessels here to awaken that knowledge in those who choose to hear the lessons we bring – or to drink from our consciousness. He suggested I should liken his work to that of a large electricity company. He puts in all the necessary wires and cables to bring electricity to my home. But once he has done his job, to turn on the supply I would need to flip a switch myself – through meditation or prayer.

Was he suggesting that direct prayers are not effective?

He looked frustrated for a second and added, 'Of course, if a person prays to help others or themselves with a pure intention in their heart and soul, then anything is possible – but gurus are here to awaken everyone's innate power so that you can awaken the ultimate God within yourselves, and thus the ability to manifest what you want in your life. But, for instance, if I wanted to help my son get into engineering college, I could not do that; he must do it based upon his own merits. He has to do the work first and then reap the rewards. But if something becomes **My** pure wish – then this would be possible.'

On the subject of prayer, he gave me another example, saying, 'A farmer prays and prays that he can grow mango trees on his land. But just by praying, he will not get a mango tree. First he has to plant a seed – and value that seed – by giving it water, light and nutrients to grow and thrive. In the same way, a guru cannot do everything for you. **I** plant the seed within you, or you could say **I** germinate the seed that is already within you – and the rest is up to you. **I** help to speed up the process *if you ask for **My** help*. (Please keep in mind here that when Swamiji says **I** and **Me** in this context he speaks as God.) 'But **I** am not attached to any outcome; I don't sit and worry all day as to whether you are nourishing that seed. That is your choice. If you want to become self-realized, you have to be willing to participate in the process.'

This made sense, as when I began my spiritual journey more than 15 years ago, I prayed and prayed for an acceleration of the process. Then a friend had told me about Mother Meera in Germany and three months after my visit, I had undergone my spiritual emergency. I had received her energy – which definitely accelerated my 'seed's' growth – but my physical body and mind had been far from prepared for the ultimate harvest. I had not done my part, whereas Swamiji had worked for 15 years to become enlightened.

Then I had dreamed of Sai Baba in India, met him, and ended up being disappointed – but I went looking for a single magic bullet from him rather than doing the necessary work myself. Looking back, I believe that Mother Meera accelerated a process that was meant to happen to me at that time, otherwise *Divine Intervention* would never have been written. However, on a deeper level I also believe that my experience seemed to be the result of a pre-agreed pact between myself and Diana before incarnating into this life. But of this I still have no proof.

Thinking about 'dead' gurus, I asked Swamiji how he feels about the thousands of religions currently practised on the planet.

'If a person has a pure wish to reach God, then this can be done outside of religion. Many people think that their specific religion is the only religion and that their truth should become everyone's truth – no matter what the cost. Consider that the word religion derives from the root word *religiere* meaning 'to connect again'. Now consider this: you live in England. Does the sun shine only in England? Of course not; it shines everywhere. If you only believe in one religion then it can be difficult to comprehend the vastness of God. To experience true liberation, to feel God and become as God, you need to rise above the restrictions of religions and think of yourself as belonging to a new whole-world religion.'

I agree with him entirely and have often read such sentiments, but to hear them from a fully self-realized being re-affirmed my views.

'And so,' I continued, 'if you are able to activate someone's kundalini energy, won't they end up in the same situation as I did, or will they then be totally enlightened because of your intervention?'

Peals of laughter followed. He really is quite a character.

'Just because your kundalini becomes activated, this does not mean you are enlightened. Yes, you have a greater opening or connection to the divine, but then you need to learn what that means and understand the gifts this connection brings. It is like saying that a person accepted to study at medical school is already a qualified doctor. They must study first and learn from experience. And I encourage people to become liberated slowly through regular meditation. It is every soul's ultimate desire to once again join with the whole – God. But so many people try too hard to have an experience and they feel let down if nothing happens.'

How right he is.

He then told me the story of a young man who had come to Swamiji's talks several times, but who after three years had become disillusioned as he had felt nothing. Finally, he decided to visit Swamiji one last time, but he no longer cared whether he had an experience or not. But because he had totally let go of expecting anything to happen, he had a fantastic experience.

'And so,' smiled Swamiji, 'in meditation the secret is to feel total *surrender*. Not like an army surrendering in a war – by surrender, I mean to offer yourself wholeheartedly to God – and then you will see changes.'

'Such as?' I prompted.

'The more you meditate, the more you will balance and clear your charkas. The more your energy field becomes balanced, the more balanced your whole life becomes. Slowly but surely you will begin seeking out healthier food, and you will become less selfish as you connect with the soul part of yourself which knows what is best for you – in mind, body and spirit. Also, you are less likely to become ill or have accidents, and you are more protected as you are resonating with the ultimate divine – which is perfection. You are then in tune with nature; the same power that is outside you is inside you. And, for example, once your solar plexus chakra is totally clear, you cannot harm yourself or others. It would no longer be in your nature. And when your throat chakra becomes totally clear then you can become more successful at whatever you choose to do in life, and so on.'

As he spoke I remembered again that summer of 1998 when I could not have swotted a fly or killed a spider. I was incapable of telling a lie. It was incredible.

When I had met Dr David Simon and asked him how I could return to a heightened state, he had recommended daily meditation. Dr Deepak Chopra a year earlier had said if we could all do just one spiritual practise daily, it should be meditation. Serena had told me that through regular meditation you can access more of your potential capabilities.

On a physical level regular meditation stills the mind and helps to regulate the thyroid gland, which in turn helps regulate hormone production. It reduces the release of stress chemicals that can destroy one's health, helps to lower blood pressure and the heart rate. It helps to re-alkalize the body, which slows ageing. Stress makes the body more acid, which triggers disease. Meditation encourages production of the hormone melatonin, which encourages deeper sleep. It helps stimulate the pineal gland situated in the brain – which is often called the third eye. And *if* – and it's a big *if* – you can go beyond thoughts, time as we know it would stop. You would no longer age. Now consider how great yogis are able to stay alive in the same body for hundreds of years …

On this subject, I asked Swamiji how old were the living saints that had taught him in the caves of the Himalayas?

'They were 800 years old, and they have remained in the same physical bodies – and yet they look in their mid-twenties and have truly beautiful auras.'

I thought about how for a short time. I had experienced the ability to look older or younger *at will*. It was awesome and I know it can be done through the power of the mind. Thinking of this 'power' I once possessed, I asked Swamiji feebly, 'Was I even close to enlightenment?'

Looking directly at me, he pointed to his third eye and said with compassion, 'Your kundalini stopped here at your third eye chakra, so you could say that you were partially enlightened. As you know, this can be a dangerous time, as your thoughts and realities become confused. This is why for the kundalini to move from the third eye to the crown chakra and beyond, the help of a living guru, or Satguru (a teacher's teacher) is required. We are like the doctors who teach the young students at medical school. We only have your well being in mind.'

I did not need to ask how I could connect more fully to him, as just looking in his eyes and being in his energy field was the connection. I remembered the pure energy that had pulsed through my eyes, and how my eyes too had become like large dark pools. People wanted to simply sit and receive the energy that was pulsing through my eyes and from my whole being. We don't necessarily need physical eyes to see, know or absorb this pure energy.

Our time together was coming to a close … and I had a train to catch. Yet I still had so many questions and suddenly my appointments back in London paled into insignificance.

Before finishing, I quickly asked if any of my chakras were blocked and he pointed to my heart and my throat. How would I clear them? I wondered.

Emma reminded me that I had been asked to bring an ordinary pebble. Quickly I rummaged around in my briefcase and found the pebble, and laid it near Swamiji. He asked me to lay my hands just above the pebble and feel its energy, but I felt nothing at all. I sat down again. Swamiji held his hands over the pebble making swirling movements for about 20 seconds, and then asked me to place my hands near the pebble again. Even I was amazed at how intense an energy I could feel. Srila told me that I should keep the pebble and that every time I held it I would feel Swamiji's energy. I held it as though he had just given me a priceless diamond, rather than a pebble which I had found behind a dustbin near the station!

It was a magical couple of hours, and as Emma took me back to the station I asked her how I could clear my heart and throat chakras. 'You could have asked,' she smiled. I felt like kicking myself.

The next day I was literally full of joy at being alive. Every word I said or thought was positive. Even my husband had asked, 'What has got into you?' I laughed.

As I typed up the tapes we had recorded, I wondered if I might ever see Swamiji again to finish my questions. Two days later Emma called and told me that Swamiji was leaving for Germany within 10 days – but he was teaching a small group at a retreat in Surrey for two days before leaving – and if I had more questions, then he would be happy to answer them.

Yet again I was amazed at the synchronicity if it all. Two whole days. Swamiji had said, 'If it is **My** pure wish then it can happen …' and he wasn't kidding. I was being granted a second chance, a rare gift indeed.

Meanwhile, I needed to find a scientist who could explain the difference between an enlightened being's brain and my own. I was in for several Ah-ha moments.

Meditation, the Brain, Another Scientist and a Mega Ah-ha Moment ...

All human evil comes from this; a man's being unable to sit still in a room.

BLAISE PASCAL

I surfed the net in the hope of locating an accredited scientist who has researched what happens in the brain when we meditate, or become enlightened – and why so many people recommend meditation as being the best practice for opening the doors to higher states of consciousness. Eventually I came across the site for the Maharishi University of Management in Fairfield, Iowa. This is no small hippie commune, but a highly acclaimed university campus, with several hundred students from 60 countries.

Dr Frederick Travis, Director of the EEG Consciousness and Cognition Laboratory, based at this facility, has spent almost 30 years researching the functioning of the brain. Along with several other eminent colleagues from Fairfield and Boston College, he has published a paper stating that they have identified specific and measurable changes in the brains of people who are enlightened. As the study's lead author, Dr Travis is quoted as saying:

'This is the first time, to my knowledge, that people who have integrated the experience of transcendence into their daily lives have had their brain wave patterns studied as they engage in mental tasks. Our results are important because they validate via Western science the experiences of higher consciousness – which have been esteemed throughout the ages.'

And Alaric Arenander, Director of Brain Research at the University, reiterated this statement by saying, 'Modern science, for the first time, has documented the existence of what ancient traditions have spoken of for millennia as the state of enlightenment, a state of total brain functioning.'

Just the kind of scientists I needed. Several phone calls later I tracked down Dr Fred Travis, and he kindly agreed to speak with me.

Firstly, I asked him which part of the brain is involved in enlightenment.

'What we have found,' he began, 'is that when people meditate regularly the frontal part of the brain – known as the pre-frontal cortex – becomes more synchronized, more coherent.'

That word again – *coherent*.

'So what is this frontal part associated with?' I asked.

'Think of this area as being like the Prime Minister of a country. The PM sits there in his or her office, and everyone sends information to the PM, who absorbs it, and then sends it back out again with comments and decisions.

'Initially, all information comes into the back of the brain, is processed in order of priority and then is sent on to the front where you do your planning and decision-making, your moral reasoning, and where your sense of self is located. By the age of 12 or 13 the rest of the brain is fully developed in that the connections between brain cells are 'myelinated' – insulated in the fatty tissue, which allows information to travel more quickly to other cells. However, the connections to the frontal cortex begin to mature around the age of 12 and this is one reason why most teenagers do crazy things – because this part of their brain is just coming on line. The teenager may have a wild thought and act upon that thought, before their frontal lobes – the judgement areas – can say, "Stop!" It's rather like being in a car without any brakes.

'Connections to these frontal lobes grow naturally until the age of about 30, and experiences that require integrated thinking, such as reading a book and understanding its underlying message, continue to help accelerate this growth. And meditation helps to directly increase coherence in these frontal areas.'

'But,' I asked, 'what does that mean to the average person?'

'It means that the peaks of brain waves begin to occur more in phase after regular meditation – in other words, the activity of different parts of the brain rises and falls together. Try to imagine this frontal area as being like the conductor of an orchestra, and if the conductor is integrated and harmonious or coherent, he or she can take any degree of input (meaning as difficult a musical score as possible, plus a huge orchestra) and yet still create a harmonious output.'

'And what effect would these coherent brain waves have on me on a physical level?'

'You have already mentioned many of the positive physical effects that this change in brain patterns triggers – lowered blood pressure and heart rate, an ability to cope more efficiently with stress and so on. But also, oxygen consumption becomes as low as during deep relaxation and, as well as measurable improvements in physical health at every level, this increased coherence changes the *quality* of the functioning of the brain, including intelligence and creativity. Eventually, what we can see is that the left frontal areas of the brain – and the right frontal areas of the brain – are working together. *They become coherent.*'

'So is meditation similar to trance or hypnosis?'

'It's simply a different state. Firstly, you need to know that during sleep these frontal areas become disconnected, and that they also become disconnected during trance and hypnosis. At such times what you think of as being your 'individual self' is no longer a part of the process. This is why when you are woken from a deep sleep it takes you a minute or two to get your act together, as the frontal area needs to re-connect. Think of a trance as when you drive from A to B – but at the end of the journey you don't remember the actual journey.

In hypnosis, the therapist relaxes the patients and gives them various suggestions. The brain at that time cannot tell the difference between a real event against an imaginary one; if you tell that person you are placing a lighted cigarette on their body, the sensory area at the back of the brain and the brain stem *physically* react as if this event or suggestion is *really* happening – and in the majority of cases the patient will awake to find themselves with physical burns, but none have been applied.

'However, during deep meditation – when you find the space between your thoughts and you connect to the infinite mind – the frontal area is connected and there is increased co-ordination between frontal areas and other brain areas. The individual remains alert and yet calm at the same time. This is why meditation triggers a unique state of being.

'Meditation is not a relaxation therapy as such, but relaxation is one of the side effects of meditation. During this time, the brain produces more alpha waves (which are produced when you become more relaxed). And the frontal areas gradually become more synchronized, both during meditation and during everyday life as a person begins to experience higher states of consciousness. Over time, one's so-called psychic powers begin to wake up as their sixth sense becomes more active.

'But the crucial point here is that the more you meditate, the more coherence you can see in *all* parts of the brain. And when you measure the EEG (electroencephalograph) of the brain of an enlightened being, we have found that their *whole* brain can function at a coherent level *all the time*. And yet, their brains can also function at an everyday level – even though they are producing totally coherent broadband waves including theta, alpha, beta and gamma frequencies *all at the same time*. And when this happens the enlightened person experiences inner, immovable, unbounded silence, along with specific streams of blissful experiences. This inner experience, based on highly coherent brain functioning, is the basis for external phenomena that are often called "miracles". The point here is that the brain is able to remain totally coherent (in bliss) – but also it is able to function at an everyday level. To the average doctor this phenomenon may seem impossible, and yet we can now measure it and see it, Enlightenment is very real.'

I was trying to grapple with the enormity of what he was saying and needed to get my thoughts together. For years I have known that during our normal waking day, our brains emit beta waves – I call them busy waves. Like, you are reading this book in beta – 14–28 cycles per second. And in meditation we work towards an alpha state – 7–14 cycles per second – so alpha waves denote that we are a little more relaxed. Then we come to theta waves at 4–7 cycles per second, which are produced by the brain during drowsiness, deeper meditation or hypnosis. Also, it's worth noting that young children produce more theta waves – and as children have up to twice the amount of physical connections between their brain cells than adults, Dr Travis believes this could explain why they tend to be far more psychic than most adults. Delta waves, at 0–4 cycles per second, are produced in very deep sleep or when a person is in a coma, but not usually during hypnosis. During meditation, a range of 7–10 cycles per second is recorded, which is the upper end of the theta and the lower end of the alpha bands.

I recalled that when I had discussed these various brain waves with a highly successful psychic surgeon, he had told me that when he was working he could switch his brain into a delta state – and yet he was able to work and function at an everyday beta level at the same time. And this had been measured in a laboratory. With what Fred was telling me, everything was beginning to make more sense. In ancient Buddhist texts it is written that with enlightenment the brain becomes seven times clearer than what we experience in normal everyday life. Everything in 1998 had indeed become far clearer to me. And as Fred spoke, at long last I truly began to comprehend how this feeling of being 'in bliss' all the time whilst going about my business had been possible. Therefore, as we chatted, I just wanted to be sure that I was understanding him correctly.

'Let me be really clear here,' I spoke slowly and deliberately, 'are you saying that the most fundamental difference between an enlightened person and myself and the majority of people on this planet is that enlightened men's and women's brains are totally coherent. *Is that it?*'

I could almost feel him smiling. 'It is,' he said quietly, 'but it takes a while, with regular practice, to be able to increase this coherence. Most people experience total coherence for a second or a minute, and others think that if they have a sudden or intense kundalini awakening that they are totally coherent, but this is rarely the case.'

'And does the kundalini need to burst before you experience this coherence?' I asked.

'It can, but it doesn't have to. What is needed for total enlightenment is for the brain to function in a specific way. If it happens spontaneously, as in your case, and the kundalini bursts, the experience usually lasts for a short period but then it's gone – and the person then spends the rest of their lives looking for it again.'

He was reading my mind!

'But I always thought,' I argued, 'that your kundalini energy had to be fully connected or functioning before you could become enlightened?'

'It does – but it does not have to blow like it did with you and others who go through an intense spiritual emergency. When the brain becomes totally coherent, which usually occurs after years of spiritual training, it naturally organizes all the systems in the body to function in balance, and this would also include the kundalini.

'The kundalini energy flows through what most people refer to as either a very fine pipe, thread or channel that starts at the base of the spine and runs through to the top of the head. And the more you meditate, the more the universal energy can gradually rise up through this channel until eventually the energy moves freely back and forth. Just like the conductor of the orchestra, the body can then naturally cope with more input (universal energy) and create a harmonious output! But what happens during a spiritual emergency is like a dam bursting – the banks overflow and you experience havoc. And if people claim to be fully enlightened during such an experience, we now have an objective way to measure whether this is actually the case – or not.'

My brain was working overtime. I started to think about miracles, instant healing and coherence and asked, 'Okay, is brain coherence the trigger for spontaneous healing? When a sick person *knows* that they are healed and becomes well in a single moment – does this happen because the coherence within the brain is instantly communicated to every cell in the body to also become coherent? And so they are healed in an instant?' I almost squealed excitedly, holding my breath in anticipation.

'You've got it,' Fred laughed.

Blimey – this was another *real* Ah-ha moment for me. Fred continued: 'When the brain becomes coherent – totally in balance – then automatically the cells become coherent too, and the healing occurs. And as the most cohesive brain patterns always prevail, the coherence appears to reset the mind, body and spirit at *every* level.

'However, in a non-enlightened person, the individual would be completely healed for *that* moment. But if they returned to thinking negatively, lived on junk food and were exposed to carcinogenic chemicals and so on, they may become sick again. For some people the reset lasts the rest of their natural lives, and for others it doesn't.'

I thought about Swamiji and my question as to whether he needed to eat, and how careful he is with his diet. So, what would happen, I asked Fred, if an enlightened person were to eat nothing but junk food all the time?

'My concept on this one would be that they could raise the energy within junk food, eat it and suffer no side effects – *for a time*. But if they lived *only* on junk, then after some time their physical bodies would begin to suffer. Also, if in one specific moment they consciously and in a fully coherent state decided, for instance, to drink poison, they would have the ability to do this with no ill effects. Of course they would not go on doing this day after day, but if for some reason they did then their physical body would suffer. Anyway, what would be the point? Fully enlightened people are not circus acts – they are *totally* connected to and at one with an infinite level of intelligence, which automatically desires and acts for the good of the whole – on every level. This is the key to full enlightenment.'

Listening to Dr Travis I also considered how certain enlightened beings have the ability to convert water to wine, water to oil and so on, in which case they could change the poison or junk food into something safer (I discuss this alchemy in Chapter 14). But as Fred says and I too think, why bother? It's so much easier to simply eat healthier food and avoid poison in the first place!

'When people are not fully coherent,' Dr Travis continued, 'or, let's say they have an experience that triggers coherence for a short time but they have not sorted things through in their minds, this is when they may desire things or events that are not for the whole good. Such people are not what I would call *fully* enlightened – as any coherence is either a passing phase or the whole brain is not *completely* coherent.'

But what about people who are healed that have not meditated or prayed, but had still experienced a moment of absolute 'knowing' that they were healed? I told Dr Travis about the case of several Sai Baba devotees I had interviewed who had asked for Baba's help to heal a terminally ill child who was in hospital in the UK. Sai Baba had instructed his devotees to visualize him in their mind's eye for several minutes every day at a specific synchronized time. Within four weeks all traces of the child's cancer had disappeared ... how had this been possible?

'Think about it for a moment,' instructed Dr Travis.

Multiple-level thinking was definitely called for here. I have often interviewed people who became healers after having their own Ah-ha moment – when during their illnesses they experienced a personal miracle and suddenly became well – and people who experienced spontaneous cures whilst at places like Lourdes. Also, similar 'miracles' can happen after healing from a hands-on healer, a healing therapy, meeting an enlightened being, through intense prayer or even swimming with dolphins. And I know that if the healer's range of frequencies is compatible with those of their patient, then miracles can and do occur. Healing happens when frequencies are pulsed into a person's subtle energy body, thus helping to rebalance their energy field, which in turn encourages the body to heal itself.

'But what am I missing here?' I asked aloud.

Fred broke in to my thoughts. 'People need to fully understand that *in that moment* of total coherence, when spontaneous healings and phenomena occur, time no longer has any meaning. Neither does karma. Whatever baggage you are carrying to that date can no longer touch you. In that moment you are outside of the field of cause and effect, you can take a new direction and begin again.'

This was another wonderful Ah-ha moment. In the meantime I returned to my theory as to how the child's healing could be explained.

'Of course,' I proclaimed, 'organized and focused intention.' Gary Schwartz had said, 'Mind and intention form patterns which form matter. And when I had asked how I was able to partially materialize a ring – he had told me that I had been in a hyper *coherent* state, and I had known with every fibre of my being that such a feat was possible – and so instantly it became my reality ... which means that if a master of the self wanted to, say, materialize money – they could?'

Fred broke in again. 'This is a possibility, but why would they do this? After all, true enlightenment is inviting everyone to learn to act for the good of the whole. If someone came along and just manifested a stack of money and made it easy for everyone, how would that help people to grow and realize their own infinite potential?'

This reminded me of the phrase 'Give a man a fish, you have fed him for today; teach a man to fish and you have fed him for a lifetime.'

After a few moments, I finally offered Fred my theory on the healing.

'The child became well because of the focused loving intentions of her relatives, and because Sai Baba held it as his pure wish (which is a 100 percent focused intention) and sent 100 percent coherent signals – which were received within the young girl's brain (as the brain is a transmitter and a receiver), thus triggering coherence and therefore the cancer disappeared. How's that?'

Fred laughed. 'Not bad, not bad at all. The key point here is that the healing happened from the universal level of being that is common to us all. From the level of pure unconditional love.'

I was on a roll. It was time to talk about mass focused intention. It is common sense that if one person can make an intention become a reality over time, then the larger the number of people setting and sending out a specific intention, the greater becomes the effect. Therefore I asked Fred if there are any published scientific experiments that prove that what lots of people think at the same time can have a physical effect.

'Of course there are,' he replied, 'over 50, in fact.'

I was really beginning to like this guy.

'There was a study on transcendental meditation carried out in Lebanon over a two-and-a-half-year period during the 1980s, in which several groups of meditators – totalling over 200 people – had the single intention of 'waking up' the underlying field of wholeness or pure intelligence in a specific area. And when all the data were examined very carefully using strict scientific protocols, taking into account dozens of variables such as holiday periods, temperature, stress levels, weekends or other explicable variations, there was a measurable significant 66 percent increase in co-operation, a 48 percent reduction in conflict and a 68 percent reduction in injuries. Such results have been rigorously tested again and again by numerous scientists in multiple war zones, including Israel and Croatia – and similar results have been found each time. What you are experiencing here is a greater coherence within the *underlying field*, and as the coherent patterns always prevail, we can measure a definite impact.'

'But does this mean,' I considered, 'that if a million people in a concentrated area were to send out a negative intention, it could trigger a war?'

'Indeed it could,' agreed Dr Travis. 'This is why we all need to be more careful with our thoughts.'

So can thoughts create anything?

'Basically, yes. The main criteria here would be that people (unless they are totally enlightened) would need to sustain their focused intention regularly over a period of time to sufficiently imprint their 'wish' into the collective consciousness, in order for it to eventually happen.

'But another important fact to get across here is that if only 1 person in 100 meditates regularly, and simply experiences the infinite field of intelligence at the source of thought (the space between your thoughts is a window into this field) then *their attention alone* can somehow 'unfreeze' the expression of pure intelligence in their environment. And once 'defrosted', this intelligence begins to function more significantly in one's environment, and automatically affects neighbouring environments. This is really important as it means that once you can help your own field to become coherent, then this coherence will automatically transfer to other people's, (or group's, or country's) environment. You can literally change your world for the better − if you act from that underlying field of intelligence at the source of our thoughts.'

This was indeed great stuff. But again, I needed to find someone − a highly respected and experienced scientist − who could scientifically explain what Dr Travis was now sharing with me as provable fact rather than theory.

And a couple of months later, thanks to yet another 'coincidence', I would speak to Emeritus Professor William Tiller in California. Tiller, the world's most acknowledged scientist in this field, has now proven these theories in science. Find him in Chapter 14.

In the meantime, a week before my chat with Dr Travis, Dr Sangeeta Sahi (who is today a good friend that I had met by 'coincidence' just after I had agreed to write this book) had told me about the Global Consciousness Project, which also offers more direct evidence regarding how our thoughts can be measured – that they go somewhere.

She told me that this project was begun in the early 1990s by a co-ordinating team of scientists at Princeton University in America who wanted to know if world events such as the death of a major world figure or a large-scale catastrophe, for instance, causes any measurable effects in what most of us think of as 'empty space' in the environment all around us. Thanks to the internet, this project now has a global network of more than 50 sites, which record second-by-second data. Their delicate measuring devices are sensitive to any common mass focus, resonance or coherence in the mental domain.

We are only in the physical domain – there are lots of others. This means that if enough of us are thinking the same thing at the same time, this effect can be detected, measured and recorded. When Princess Diana died, this effect caused the sensitive instruments to show a marked change, at a ratio of 100 to 1 against chance. And when Mother Teresa died a few days later, there was hardly a measurable effect. This was because Mother Teresa was old and had lived a full life, and the media had told us that she was critically ill several days earlier, so her passing was not such a shock. But Diana was young, vibrant and greatly admired. Therefore, to my mind what triggered that marked difference in the measurements was the amount of *emotion* behind the thoughts. As I spoke to Fred I could not prove this theory – but Professor Tiller could …

If you would like to take part in this exciting Global Consciousness Project, log on to http://noosphere.princeton.edu/

It was almost time to end my chat with Dr Travis, so I asked him light-heartedly, 'Did the guru whom your university is named after have anything to do with the man the Beatles went to meet in India during the 60s?' And

I was surprised when he replied, 'Yes, it's the same man.'

H. H. Maharishi Mahesh Yogi is apparently now in his late eighties and lives in Holland. He has dedicated his life to helping people understand who they really are. If you would like to hear His Holiness speak, then every Wednesday, along with other scientists, Maharishi speaks on line about enlightenment on www.mou.org – and for more information on Dr Travis's work, log on to www.mum.edu

Before finally saying farewell, I couldn't resist asking Dr Travis, rather tongue in cheek, 'Well, if you've been meditating for 32 years, are you totally enlightened yet?'

He laughed and then paused before replying, 'The thing about enlightenment is that it's not a place you get to and stop – even enlightened masters are still growing – just like the universe. But I like to think that I have come to a peaceful space, of knowing who I am and how I relate to the world.'

We couldn't ask for more, could we?

12

Magic with a Master

The master stands, literally, at the exact point where two worlds meet; the world of awakening and the world of sleep.
PURNA STEINITZ

April 30, 2004 – London

As I drove through the grinding late afternoon Friday rush hour and observed the weary commuters making their way home, I thought about Swamiji's words a few days earlier in Cheltenham – that so many of us have forgotten happiness. Thankfully, on that day I wasn't one of them.

When I had told my husband that I was going to spend two days in a wonderful energy field that would help lift my spirits and give me inspiration to keep typing he had joked, 'People still joke about Prince Charles talking to his plants – so if I were you, I wouldn't talk about what you are doing to many people.'

In the Prince's defence, I reminded Stuart that scientists in Sweden and at several other research institutes have shown that when plants are spoken to and treated with love and respect they flourish significantly better than those that are tended with emotional detachment.

Stuart smiled indulgently. At that point I should have simply let his joke drop, but his statement was like a red rag to a bull. I argued that because he is passionate about his garden and, thanks to the *attention* he lavishes on it, it looks beautiful.

'Not the same thing at all,' he had replied.

Oh really? Common sense should tell anyone that anything – be it a plant, rabbit, fish or human being, will thrive better in a loving environment.

At this point I tried another approach, sharing with him some of what Dr Travis had told me about the positive effects of collective intention in war zones – but before long Stuart's eyebrows went up in that 'Oh ple*eeese*' look. The one that children give you so often when you are being uncool. I gave up …

In that moment I felt somewhat miffed, and yet his comments served to remind me of the truly enormous chasm still remaining between those who are 'waking up' on various levels and those who wouldn't have the faintest concept of what I am writing about in this book.

As I sit writing this chapter, recently the media have featured wall-to-wall stories of the Beckhams' marital problems; also about the continuing horrors in Iraq, Saudi Arabia and Israel. And when I read the shocking story of how gang rapes are now becoming more widespread in certain inner-city areas, I truly felt that the world was going mad. What I should have thought was, 'How can I help to change this?' But in that moment, as I read about boys and men who consider gang rape 'normal', I was in despair. Cause and effect at every level is making our world what it is today. And all it takes for truly evil men to thrive – as the famous saying goes – is for good men and women to do nothing. If you ask law-abiding, hardworking people why they allow such insanity to continue in their communities, they tell you of the appalling fear and violence in which they live. If they had a choice, most of them say they would move away from the mindless cruelty; others are actively trying to make a difference, and I admire their tremendous courage.

But when I awoke this morning and sat down to begin writing again, I thought, 'Well, I *am* doing something. Be it ever so humble, I am trying.'

And so can we all – if we choose to. What science is now telling us (and you will read more of this in Chapter 14) is that through our *intentions alone*, we can make a difference. There is always hope.

This is why people like Swamiji Shivkrupanandji have incarnated through the ages. They come to offer the pure universal consciousness that flows through them, to encourage us all to take an active part in 'unfreezing' the expression of pure intelligence and love that we call God *which is everywhere*. What we think of as God is here now, inside and around us all – but most of us don't know it!

Dr Travis had told me that we only need 1 in every 100 people to help awaken, or unfreeze, this highly evolved pure intelligence into our environment by sitting in a quiet and peaceful state. This means that if 60 million people (1 percent of the world's population) could meditate daily, then this underlying field would unfreeze everywhere on the planet. Dr Travis also pointed out that if a large group of enlightened beings could sit at one moment with the intention for peace, far fewer would be needed as *they are* that pure field.

Millions of people buy a single lottery ticket every week or month, hoping that they can win lots of money in order to escape into what they consider to be their idea of a perfect life. And for every ticket sold, the chance of your winning is greatly reduced. But in the case of unleashing the spiritual lottery, the more people who sit and meditate – which costs nothing – the sooner we can all become winners in the grand spiritual lottery. And how can we achieve this aim?

How do you begin a great journey? Just one step at a time. Just one soul at a time …

And so as I drove into Tekels Park to spend a couple of days with Swamiji, I was simply another cog in this great wheel. And yet the day could soon arrive when just *one more person* meditating and becoming at peace within themselves could tip the scales of our existence into another world, another dimension. And when you start to think in such a way, then you really begin to understand just how important **you** are.

Tekels Park is a 20-hectare (50-acre) private estate which was bought around 1928 as the headquarters of the Theosophical Society - a charitable foundation started in 1875 by Madame Blavatsky, a renowned Russian medium and psychic who was keen to encourage research into the science of spirit.

Today, the main centre, a 1960s-built, two-storey affair, is used for all types of conferences and gatherings. Much of the land has been sold for private housing, but the new houses remain within the perimeter walls of what must have once been a very grand estate. Hundreds of tall, majestic trees are scattered around the estate and the walled gardens that once served the main house are now planted with lawns and roses and have fountains. Much magic from a bygone age remains.

But alas, not in my room – a small double bed, a basin, two chairs and a tired closet greeted me. It was cold, too, as my radiator was not working. And horror of horrors – there was no loo. That was along the corridor and eight rooms would be sharing one bathroom and one toilet. Mornings would sure be busy. I wondered what Michael Winner might make of such a hostelry!

'Don't act like a princess,' I reminded myself, 'this room is perfectly okay for all your needs ...'

At least they had supplied a kettle, coffee and teas. I brightened. My guest, Dr Sangeeta Sahi, popped her head around the door – and I asked what her room number might be.

'This one,' she replied with a cheery smile. Whilst my mouth hung open, one of Swamiji's helpers also arrived. Perhaps we should have a party.

Apparently because I had so wanted Sangeeta to meet Swamiji, he had agreed that she could come, but there were no rooms left – except mine. We would have to share. He had granted my wish, but not in quite the way which I had expected!

We unpacked and went down for supper. Whatever in my 'princess moment' mode I had considered lacking in my room was more than redressed by supper. Local ladies had prepared a fresh vegetarian feast, which was served in the magical restaurant area overlooking a walled garden. Around 34 of us from all walks of life queued as strangers, but by the time we returned for dessert we had become friends. After all, we had come with a common purpose: to be with Swamiji and to hear his wisdom.

After supper we filed quietly into the meeting room. Some people sat cross-legged on cushions on the floor, but with my chronic back problems I chose a chair. At the far end there was a small painting of Swamiji surrounded by candles and a simple chair with his favourite cloth laying across it. Srila, his interpreter, duly arrived and took her place near his chair.

Silence reigned. A few minutes passed, then in walked Swamiji looking very serious in a flowing white robe. In our instructions we had been advised not to wear black because it absorbs negative energies; also, to have a salt bath – as salt helps to ground one's energies.

And as Swamiji sat and surveyed his audience I could sense why we had needed the salt. There was a subtle and yet noticeable breeze flowing through the room. As I sat silently I understood that all information I could ever need was being emanated through his energy field, all I had to do was to be open to receive it. But, as most people expect to hear wisdom rather than *feel it* – Swamiji also began chatting to us.

He told us that most medical conditions are linked to our negative thoughts and that there is still no modern medicine to clear thoughts. There are, he added, very few people who can understand the language of silence. He compares himself to a loving mother or father who prepares a delicious meal and keeps it warm in the hope that very soon you will eat that meal and enjoy it. But he cannot give us too much spiritual 'food', as the majority of humanity cannot even digest 10 percent of what he is offering. But by learning to be silent, we can increase the body's ability to absorb more. The more you learn silence, he said, the happier and more contented you will become.

This was almost exactly what Dr Travis had told me.

Swamiji went on to tell us that just by being in a room with us he was able to automatically absorb any negative energies that we might be emanating. To do this, he does not need to concentrate or focus his attention – it just happens. Because he absorbs a lot of negative energy at one time, on occasion there is a physical residue, in which case his liver can become very 'hot', or his feet may swell and he experiences a burning sensation. He made it clear that if he were to store all the negative energy that he absorbs he would die, so he passes it on to his gurus and ultimately to the 'all that is'. And he laughed his magical laugh when he proudly told us that he has not had need of a medical doctor for over 40 years. I wish I could say the same!

He clarified that he can transform any amount of negative energy, but he automatically absorbs only the negative energies that are appropriate for each individual at that time… sometimes he says people need to hang on to various aspects of their negativity as it serves a purpose for them.

This resonated well with me, as when I was in a heightened state I somehow automatically knew when it was appropriate to help remove someone's illness or when to simply offer the energy of pure love that flowed through me and allow the illness to run its course. It was a state of bliss, humility and love – but with total detachment. I also thought that any doctor worth his salt should know that anger affects your liver. Not speaking up for yourself affects your throat, feelings of restriction in your life affect your lungs and lower back pain can denote that you are feeling unsupported – and so on. Emotions emit frequencies that have a huge impact on the physical body and your energy field.

Once again I remind you that Swamiji is a pure field of intelligence; he has no existence of his own – God flows through him. With enlightened beings there is no separation between them and the Guiding, Organising, Designer. Swamiji asks that we do not worship his physical body, but simply connect to the whole divine energy that flows through him.

He also reminded us that peaceful meditation brings our individual energy fields into balance, thus reducing illness and anger and creating more emotional balance. And with regular practise, we can also learn to accept more calmly those situations that would usually bother us a whole lot more.

At this point I invite you to consider once more what Dr Travis said: if you help your individual energy field to become more coherent, then you become healthier at every level.

And science agrees.

Then think about thousands of people meditating and becoming balanced; not only their bodies but also their environment, then their country, and on and on until the whole planet could become balanced or coherent. But where there is a lot of anger, negative intention, thoughts and therefore actions, the body first becomes ill, then this negative energy accumulates and you have explosions of energy, which can turn into an argument and eventually a war.

And so I asked Swamiji via Srila, 'But *if* an enlightened person does absorb too much negative energy or negative karma at one time, could they become really ill?'

'This is indeed a possibility,' he smiled. 'We come to absorb negative energy and transform it. Too many people keep their attention on disease and disharmony, which makes our job more difficult. Also, what you bring before me is what I will mirror back to you, except that this energy will be amplified. Therefore, always try to come before your guru in a positive and happy state of mind.'

As he said this, I thought about the number of times I have sat to meditate in a foul mood, hoping that by sitting my anger would pass – but my day only got worse. And of course when I'm angry the one thing that eludes me is a quiet mind! I became a boomerang. What you give out is what you get back.

Swamiji continued. 'Worrying just increases the amount of negative energies around your body, so you are more likely to become ill. Take your attention to harmony through meditation and automatically you are inviting more peace and happiness into your life. Work on staying in the "now", as this helps to balance all your energy centres – your chakras – and then sickness can fade away as you become more harmonic. If you are thoughtless, there is no fixation on past or future, just the present moment. And once the space between your thoughts becomes longer you begin connecting more at a soul level, and at this level you will automatically come to know what foods you should be eating and which you should leave alone. Also, if you cook with negative intention, this will pass to your food, if you speak with a negative intention, this affects others. Your energy mingles with theirs.'

Then he sat up straighter and looked at us all intently and said, 'But light always comes before dark; you cannot bring darkness into a pure light. Light will always prevail.'

I thought of Dr Travis saying, '*Coherence always prevails.*'

Uhmm. Returning to the subject of absorbing and transmuting negative energy, I asked, 'Is this what Jesus did in his life and during his crucifixion?'

'To an extent, I would say yes. He did forgive sins, but in those days no one understood the concept of karma, and so today I would say Jesus came to absorb and transmute a lot of negative energies and karma from those around him. By suffering that amount of pain Jesus was taking on and transmuting a huge amount of negative energy. But there really is no need any more to "crucify" yourselves. Learn to forgive and forget – growing spiritually does not mean you have to suffer; yes, you learn by experience, but connecting with God is a joyful experience. Learn to be happy. If you have done something in the past for which you feel guilt or regret, if you truly and with your whole heart ask me for forgiveness and surrender your guilt, and you can also forgive yourself 100 percent, then any karma that it caused can be neutralized. And when people come into the presence of a liberated guru, satguru or teacher and they *totally* surrender all their problems to us, we can transform their negative energy and lift their burdens. In this way some illnesses and situations can be completely resolved, and around 50 percent of negative incidents that were heading your way could be avoided and your life can become a little easier. But even better is that people should all become liberated themselves, which neutralizes their karma – and then they can begin again. And from that moment they become aware of instant karma (cause and effect) and therefore become more careful with their every thought, word and deed.'

Just as Dr Travis had said, this was wonderful verification from a man who has never read a spiritual book; nor is Swamiji a scientist.

Other questions flowed from his audience, many of which we had already discussed in Cheltenham. After an hour or so, Swamiji retired and Emma asked us to reconvene on Saturday morning.

For most of that night poor Dr Sahi had to put up with me continuously switching on my bedside light so that I could write more questions ready for the next day. By 5am as the dawn light crept through the flimsy curtains we abandoned hope of further sleep. The good news was that the loo and bathroom were free and so in that sense we got up at the perfect time.

Over breakfast I met Honey Kalaria, a young 20-something choreographer who lives in London. She told me that the last time she had seen Swamiji was in Gujarat, near Bombay, which is where he has decided to base his ashram. Talking ten to the dozen, she told us, 'The day was very hot, with totally cloudless skies and Swamiji sat under a simple canopy and we all sat before him. Suddenly I could see that soft rain was falling – but only on Swamiji. We all looked for clouds or any possible explanation, such as nearby pipes, but there was nothing. It was amazing.'

And as Honey finished her tale, another devotee, who had come from Japan especially for the weekend, showed me a picture of some clouds in the shape of an OM that had appeared in the sky directly above where Swamiji was sitting in front of thousands of people. There were others who told of miraculous healings that had taken place with Swamiji – and such stories are legion when you are dealing with any truly enlightened being.

But as Gary Schwartz had said, people's stories are not scientific proof. Yet within a few weeks, Professor Tiller was to share with me how such feats are possible …

Meanwhile, it was time for our next lecture.

When Swamiji invited questions, someone made the mistake of telling him that she found it difficult to make a space for 30 minutes' meditation every day. He was not angry, but let's say that his stern reply came very quickly.

'When I was passed from guru to guru, in all those 15 years, every discipline that was set for me I obeyed without question. I lived in caves through many freezing winters and boiling summers. I stood night after night in freezing waters as part of the mastery – and many more tests that were set for me. And I never once said, "I don't have time." A lot of people these days live in comfort. Living in peace and comfort is in itself a miracle. But once you have these things you want more, you want miracles, you wish for an even easier life – and you want such things from God. And yet you are not willing to give back half an hour a day to allow God to do His/Her work.'

We all got the message.

He continued by telling us many things that I have written about over the years – that everything is vibration and energy, and not to give attention to things that you don't want in your life, but to concentrate on what you do want. If you have a problem and you keep paying it attention, then it will expand, so we need to concentrate on other things which take our attention away from what is bothering us, which reduces its power. Swamiji also talked about how spiritual enlightenment makes you rich in ways that go beyond physical wealth. He agrees that money is necessary as we live on a physical planet, but he also says that although many people meditate and set their intention on having more money or more stuff, we should never meditate for money – more that we should simply find that space between our thoughts and, once we have access to and can integrate this energy, then the God within us can create all that we need! Again, these are similar comments to those made by Dr Fred Travis.

He told us that he has no wish for personal wealth, and that his devotees have set up a foundation so that if anyone wishes to give, then they will pass these funds on to those that need it most, which is what Sai Baba and many other enlightened beings do. His devotees are also planning a lovely home for Swamiji within his ashram, as they want him to have somewhere special to live and entertain people who come to visit. They say it's like building a home for a beloved parent. Swamiji has not asked for this home. But I must say if I had lived in caves in the Himalayas for almost two decades, then a working bathroom would definitely be on my wish list.

It's strange, but I have never considered giving money to an enlightened being. Mother Meera gives her *darshan* for free, but we would all buy books, photos and prayer beads, the income from which allows her to pay her bills and enables her to keep giving the light that pulses through her. And of course many of her devotees, who love her, give if they wish to. There is a huge difference between giving a loved relative or friend a gift or money because you want to and being asked or coerced. There are gurus who do ask you to give money, but unless you are free to choose, think again.

Also, when I was in that heightened state and I saw healers smoking, I felt that their unhealthy habit grounded them. Several enlightened men and women have lots of cars and jewellery, for example, which may have the same effect – I have always said that shopping is grounding! On this issue, I try not to be judgemental. And anyway, if you don't like what a particular 'master' spends donated funds on, then don't give. It's that simple.

Later that same day, Swamiji told us that many highly evolved souls are waiting to reincarnate. The need for their energy is great, but they have to wait for parents who are on a suitable wavelength. He says that in India a lot of young children are now being made ready for liberation, or that they have reincarnated already enlightened, because the reality of enlightenment is better understood as a part of their cultural heritage. This is why many enlightened beings on earth today were born in India and the East. Interestingly, Swamiji also told us that when he has met all the souls that he was sent into the world to connect with and help, he will return to seclusion in the Himalayas. When I heard this I was initially saddened. With the state of our world today, we need all the help we can get … and yet, as I recalled Dr Travis saying that if enlightened beings were to congregate, only a small number would be needed to have a greater impact on 'unfreezing' the universal consciousness of pure love. So I began to understand that wherever Swamiji is, the work is still being done.

Before retiring, Swamiji explained his meditation. Firstly we were asked to chant his spiritual name, *Om Shree Shivkrupanand Swami Namo Namah,* for a few minutes while concentrating on our crown chakras; as energy flows where our attention goes, he is keen to help as many people as possible to connect the third eye chakra with the crown chakra. For several years I have found that a few minutes' chanting helps to prepare me for meditation, and then once I sit quietly I seem to go deeper more quickly. When I had asked Dr Travis about chanting, he had said that the effects of chanting can be similar to those of meditation, but that the effects are variable depending upon where one's attention is. If, for example, a person is only focused on the sound itself, this would not encourage the frontal areas of the brain to become coherent. In general, Dr Travis said his research shows that meditation releases more universal energy than chanting.

Then we were instructed simply to sit in silence and allow our thoughts to come and go. Eventually, through this simple, regular discipline, our brains would become quieter. Swamiji asked us to meditate every day for around 40 days as this would help us to form a regular pattern, which should then become an automatic habit like brushing one's teeth.

Because we were in a group the meditation was more powerful, and in my mind's eye I could see a huge eye appearing before me. This is very common, and I presume these days that the 'eye' belongs to the 'all that is', the infinite part of ourselves that we call God. At some level I am looking at myself! And when the meditation finished, we said a simple prayer asking that all people might live in peace.

After Swamiji had left us, Srila, his interpreter, told me that Swamiji had granted me another one-on-one interview, starting at 6am the next morning, to finish any remaining questions. Inwardly I groaned at the thought of getting up so early again, but realized that this was a great opportunity. As we made our way back towards our rooms, Srila whispered, 'And don't forget to ask him to clear your chakras this time.' I vowed not to make the same mistake twice.

I set two alarm clocks for 5am … my room mate, Dr Sangeeta Sahi, would be woken early for a second time. Sangeeta is a highly qualified medical doctor who has worked in India, America and the UK – she specializes in energy medicine and has a specific interest in the subtle energy aspects of spiritual emergency. Since we had first met in the autumn of 2003, several people, including a 14-year-old girl, who had read my book *Divine Intervention*, had emailed asking for urgent help. Sangeeta had been an invaluable help to the girl and her family. She is a magical soul who has met many enlightened masters all over the world, and so before we said goodnight I asked for her opinion on Swamiji.

'I like his honesty; if he doesn't know the answer he says so, which is a sign of having no ego. He is humble and his energies are very pure and loving.'

I agreed. It had been a long day. As I turned off my bedside lamp, I prayed that my alarm clocks would work.

Sunday, May 2, 2004 – Surrey, England

At exactly three minutes to five, a voice in my head said, 'Get up – 'it's time to get to work.' It was so clear. I sat bolt upright in bed and then spent a couple of minutes gearing up my frontal lobes so that I could focus! Obviously, Swamiji has his own way of waking people up.

After a miserable overcast and cold Saturday, Sunday dawned with clear blue skies. My step had a definite skip as I made my way to his room. Srila let me in – and I sat once more before an enlightened being.

I began by asking him what other rules he applies to meditation and how he suggests people should live their lives.

'I don't have any rules as such. I don't judge right or wrong, I accept what is. I give my light and if a person is ready to receive it, then this is fine. If not, this is fine too. If you keep saying to people, don't eat, don't smoke or drink, don't do this or that, then most people fall by the wayside. All I ask is that anyone who wants to link to me should concentrate on the divine energies that flow through me every day during their meditation. The more they do this, the more I can help.'

Back in Cheltenham, Emma had given me one of the first formal pictures ever to be taken of Swamiji and I must say the energy emanating from his eyes in that picture is incredible. For a few weeks during 1998 I had been physically unable to look at people's eyes in magazines as I could see the light emanating from them, but because I was already full of light I could not cope with more. Therefore I asked Swamiji, 'If people sit and look at your picture, would this be the same as being with you?'

He smiled his wonderfully innocent smile and said, 'Yes, it would.'

I knew it. Then I moved on to the clouds that appeared in the form of an OM above him at one of his meetings. How had he done that?

'How do you think I did that?' he questioned.

'Well,' I surmised, 'because it was your pure wish, your intention?'

He laughed. 'Many people learn how to have power over their physical body, but I have also learned how to control my subtle energy body, my mental body, and so on. We are far more "bodies" than you "see" at this moment. In this way, I can utilize my subtle body and take any form I choose or appear anywhere I choose. But I have no specific wish to show miracles, I have no ego, there is no personal wish — I am detached. If it is a devotee's heartfelt wish to have something happen, then their intention gets my attention and it's this combination that helps create what you call miracles.' He was keen to clarify this point — 'Firstly, you have the devotee's or person's wish or prayer. Secondly, you have my physical body (and other bodies) as a medium of the "all that is" … and the two combined causes the symbol of the OM to appear in the sky.'

'Okay … so if you or any liberated being wants to appear before a devotee thousands of miles away, you can do that?' I asked.

'Of course. Also, if people have a very strong intention which gets my attention – then this can happen. Anything is possible.' I could hardly wait to hear Professor Tiller's scientific explanation on this one.

It was time for me to go and join the morning meditation, but before leaving I asked if Swamiji would clear my heart chakra. This he did by placing his hands near the top of my head, and then slowly down my spine, and finally he blew energy into my crown area. My whole body began to tingle as I felt the energy flow through me and around me. An overpowering emotion overwhelmed me and tears filled my eyes – it was an amazing experience.

At midday, Swamiji invited us all to join him in the magical gardens of Tekels Park. Under great oak trees we formed a large circle and Swamiji demonstrated a simple method of eliminating negative energy that I had long forgotten. Off came our shoes and socks, and we stood with our feet shoulder-width apart and our palms facing down towards the earth. We stood silently whilst Swamiji instructed us to allow all feelings of negativity and anger to flow down our bodies and out into the earth and to ask the earth to please accept this energy and to neutralize it. I could feel a river of tension simply flowing from me and when we sat down, I felt really refreshed.

Then it was time for Swamiji to demonstrate the energizing of a stone. Everyone was invited to go forward one at a time and feel the energies of a largish stone (about one third of a metre – 12 inches or so, in diameter) that was set in the midst of our circle. Afterwards, Swamiji vibrated it and again asked us to go up and feel it. The difference was unmistakable. He then explained how through the ages great saints and gurus had placed their pure universal energy – which contains knowledge – in many great stones, monuments, statues, temples and so on; and that if people wanted to access this energy, all they had to do was tune into such places. He made us all laugh when he said that it's far easier for him to pulse his knowledge into a stone than it is for him to do this to a human being, because stones are not thinking all the time! Now that should really make you think ...

Several weeks after Swamiji had said this, I read about the mummy of a 500-year-old monk found in the Himalayas. No embalming had taken place and scientists, led by Professor Victor Mair, were astonished to discover that the monk had remained exposed to the air for 500 years, but his body had defied the natural process of physical decay. His body was curled up in an advanced yogic posture and tests showed that he had deliberately and slowly starved himself to death. I wondered if this mummy might once have been an enlightened being who consciously chose to die in such a way that his body, with all its knowledge intact in its energy field, could remain to help future generations. At the end of the article it listed many miracles that are happening around this revered mummy — and now you know why.

Finally, Swamiji asked us all to walk through the gardens and then to walk slowly back towards him, five people at a time, with our palms facing him. As we gingerly approached, within about 270 metres (300 yards) of where he sat, we began to feel that we were pressing against an invisible energy, like a barrier slightly pushing us away — and the closer we got, the more powerful it became.

And once we walked to within 6 metres (around 20 feet), the energy was so obvious that there was no need to walk closer and so we moved off to the side. As I slipped quietly away, my abiding memory of that magical day was of waving goodbye to the tiny, delicate, china-like figure of Swamiji as he sat quietly in complete peace in the sunshine. It was hard to comprehend the enormity of the power that flows through his tiny physical body.

I was very pensive for the rest of that day and found it hard to explain to my husband the joy of spirit that I felt. Once again, I longed to be able to show Stuart what kundalini energy looked like, and what a chakra energy centre looked like — as to him seeing is believing. Little did I know that within two months my wish would be granted.

And before leaving Tekels Park, Sangeeta had told me about a woman from America who could 'see' inside people – and how biophysicist Harry Oldfield has been doing this for years using a specialist scanner. Yet again, the universe – the conductor – was guiding me towards my goals. What I wanted was also what the universe wanted – and so it was coming to pass. It seemed as though many aspects of my life were becoming more coherent.

Seeing Through You

We are experience-starved ... A person who has some attainment can 'zap' people, and it is very seductive. It's like taking drugs. People want that hit again and so they hang around the teacher.

REGGIE RAY

During early spring of 2004, I was again reminded of how behind the times most people remain, especially when it comes to truly understanding that we are electrical beings in a physical shell. Healthy scepticism is a valuable trait, but it became virtual total cynicism when the press and TV featured the story of a 17-year-old Russian girl, Natasha Demkina from Saransk, a city 400 miles or so east of Moscow, who claims to be able to diagnose illnesses and health problems by looking inside people's bodies. Most of the orthodox medical doctors asked to comment dismissed her unusual ability as being utter nonsense, or suggested that she was reading people's body language or even guessing their health problems.

On live TV, Natasha gave readings to several strangers with a medical doctor present, who had initially told the viewers that claims of 'seeing through' people were ridiculous. However, he soon changed his opinion after witnessing Natasha's descriptions of what she saw inside various bodies. 'Sand and gravel' correctly described one man's kidney stones, and she also saw old surgery scars and heart problems. Natasha also correctly told one amazed woman that she had suffered from breast cancer – even describing the physical after-effects of surgery. The list went on and on.

This ability manifested in the young Russian after a botched appendix operation in which swabs were left inside the ten-year-old child's intestines. A month later, Natasha told her amazed mother that she could see two beans, a tomato and a vacuum cleaner inside her mother's body. Natasha, with no medical knowledge, was trying to describe her mothers kidneys, heart and intestines. A psychiatrist was quickly called, but he too was perplexed when the young patient correctly 'saw' his stomach ulcers.

It's hardly any wonder that Natasha has decided that she would like to become a doctor. The press and media in the UK were either very cynical, or grudgingly impressed. Meanwhile, poor Natasha was made to feel like some kind of freak.

In Russia, hundreds of people wait outside her family's cramped two-room apartment, hoping that Natasha can help them. For almost seven years, the child gave her gift free of charge – which left little time for her school work. Today, she is widely known and now charges a small fee to help save towards medical school.

Over the years I have become fed up with people saying, 'Oh, that healer or psychic or medium is really grasping, he/she had the gall to charge me – but if they have this kind of gift, they should offer it for free.'

Why? Healers, psychics and people like Natasha have bills to pay like everyone else. If you go to buy food, do you say at the check out, 'This is a gift from God, so it should be free?' No, you don't; you pay for it. Russell Crowe and Morgan Freeman are great actors, they have a gift – and do they work for free? Do you? If a person chooses to give their time and talent for no remuneration that is their choice, but if they choose to charge, they should not be made to feel guilty. Healers have mortgages, too. Just because they are sensitive or gifted in areas in which you may not be, their work and time still has value.

By my bedside I always have a small vase of fresh flowers. Before I switch off my bedside light I look at them and marvel at the miracle of nature. When you see microscopic pictures of the moment of conception, or the growing embryo, you are witnessing a miracle. All of life is a miracle, yet we take for granted so many of the daily miracles around us, and if 'new' ones are publicized, like Natasha's X-ray eyes, they are often labelled as witchcraft, nonsense, magic or a con trick. Some phenomena are indeed designed to deceive, but many scientists are finally beginning to understand how even the most controversial of so-called 'miracles' are possible.

Thanks to Professor Gary Schwartz and others like him, we now know that there are thousands of people who are super-sensitive; they can hear more, see more and understand more than the rest of us. And enlightened masters are, in most cases, the most *super*-sensitive of all.

Back in October 2003, Professor Gary Schwartz had reminded me that what we think of as being matter, including our physical body, is actually 99.99 percent empty space. And if I were to tell you that your brain and body contain trillions of electrical circuits, would you think me mad? Yet this is a scientific fact: you are a ball of electrical energy held together by an electromagnetic energy field, in a combination sufficiently dense that you can be seen and other people can see you. You emit your own unique signature range of frequencies and, in turn, you are affected by frequencies all around you – from other people's thoughts and feelings to mobile phones, computers, satellite dishes, microwave ovens, the TV and so on. Everything is frequency, and most importantly, therefore – information. Every cell or clump of cells such as your heart, liver or spleen all emit frequencies that can be read and detected on specialist equipment – this is done in hospitals every day with EEG and EMG machines.

Keeping this in mind, stretch your imagination and ask yourself, 'If we are 99.99 percent empty space and we are electrical beings in a physical body, then might it not be possible for a sensitive person to see inside our bodies, which are standing waves of multiple energy fields, rather than seeing them as dense, solid physical objects?' Of course it is. It's been happening for centuries and now there is research to confirm that this phenomena is a reality. Read on to find it.

During the past seven years I have met several people like Natasha who can 'see' inside the body. Most of these people have suffered life-threatening illnesses which triggered psychic abilities in varying degrees. One particular healer, Robyn Welch from Australia, suffered appalling head injuries after a car crash in 1981 and lay seriously ill for more than a year. But when she finally recovered after five years of rehabilitation, she found that she could see people as pure energy – and therefore could see right through them. Robyn 'sees' a tumour or health problem inside the body as varying colours of frequency. By switching her brain into a more coherent state, she is then able to 'laser' any blockages directly into a patient's energy field, which encourages the body to heal itself. Robyn and I met several times in London and on one occasion when I was stranded in America with a severe infection in my bladder and congestion in the lymph node in my groin, in desperation I had called her in Australia and she had scanned me over the phone. Not only was she spot on with her diagnosis, but after her 'lasering' of my energy field down the phone, the next morning I had felt 90 percent better! The doctor who had prescribed powerful antibiotics only 14 hours earlier scratched his head and wondered how his pills could have possibly worked so quickly.

The medicine of the future is here today, and I hope that one day Natasha can extend her abilities to working at a distance – as your mind can be anywhere and can know anything. This is how remote viewing works. More on this later.

May 20, 2004 – Luton Airport, England

In the meantime, thanks once more to a personal introduction via my friend Dr Sangeeta Sahi, I was on my way to meet Vianna Stibal, an American woman who has developed X-ray vision to a very high degree.

When we met at a quaint country inn near Luton, and our eyes locked, I knew instantly that this woman was for real and that she could pretty well read my thoughts. Her beautiful green eyes are like intense laser beams – she is full of light and living the light.

Before testing her abilities, I was keen to hear if she too had gone through a life-changing experience.

Today, at 41 with three children, Vianna has been psychic all her life, but she did not begin exploring her full potential until the early 1990s. She told me, 'I had this dream of becoming an artist – and at work, my colleagues would ask me to sketch them during our lunch breaks. As I did so, I would tune into their energy fields and intuitively tell them about their health. Because I had done several years of naturopathic training in my spare time, I was also able to suggest dietary changes and various supplements or herbs that I knew could help them. Before long, they would be back telling me that my "diagnosis" had been correct, and their doctors could not figure out how their patients suddenly knew so much and were recovering so quickly. Prior to each reading I would always ask for God's help and the more readings I did, the better I became until I realized that I could put myself into an altered theta brain wave state, which enabled me to literally "see" inside people's bodies and describe what was happening.

'One day, a friend introduced me to a psychic who was supposed to be really good. She held my ring and began telling me all this stuff about myself which wasn't very accurate. And so I asked for her ring and I gave her a reading. She said to me, "You should be doing this for a living." Because I have always been very psychic, it never occurred to me that people would pay to hear what I had to say about them or their health. This is when I decided to become a full-time medical intuitive. And pretty quickly my business grew.'

Fate intervened during August 1995 when Vianna's leg began to swell to almost double its size – and as the pain grew in intensity, her doctor finally sent her for tests.

'They found a rare type of cancerous tumour in my right femur and the specialists told me that they had only seen two other cases like mine. It was devastating news, and doctors at the University of Utah told me that if I walked on the leg it would shatter. I was incredulous when they gave me a couple of months to live, but suggested that I might live a fraction longer if they could amputate my leg. It was horrendous. My life seemed to be falling apart, and the pain was beyond anything I imagined a human being could endure. Local healers came and helped to ease the pain and others prayed for me every day, but still I remained seriously ill.

'Most of us presume that if we are dangerously ill it's going to take a long time, if at all, to become well again. At that time, I had no idea that we could heal in an instant, and so I began spending up to four hours every day in a sauna to sweat out toxins. I changed my diet, did lemon detoxes and prayed and prayed. Intuitively I felt the orthodox diagnosis was wrong, and when I was referred to The Mayo Clinic in America they too said I had a tumour, but also that I had lymph cancer.

'This felt correct to me, and when I tuned in and asked God what had caused this, I was told that it was mercury poisoning. More detoxes followed. And somehow in the midst of so much heartache and chaos people would still come for readings, as we needed money to keep the house and children going.

'One day, my aunt popped in with a really bad case of 'flu accompanied by stomach pains. She asked me to look at it intuitively for her. I placed myself in an altered state, then moved my consciousness out of my body via my crown chakra and entered her body the same way. I commanded the Creator to eradicate her pain, and when we both opened our eyes her intense stomach ache had disappeared. I tried this command-type treatment on one other person in an acute situation and they too were healed instantly. And so I concluded that if I could do this for others, then with God's help I could do it for myself.'

And by a 'miracle', she did. Her brain became coherent – and thus her cells followed suit. Her life-threatening cancer disappeared instantaneously.

Time and again, I have found that in the majority of cases in which profound 'miracles' and phenomena have taken place, the person has often undergone some kind of trauma or illness. In my case, it had been a profound spiritual emergency and I clearly recall nutritionist Patrick Holford saying to me, 'I don't think you had a breakdown as such, more a breakthrough ...' and now, thanks to scientists like Dr Fred Travis in America, we know that as the brain becomes more coherent then virtually anything can become possible. I believe that for a time I experienced this total coherence, which came and went depending on how my brain was functioning in each moment. But people like Vianna and Robyn and many others are able to switch this coherence on and off as they please.

Vianna spends her days offering healing to sick people in her home state of Idaho in America, and she regularly gives workshops in America and around the world to teach others her unique method of healing. When her brain waves were measured, it was shown that she does indeed produce theta waves during her healing sessions.

After lunch, Vianna asked if I would like her to have a look at me – and of course I said yes. Back to her hotel we drove. In her room, she invited me to sit opposite her, and she asked permission to enter into my energy field and then closed her eyes for a minute or two.

'Okay,' she began, very matter-of-fact, 'you have scar tissue in your right cheekbone, you have an astigmatism in your right eye and you may need glasses; there are problems in your right jaw area – you are losing bone. You grind your teeth. Your neck is out in two places, and there is scar tissue in your breasts, also in your pubic area. You also have a problem in your right groin, possibly inflammation or a tear of some kind. You are carrying too many toxic metals, some of which came from your mother. The whole of your lower spinal area is inflamed, it looks like there is some structural damage down there ...'

On and on she continued.

It was astonishing. She was 95 percent correct. I have had several operations on my upper jaw area going into the right cheekbone, which has left me with persistent pain, and I wear a brace at night to prevent me from grinding my teeth. Where teeth were removed in my youth there is indeed bone loss. With so much computer work, I have come to need glasses. There is scar tissue in my breasts from implants that were put in 15 years ago. The scar tissue in my groin related to a hysterectomy I underwent at 32. In my lower back I have two slightly prolapsed discs, the result of two bad falls in my thirties, which do indeed cause me continuous pain – and on many days I feel as though I am carrying the world on my shoulders.

Vianna, it seemed, was reading my thoughts. 'Do you feel as though you are carrying a burden?'

'Yes,' I replied, somewhat taken aback.

'What is it?'

'Well,' I moaned, 'I'm desperately trying to finish this book – and my daughter has just imigrated back from Australia but says she has made a huge mistake and wants to go back.' It was just all my stuff.

'And what's your biggest fear in all this?'

I rambled on about no longer being able to hear Princess Diana clearly, generally whined on about my life and even ended up sharing some of my lifelong fears.

'Okay,' she smiled. 'Everyone needs to understand that every cell carries a memory, and with this type of healing you can repair genetic programmes, you can repair cells. You can destroy parasites, viruses and bacteria. You can repair and heal deeply ingrained beliefs and health conditions that you may have brought from past lives. You can even clear beliefs that have been held genetically through many generations such as, "To be nearer to God, I need to be poor," or, "Life should be a struggle." Such misapprehensions can be neutralized so that future generations don't carry so much emotional baggage. But to achieve these aims, we all need to really believe that such things are possible. There are laws governing the universe, but if you know how, you can manipulate these laws. When a patient has absolute faith that the Creator can heal them in an instant, it happens. But if people run into old subconscious beliefs that such 'miracles' are not possible, or if they have fear, or the illness serves a purpose, then I cannot help them. In my case, when I *knew* I had become at one with our creator, my cancer was healed instantly.'

Just as I had known that I could manifest objects – and the moment in which I knew it 100 percent with every fibre of my being – it happened. Total coherence.

Many of Vianna's questions touched me to the core, as she has the uncanny ability of getting to the heart of the matter very quickly. At one point I'm embarrassed to say that I began to cry – as she was seeing emotions, fears, and deep beliefs that I have kept hidden all my life.

Vianna gave me healing using her 'command' technique, which included muscle testing (kinesiology). But when she came to working on the inflamed area in my lower groin, which had steadily worsened during the previous weeks, she told me that for some reason I was hanging on to this pain – and that I was going to have an interesting weekend …

'Now what?' I frowned.

'And does your healing work for all time, or just for a moment?' I asked, bringing myself back to the present.

'It depends upon the person,' Vianna said softly. 'Obviously, I also tell people to watch their diet and to take various supplements.' In my case, she recommended eating more fresh coriander, which helps to absorb and eliminate heavy metals from the body. She had been correct in this respect too, as I had had several mercury fillings removed a few years ago, but had never got around to doing a full detox. Anyway, our atmosphere is full of various toxic metals – from cadmium in cigarette smoke, black polythene, fungicides and processed foods to lead and copper from old pipes and aluminium found in tin foil, water supplies, baking soda, cat litter, deodorants and so on. This is why we all need to eat more fresh coriander and reduce our toxic load as much as we can through our diet, by using organic cosmetics and other more natural-based products, from paints and insect repellent to herbicides and deodorants.

By the time we parted, I felt altogether lighter and brighter. The pain in my neck and lower back was greatly reduced and I felt more positive.

My greatest sadness was that I could not return for a few more treatments as Vianna lives so far away. But if you want to know more about her fascinating work and her workshops, try reading her book *Go Up and Work With God* which can be ordered via her website www.thetahealing.com

Within two days the pain in my groin had intensified to such a degree, that on the Saturday my doctor diagnosed a hernia which she said needed fairly urgent medical attention. But when I had an MRI scan at the hospital, no hernia could be found! Vianna had indeed seen my imminent future.

A few days later, on June 4, I awoke to hear the news that Frances Shand Kydd, Princess Diana's mother, had passed away peacefully the previous day at her home in Scotland. And I prayed that on 'the other side' they would be reunited as friends. Little did I know on that day the surprise that Diana was hatching for me, which would occur within weeks of my publisher's deadline for finishing this book …

July 1, 2004 – Ruislip, Middlesex, England

Five years earlier I had interviewed London-based energy specialist Mark Lester for a feature in *The Sunday Times*. I was fascinated to see the pictures he took of my energy field with a specialist PIP scanner, which clearly showed areas of pain or congestion in my body. Here was a machine that could do some of what Vianna and others like her can do. My feature duly appeared and caused great interest, but in that moment I never dreamed that one day I would meet the scanner's inventor – biophysicist Harry Oldfield. Nor did I ever think that I would be able to actually see energy meridians, chakras, and even a kundalini on the move. I was in for a few more Ah-ha moments.

Harry Oldfield, based in Ruislip in Middlesex in the UK, has spent over 30 years researching energy medicine. His fascination with the possibility of utilizing human energy fields as a diagnostic tool was first ignited when he saw the character Dr McCoy, from the TV series *Star Trek*, scanning patients' energy fields using a small hand-held device. In the early days Harry experimented with Kirlian photography, in which specialist cameras clearly showed the energy fields surrounding humans, animals, plants and crystals. And when he started working alongside conventional doctors at some of London's teaching hospitals, he noticed that when he compared pictures of patients' energy fields before and after conventional medical treatments such as chemotherapy, the treatment often triggered distortions within the energy fields, which on average extended about 1.8 metres (six feet or so) – around the body.

The young scientist then set about developing a scanner that would photograph these energy distortions being emanated from the body. Like numerous other scientists around the world, he came to the conclusion that if these distortions could somehow be correctly interpreted, he would have made a non-invasive detection device. Later on, he subsequently concluded that if the patient were also to be pulsed with harmonic frequencies, then any disharmonic frequencies and distortions could be neutralized, which Harry theorized would rebalance the energy field and help the person to become well again. This is what healers and dolphins have been doing for thousands of years.

First, Harry developed the scanner, which he called Polycontrast Interference Photography, or PIP for short. Poly means many; contrast means that you can contrast, and therefore compare, one thing with another; and the whole procedure can be photographed using a digital camera linked to a computer. Harry took up his story.

'Basically, light enters our energy fields from our environment, interacts with our fields on a subtle level and bounces off into the environment again. I designed the PIP to give us diagnostic information from this energy-field interaction – we can observe light as it passes into the energy field, and then as it is reflected back out of the body we are able to see and analyse the effects.'

After more than 12 years as a health writer, I am already aware that every cell or group of cells within the body emits a specific range of frequencies. When a person is healthy, the cells emit harmonic frequencies which can be clearly seen as specific frequencies of colour on specialist scanners like the PIP. But if a person has a cancer, a tumour, injury sites or any areas of energy congestion, these all emit disharmonic frequencies which again are clearly visible on scanners like the PIP. Harry has now also developed a research microscope that can show energy reactions around living cells, bacteria and amoeba, that could not be seen on any ordinary microscope. When he showed me plain mud under his microscope not only could I see myriad bacteria, but also beautiful bright pinks and yellows within the mud. The mud was alive!

Meanwhile, problem areas within the body are clearly denoted by largish bright red blotches, whereas long thin red, green, blue or yellow lines indicate that energy is running smoothly around the body. And today, with more than 20 years' experience, Harry can instantly spot any health problems, old injury sites, inflammation and so on.

'In fact,' he smiles, 'we often "see" pain or potential health problems in a patient's energy field weeks or months before the physical condition presents itself, as virtually all disease begins in the energy field before it manifests in the physical body. And over many years I found that by looking at the scans I was easily able to determine where and what the main medical problems were.'

At this point in his career, Harry had begun experimenting with crystals – which make great conductors and amplifiers of frequencies (hence why they are used in TVs and computers) and he eventually found that pulsing 'problem' areas with specific, harmonic or balancing frequencies via crystal electrodes rebalanced the energy field, thus helping to resolve many health problems. Therefore, once Harry has seen the PIP scans, he places crystal-filled electrodes near the injury or illness site and pulses patients with the appropriate harmonic correcting frequencies, which encourage the body to heal itself. Today his scanner, in conjunction with his electro-crystal therapy, is used worldwide by alternative practitioners, hospitals and doctors alike.

As it had been more than five years since my last scan, I asked Harry if he would have a quick look at my energy field. His ex-wife, Eileen, who works as his assistant, asked me to strip down to my underwear ... thank goodness it was matching! And as I breathed in for England, Harry scanned me from head to foot with a small hand-held digital camera linked to a computer. Almost instantly I could see myself on the screen as a mass of green, yellow, purple, pink, blue and red zigzag lines. It looked as though a small child had gone ballistic with a crayon set.

'See here,' he began, pointing to my jaw area. 'Look at all this red in your jaw and neck − this is severe compressed energy and looks like post-operative blockages. There's your solar plexus chakra pulsing away − but it is showing signs of energy depletion; you are quite run down.'

It was like being with Vianna all over again − she too had told me that my energy levels were very low, and I had promised to take myself off to a health farm when the book was finished. As he continued examining my pictures I asked him about people like Vianna. 'Of course humans have this ability,' he laughed. 'Think of it this way. If you want to log on to the internet, you need a computer to access it, to see and receive information. But if you were to destroy your computer − which you could pretend is a human brain − it doesn't mean that the internet connection that was on your screen or the knowledge within your brain has disappeared into nothingness. In the case of the internet, all that information is still there in cyber space; in the case of your brain, all the information is still there in consciousness. The human brain, through which the 'whole mind' can work, is far more powerful than my scanner or anything that is currently available in science. My PIP scan is only capable of a fraction of what a fully enlightened brain or mind would be capable of.'

Within hours of Harry telling me this I was to chat with Professor Gary Schwartz, who was in the UK attending a conference. When I had talked to him about Harry, Gary had told me that double-blind scientific trials on several medical intuitives, one of whom is a PhD scientist working in his centre, were in progress to determine whether the 'gifts' that Vianna, Robyn and others display could be documented.

Back in Ruislip, I was full of admiration for Harry's humility and honesty. He turned his attention back to my scans.

'Look here,' he showed me a large green area that was pulsating like a jelly fish. 'It's your heart energy field, clearly visible. This chakra looks very healthy.'

I was pleased that something was okay, and was fascinated to actually see my chakras.

'The heart,' Harry went on, 'is the largest generator of electromagnetic signals in the body, which then radiate back out through the body and into space. As the human body is around 70 percent water (made up of blood plasma and lymph), which is a great conductor of electrical energy, with every heartbeat the electrical signals it produces travel to every cell in the body, and every cell is automatically bathed in the electromagnetic energy produced by the heart. This is why if a person was very stressed or angry we would easily see it, as they would emit a very high electrical field, capable of affecting electrical equipment and people around them.

'Every cell holds a memory of everything that has happened to it for years. So when a person receives someone else's heart in a transplant operation, they are, in effect, receiving a lot of information about the person whom the heart came from. We hear of cases all the time in which a donor heart recipient begins craving foods or music that the deceased donor had. This is because they have a new energy field inside them that carries information.'

Fascinating.

We moved on to my groin. Harry showed a blotch of red in the exact area in which I was suffering extreme discomfort that the doctor had thought was a hernia. Harry suggested that this could be linked to scar tissue from an old operation, or that I might have a trapped nerve in my spine. On the side of my legs were large red areas, which Harry said was severe pain tracking down my leg. As he said this I was confused – yes I suffer from back pain, but not leg pain. But within a month of meeting Harry, I started to suffer pulsing pains in my legs which started out of the blue one morning as I stood in the bathroom ... and my chiropractor diagnosed a trapped nerve in my upper back! Like Vianna, Harry had also seen the future of my health. However, during our meeting he was keen to make it clear that he never offers a medical diagnosis as such – he tells people what he sees in their energy fields and what his analysis denotes, but he is keen for people to also consult their doctors, to have blood tests or whatever is necessary to make a conventional diagnosis. After all, it's always a good idea to receive two opinions.

In my lower back area Harry showed me how an energy bubble had formed at the site of my original back injury which was 'leaking' energy.

'Energy comes and goes all the time,' Harry continued. 'Pain doesn't stop at your skin – energy just flows out into your energy field and from there, out into the universe.'

And as he studied my back more closely, he said, 'And here is your kundalini energy. Look at this configuration tracking up your spine.'

Suddenly I was all ears. 'You mean,' I asked incredulously, 'that you can actually see the kundalini if it's active?'

'Good heavens, yes, we see it all the time. In your case what we can see clearly is the residual *memory* of your kundalini experience. It's like when I look at the energy field of someone who has had an arm or a leg amputated – you can still see a clear, well-defined energy field that remains in the shape of an arm. We would see the same phantom effect if we plucked a leaf from the stem of a plant and then looked at that plant using the scanner. This is why an amputee can still feel pain. The energy field remains for quite some time and therefore the brain will still register feelings as if the physical limb were still there.'

Before I could say a word, Harry rushed off and returned with a scan that clearly showed a funnel of bright white light all the way up a patient's spine.

'Most people think of the kundalini, the chakras and the meridian energy channels as an abstract theory or a figment of some ancient philosopher's imagination. But they are very real and they can now be seen. Thousands of years ago, enlightened people sketched the kundalini like a coiled double serpent spiralling up the spine that became the symbol of medicine − a caduceus. In fact, they were sketching an exact replica of our DNA which scientists did not discover until several thousand years later.'

'Does this indicate,' I asked breathlessly, staring at the zigzag column of white light that resembled lightening in reverse, 'that these people are in the middle of some kind of kundalini awakening and going through a spiritual emergency?'

'Absolutely.' Harry smiled as if he had just told me something startlingly obvious, like the sun comes up every day.

'And how often do you see this phenomenon?'

'Oh, at least once a month. We see it especially in people who have taken ecstasy, forms of marijuana or other "social" drugs − like the stuff that Zulus use as snuff to make them more aggressive.'

'And are these people in a very heightened state?'

'I should say so,' he chuckled, trying to look suitably serious at the same time. 'We try to explain to them what's going on, what they can do to ground their experience. We help them to understand that they are not the only person in the world this is happening to. It takes time, but like you, if they can keep going without blowing a fuse such as developing high blood pressure or having a stroke, then they tend to eventually figure things out.'

Harry is keen for people to realize that he does not advocate attempting to induce a kundalini experience through drugs; he wisely suggests that if a person wants to experience heightened states they need to explore a more spiritual pathway.

I wondered what Harry would have done for me if he had seen me at the height of my experience. 'We would,' he explained, 'have applied really calming frequencies to help slow down the huge energy surge that was pulsing up your spine and through every cell in your body. The electro-crystal therapy acts like a tuning fork, helping to balance out your energy fields, and thus automatically it would have helped bring you back into balance.'

Harry also explained that when he has scanned healers whilst they were giving hands-on healing, he could clearly see a transfer of energy from the healer to the patient.

'And does this healing,' I asked, 'emanate from the healer's body, or is it channelled through the healer and into the patient?'

'It can be either. Sometimes we see the energy emanating from the heart chakra or the solar plexus area of the healer, but on other occasions we see full-spectrum white light entering the healer's energy field and then we can watch it being transferred into the patient. But whichever way it happens, I need to make it clear that, in the majority of cases, if the healer does not have the intention to heal then we usually see nothing. First comes the intention.'

'And so,' I pressed, 'if you can see these subtle and yet very powerful energies, can you also see ghosts' energy fields?'

'We have on occasion.'

Harry showed me an amazing image of what looked like the energy field of an elderly bearded man whom he had photographed in a mortuary, which he suggests could well be some kind of guardian angel or a spirit that helps people to move on.

Before I took leave of this highly energetic and passionate scientist, I spoke with several patients who have been healed from conditions as diverse as severe back pain and insomnia to irritable bowel syndrome and some cancers via electro-crystal therapy. Just in case you think that all this is in the patients' minds, bear in mind that Harry also treats animals. One patient told me about her cat who had suffered severe nerve damage after being hit by a car and whom the vet had said would have to be put down. But after several treatments the nerves had reconnected and the cat was fine! There is no doubt in my mind that energy medicine in its many forms is the medicine of the future – which can be found today.

As Harry showed me out, my mind was full of questions and I quickly asked him about the anecdotal stories of adults and children who have 're-grown' partial limbs after amputation.

'Oh yes,' he smiled, 'I've seen this several times. Orthodox doctors and surgeons regularly see fingertips that have been cut off in accidents grow back. This generally happens when the wound has not been stitched, as the finger would naturally grow back into its original energy-field pattern.

'Salamanders grow new limbs all the time, and there are documented cases in which people's limbs have started to re-grow. My theory is that if we were able to keep any amputated area in a sterile environment and somehow control the bleeding without stitching, then we could stimulate the area by either pulsing electromagnetic fields or using stem cells or possibly hormonal growth mechanisms as well as the electro-crystal therapy – then I believe the limb could re-grow.'

A week or so after Harry had told me this, I read in Professor William Tiller's book *Science and Human Transformation* that a paranormal scientific researcher in the States – one Jack Schwartz – could thrust needles through his body, then mentally, through the power of his intention, either allow his body to bleed or not … it was simply his intention that created the desired outcome.

It seems that intention holds one of the most vital keys to truly understanding not only our capabilities, but also to explain how the universe evolves. And I was about to speak to one of the world's most accredited scientists on the subject of matter and consciousness.

Hold on to your hats.

If you would like to know more about Harry Oldfield's work or receive a list of the therapists he has trained, log on to www.electrocrystal.com or read *Harry Oldfield's Invisible Universe* by Grant and Jane Solomon (Campion Books).

14

How Miracles are Made

What we can see with our eyes comprises less than 10 percent of the universe. The real power sustaining its architecture is the energy contained in the 90 percent of the unseen.

EMERITUS PROFESSOR WILLIAM A. TILLER

Down the millennia, thousands of so called 'miracles' have been reported. There are documented cases of enlightened masters who can sit and stare at the sun for hours or they can be locked away in a confined space with no food or water for several weeks or months at a time and remain in perfect health. There are monks and spiritual swamis who can move small and large objects using the power of their minds; and phenomena such as levitation, plus instant healing, would to them be a normal occurrence. Jesus and others like him have been reported to have the ability to turn water into wine or oil. At Lourdes, several 'miracles' of spontaneous healing have occurred, and at Medjugorje in Croatia, thousands of people throng to a hillside in the hope of seeing visions of Mother Mary. Some mystics and psychics can predict the future with amazing accuracy – whilst others can retrieve precise messages from the deceased. A comprehensive list of such phenomena would fill a large library. Some of these have been well documented, whilst others reflect historical accounts that have not been verified.

It's one thing to relate your own experiences of 'miracles', but proving such anecdotal evidence in science is one of the greatest challenges facing open-minded scientists today. And yet there is a huge amount of definitive, well-researched and, even better, well-validated evidence out there if you are willing to go out and find it.

During my stay at the Chopra Center in California, the medical director, Dr David Simon, had told me that the way to create your reality is to bring your attention to something and then to introduce an intention – and when this is done by people who have greater levels of control over their minds, then virtually anything is possible. To illustrate his point he referred to the studies carried out by Professor Herbert Benson, based at Harvard Medical School. Professor Benson studied Buddhist monks in India's northern foothills, where the outside temperature was just -6.6°C (20°F), which is below freezing. The monks were stripped, and wet sheets at a temperature of just above freezing, 4.4°C (40°F), were wrapped around their shoulders. Within 15 minutes steam had begun rising from the wet sheets as the monks' body temperatures rose as much as 17 degrees above normal; and within 45 minutes the sheets were completely dry, thanks to their focusing of attention and intention.

Back in 1968 Genagy Sergeyev, a neurophysiologist at the Utomskii Institute in Leningrad, tested a healer, Nelya Mikhailova, by attaching her to an electroencephalograph (an EEG machine that measures brain waves) and a heart monitor. The scientist then broke an egg into a saline solution in a large container 1.8 metres (about 6 feet) away from the healer. Whilst he and his team recorded any unusual activity in Nelya's brain, heart rate and so on, they asked her to attempt through her attention and intention to separate the yolk from the white of the egg. Not only was she able to do this – and it was recorded for posterity – but she was also able to move them back together. The main movement occurred when her brain waves shifted into theta – the same waves that Vianna Stibal and others produce during healing.

It's great to know that such phenomena are verifiable and at times repeatable under scientific conditions, but the next step is to find out *how* such feats are possible. Thanks once again to my friend Dr Sangeeta Sahi, I was about to find out.

A few months earlier when I had told her I would be writing this book, she had suggested I should read material physicist Professor William Tiller's book *Science and Human Transformation*. When it finally arrived I had a quick flick through, noted all the complex scientific data and mathematical equations it contained – and quietly filed it away among the 1,000 or so health and metaphysical books I have collected over the past 15 years. It was way beyond my understanding.

Then fate intervened again. One day as I had sat staring at my collection of books, I asked the universe to somehow send me a highly regarded academic who could help me to really understand how 'miracles' happen from a scientific perspective. Even though science is a long way from being my favourite subject, I had long ago come to the conclusion that a massive shift in our perception of what is possible will only take place through science.

Two days later, my husband brought me a cup of steaming tea and went to place it on my beautiful oak desk.

'Don't do that!' I had exclaimed, 'You'll mark my desk …'

'Well put it on a book, then,' he countered.

You have guessed. The random book I pulled out was William Tiller's tome, and as I drank the tea I flicked once more through the pages I had long forgotten. This time around, I saw headings such as Remote Viewing, Levitation, Dematerialization, Fire Walking, Spirit-initiated Physical Action – and so on, and I knew that my prayer had been answered. After researching his name on the web and seemingly endless calls to Stanford University in California, I finally spoke with the man himself.

After polite introductions I offered a brief overview of my work, and told the Professor that I was keen to understand how intention itself can have a physical effect on the human body and our lives; how Mother Mary can appear at Medjugorje, how Swamiji and others like him are able to shape their subtle body and appear in several places at once; how remote viewing works ... and more. And might he be willing to help me?

A deep sigh greeted my avalanche of requests.

'Young lady (I loved that), you have just asked me to summarise what has taken me 35 years of painstaking research to even begin to understand – in just one phone call.' He suggested that we would need a few hours on the phone, and we made our first date. Before we said goodbye I jokingly commented, 'It's a great pity that someone, somewhere, cannot bottle intention and then there would be some proof.'

'Oh, we have been doing that for quite some time,' quipped the amiable scientist.

Needless to say, before our first chat I did my best to read and absorb a fraction of the huge amounts of knowledge his books contain, and I also had a look at his website, www.tiller.org

William A. Tiller PhD is one of the world's leading physicists on the structure of consciousness and matter. For over 35 years he was based in the Department of Materials Science at the world-famous Stanford University in California, and today he continues his research through the Tiller Foundation. He is a fellow to the American Academy for the Advancement of Science, an Emeritus Professor who has had five books and 350 scientific papers published. You get my drift. But importantly, from my perspective, here was a world-class scientist of huge renown who also meditates, who has tried kinesiology, who advocates qigong as a great exercise, and a man who has witnessed, practised or experienced many of the phenomena – from healing to materialization – that I too had experienced during 1998. We may be worlds apart in our IQ scores, I mused, yet we still have considerable interests in common.

In the foreword to his book *Conscious Acts of Creation* are glowing contributions from Rustum Roy, Professor Emeritus of Solid State at

Pennsylvania State University; from Wayne Jonas, Associate Professor at the Department of Preventative Medicine in Bethesda, Maryland, and George Sudarshan, Professor of Physics from Austin, Texas. They all discuss the importance of Tiller's work and state that this is the first time that so much 'new science' has been so clearly explained via the language of physics. As I flicked through the pages I knew that his equations were way out of my depth, so I simply made a list of the questions I was hopeful Bill could explain to me as if he were talking to a 10-year-old. You really are as old as you feel, and I was getting younger by the minute!

Now if like me you are intimidated by science, please try to keep going with this chapter. Even better, I suggest that you read it twice to allow the enormity of what Tiller has discovered really sink in. Believe me, if I can get it, you can. Professor Tiller was to share with me not only some of his fascinating research results, but also a few of his predictions for what we will become capable of in the future. At times I have greatly simplified his information, with his permission, but please do not allow this simplification to diminish the importance of this man's message. Thanks to his awesome knowledge, I now truly understand that we really are in the middle of a huge transformation in the way we view our world and the universe. We are no longer on the verge of this transition – in terms of spiritual awakening, all the ingredients have been mixed and are now 'baking in the oven', so to speak; and thanks to scientists like Bill Tiller, Gary Schwartz, Rupert Sheldrake, Fred Travis and their many colleagues around the globe, pretty soon we are going to witness the most incredible, perfectly cooked feast of all time. That is, of course, if we choose to take a bite of this feast and digest its contents properly …

And so we began our first call. The first and most obvious question was to ask Bill Tiller to clarify his definition of a miracle.

'A miracle is an experimental or observational result that defies explanation by the prevailing world view. In other words if you can't explain it, based on the prevailing paradigm (framework), it's a miracle.'

Well that seemed clear enough, so I plunged in at the deep end. 'When we last spoke, you said that you have "bottled intention". Can you expand on this?'

'Firstly, I need to say that for the past 200 years the unstated assumption of science has been that no human quality of consciousness, intention, emotion, mind or spirit can significantly influence a well-designed experiment in our physical reality. And so I and others designed experiments involving human intention – and they show that intentions strongly influence the properties of materials, and such results cannot be explained by the prevailing paradigm, therefore by definition they are miracles.'

So far, so good.

'In our experiments, basically two small black boxes were fitted with simple electrical circuits with outputs of about a millionth of a watt, so compared to a normal light bulb their output was insignificant. One of these boxes was kept as the control box, meaning that no intention was 'pulsed' into it. The second box was placed on a table and it had a transformer that could be plugged into a normal socket to give it power.

'Okay so far?'

Just about. My idea of a complex experiment is getting the video to record the programme that I actually want to see!

'And then,' he continued, 'we asked four experienced meditators to sit around the table and go into a very deep meditative state. In that deep meditative state they cleansed the surrounding area of the box on the table, so that it became a kind of sacred space – in scientific terms, we would call this a "conditioned space". Then one of the four read a particular stated intention, focusing on the small black box in front of them. The intention we asked them to set into the box was that the device should increase the pH of purified water by one full pH unit. Keep in mind that every human body has an average pH of between 7.35 and 7.45; if you move it half a pH unit on one side, you're probably dead, and if you move it half a pH unit the other way, you're also probably dead. So if we could achieve a result of one full pH unit we would call this a very significant change, or a very big signature, because the measurement accuracy was better than one hundredth of a pH unit. Still okay?'

Kind of … and for those who are not clear what pH does, it relates to the hydrogen ion concentration. Whether a substance is acid or alkaline depends upon its pH level. For good health your blood would need to be 70 percent alkaline and 30 percent acid. This subject is well covered in my health books.

'Well,' he went on 'then we shipped this tiny box with the intention "set" inside it 1,500 miles away to a laboratory where they were all set up with the equipment to measure and monitor the pH of purified water. They plugged in our little back box, placed it near the water – and waited. And after a month or so, slowly but surely the pH within their water began changing in the direction of the requested intention until it had increased by *exactly* one full point. Then we repeated this same experiment with another black box and asked the meditators to set the intention to go down one full pH – and again it worked. And this experiment was then repeated at various other laboratories with the same results.'

'And what are the chances,' I asked, 'of this change in the pH happening by chance?'

'Let's put it this way. Without chemical additions, pH variations might fluctuate around a few thousandth of a pH unit but we were asking for one whole pH unit; that's more than 100 times larger. The probability of that happening by random chance is incredibly small.'

'So this obviously implies that intention affects physical matter. It changes an outcome.'

'Yes, it changes an outcome. Now if that little black box were a computer, you would know it contains physical software and stuff, but our software had been "placed" in the device by thought, so it's very different than anything you have ever known, because in essence we haven't touched the device. We haven't fed in any electronic information per se.'

'So ... this shows that thought goes somewhere? But on an everyday level, what happens if someone sends out horrible thoughts to someone? Could my thinking negatively of them actually harm them?'

'Of course it could. We're creating the future all the time this way, by our thoughts, attitudes and actions. We collectively do it; it would, however, take more than a few odd casual thoughts, but if you sustained such thoughts over a long period of time or if you were a highly experienced and focused practitioner, then you could achieve it. This is how voodoo works, and it's how prayer works. Knowledge as always is impartial, it's what you choose to do with it that determines the outcome.'

'So', I queried, 'if you send loving thoughts like the prayer study done by Dr Randolph Byrd in America in 1988 – in which heart patients were prayed for without their knowledge and they recovered more quickly – this is simply intention?'

'Yes, so long as you allow the hierarchy of spirit in the "unseen" to seriously participate in achieving the final outcome, the intention influences the heart patient's energy environment – and there are a lot of details as to how this happens – but in principle that is exactly what I'm saying and we showed this with our water experiments. We have also done similar experiments on liver enzymes and then on fruit flies, and again, the specific intentions that were set were *exactly* what occurred. And in the case of the prayer studies, what all this implies is that the universe is far more intelligent than we have previously understood. We can talk more about this later, but to clarify what we have done: we have shown that this unstated assumption that science has held for two centuries is *very, very wrong* ...'

What he was sharing with me was awesome in its implications, but I wanted to know how Bill would suggest people protect themselves on a daily basis against all the negative energies that are around us constantly.

'There are a variety of ways. Certainly the simplest one is to meditate and imagine surrounding yourself in a white balloon, or a shield-type structure. Over time you then basically build up a conditioned space around yourself.'

This was similar to what I had recommended to Jatinder back in Chapter 9. Again, it's great to hear verification from a scientist. Not only that, but one who knows why and how this type of visualization works.

From what I had read in Bill's book, I knew that as his experiments continued some big surprises happened – and I asked if he could explain in simple terms what they were. Professor Tiller does not do simple. Nevertheless, what he told me was astonishing. He explained that when the black box containing the intention 'imprint' had achieved its 'intention' of raising the pH in the water one full point – and it had remained at that level for a month or so – it was then moved out of the room where the experiments took place and put in a Faraday cage, which prevents any electrical energy going in or out. But even though they were separated, then the pH levels in their water *stayed exactly at the level of the original intention for more than one or two years.* In other words, there was no 'electrical' signal of any description getting through to the water.

However, if the boxes were removed whilst the pH level was slowly climbing or falling depending on the 'set' intention, gradually the water returned to its original state. It was only when the water reached the plateau of the one full point up or down that the intention remained for any length of time.

Bill continued his story. 'My point is you have to *get past a threshold*; something stabilized the conditioned state, because this conditioned space is really quite remarkable. But even more remarkable is that when we took that Intention Imprinted Electrical Device – the simple black box with the intention imprinted in it – and placed it about 100 metres (300 feet) away from the original unimprinted device (the one that had not had any intention pulsed into it) and turned them both off electrically, according to present-day accepted scientific terms no information should be transmitted. But it was. We found that within three days to a week, the unimprinted device began to act like the imprinted device. It had picked up the intention statement somehow.'

'And how do you perceive it did that?'

'Via a new magnetic type of energy that is associated with consciousness. Let me simplify this a bit ... pretend that you are in a church and people go there, let's say, every day to pray. They visualize what they want, they set an intention. Let's pretend they are all wishing for the same thing. Once they leave the church, they have begun to 'condition' that space – they have left some energy there – but overnight their thoughts disperse or decay somewhat.

'But if they return the next day and do it again, they lift the conditioning a little higher and the next day they lift it a little higher and the next day, the next week, the next month, the next year, and so on. This coherence – this conditioning – begins to build an invisible structure in their environment, something akin to builders putting up a fine lattice-like scaffold or a grid-type structure in order to 'hold' the intention. So this is how sacred spaces were created in the old days. So that's one example.

'Another example is, suppose there is a garage inventor who thinks he has an idea of how to make a free energy device, something whose efficiency is 100 percent. He works on it in his garage on evenings and weekends for years, and eventually he gets to a stage where he thinks he's got it. And so he invites in his friends and demonstrates it to them, and they're jumping up and down with excitement because they believe he's got it. They say, "Let's start a business with this, let's do something really practical with this wonderful thing you've created," and someone else says, "Okay, but before we do this we have to have it independently tested by someone else who has the testing equipment to do this." Let's say such a testing facility is miles away and they send the device to be tested. But the analyst sends back his results, saying, "Are you guys kidding, because the results just show normal sorts of things, there's no special efficiency – nowhere near the 100 percent you guys were reporting."

'What they had not realized was that while the man was working on his dream invention all these days and nights and weekends, his intention for fulfilling his dream and his goal were *conditioning* the space, and so they got the special properties because *the space was conditioned and it had become intelligent*, it had become *part of the instrumentation*. In other words, the testing facility was not a *conditioned* space, so the original data could not be reproduced there.'

Wow, this was incredible. I tried to get my thoughts together and slowly asked, 'In other words, "empty" space, as we consider it, contains lots of "stuff" and lots of knowledge?'

'Absolutely.'

We talked on for another hour about conditioned spaces, magnetic monopoles, information entanglement, and how Professor Tiller had confirmed that his small boxes are even able to communicate with each other thousands of miles apart. And if anyone needs to read all the technical data, obviously you are free to study his books and papers.

In the meantime, what I was looking for was a big conclusion ...

'*Okay, what I am saying is that there is a channel, previously unknown in current science, through which information can be communicated*. We've shown experimentally that this process is real – and the physics is there, but it's at a higher level of physics that facilitate what hitherto most people would term miracles. We are talking about a new category of universal energy that can be modulated by intention, by consciousness. It's an energy source beyond what we can imagine because it's tapping the vacuum.'

'Hang on,' I interjected, fast wishing I had a large piece of chocolate cake to keep me going through all this. 'What's this vacuum?' I had read about the zero point field in Lynne McTaggart's great book *The Field*, and I had understood from Lynne's descriptions that the zero point field is basically an ocean of microscopic vibrations in the space between 'things', the vast quantum field of space all joined together by some invisible web.

The Professor sighed, and I could sense his frustration at my lack of scientific knowledge. But he continued with gentle patience. 'Thinking of the zero point field as being the be all and end all is not correct – in fact, what's happened so far is that science up until now has only peeled the first layer of the onion; the next layer of the onion is the vacuum itself. In fact, the energy stored in the zero point field is extremely trivial compared to the total energy stored in the vacuum. Professor Gary Schwartz asked you to imagine that one atom of hydrogen was the size of the Empire State Building [see Chapter 5], and he told you that the nucleus of that atom would only be as big as a grain of sand – therefore 99.99 percent of that atom was empty space – this empty space is the vacuum level of reality. Whereas the zero point field is the electromagnetic radiation field that pulses back and forth between atoms, even at the absolute zero of temperature, and it is created by atoms. Thus, *it passes through the vacuum level of reality, but it is not the stuff of the vacuum level of reality.* The "stuff" of the vacuum is not detectable by normal present-day instrumentation. However, we have recently patented a device that does detect aspects of this vacuum "stuff".

'Gary also told you that the infinite mind is bigger than the entire universe, and it is. But the energy stored in all the physical mass of the universe is quite small in comparison to the energy stored in the "stuff" of the vacuum. The energy stored in the vacuum far, far outweighs all the energies involved in the zero point field. And even this vacuum has many levels. Stephen Hawking has acknowledged 11 dimensions in nature; what I believe is that everything up to number 10 is simply pre-school and after that you are then seriously working your way towards the centre of the onion. Let me put it this way – once a person taps into the energies within the vacuum, seeing through a human body would be very much like child's play. In fact, we have shown this in experiments in which we have photographed highly spiritually aware people using "*conditioned*" cameras, and the pictures show what is on the *other side* of their bodies. This science is already in play. And there could come a day when we could have the capability, metaphorically speaking, to birth whole universes out of ourselves.'

Now it was my turn to take a deep breath. What I was hearing was so beyond my comprehension. It was time to bring this down to earth.

Bill began again. 'Think about what I have told you. If small black boxes can "communicate" with each other across small and huge distances, what we have shown in multiple and repeated experiments through physics is how remote viewing works, how telepathy works, how a prayer or a curse can reach a specific person or target a specific location either across a room or on the other side of the world; how you can have access to the past and the future, how enlightened beings can move their subtle energy bodies 6,000 miles and appear somewhere else. What we have found is a new kind of energy, which is a highly intelligent energy. And crucially, within the human body *we have access to this new vacuum energy via the acupuncture meridian chakra system.* This is where this "new" energy flows. This is why it is imperative for more research into "alternative medicine". As we now know – and orthodox medicine and science agree – 90 percent of normal medical drugs are actually not needed if you introduce this new "vacuum-intelligent energy". This energy knows where it is needed, it knows what it needs to do. Let me give you an example.'

I quietly raised my eyes to the heavens thinking of how most medical doctors would view what Bill was telling me – which I instinctively have known is true for several years. Now, at long last, here was authoritative verification ...

'I call this new way of healing "information medicine", because it has consciousness, it has intelligence, it has patterns. The information – the pattern – is what is important. For example, if you took a glass of water and you put bacteria in it, and then you placed some silver colloidal particles in that glass, you will kill the bacteria. Anyone who is interested in alternative health will know this. However, what isn't well known is that if you were to take a fluorescent bulb or lamp and you put the colloidal silver particles on to the bulb and then focus the radiation output of that lamp on to the water containing the bacteria, then the bacteria will also be killed. It is the electromagnetic radiation pattern from the silver that is the lethal agent here. Now, by tapping into a higher level in nature, to the consciousness-influenced magnetic energies functioning in the physical vacuum level of the body, this is what will eventually provide the world with information medicine.'

'So,' I interjected, 'when Vianna stated that she could repair genetic programmes, repair cells, destroy parasites, and that the laws governing the universe can be manipulated – was she correct?'

'I cannot answer for this lady's specific abilities as we have never met and I have not tested her, but basically what all our experiments show is that yes, such things are possible. When you activate your chakras and what I call your chi/prana pump by practising techniques such as qigong, meditation and so on, then you begin accessing the energy within the vacuum level of your bodies – and the potential is limitless.'

This reminded me of what Dr Fred Travis had said: that if 60 million people could focus on a single intention at the same time, it could become a reality.

'As you say,' added Bill, 'yes, their total intention would have that *potential* in that moment, but remember what I said about the analogy of people praying every day in church – this coherence – this conditioning – begins to build an invisible structure, and what we call a "higher gauge symmetry state" could be achieved once you reach a certain threshold. But first we need to build up the "invisible" infrastructure or lattice to hold any intention and then yes indeed, if enough people prayed and kept sustaining this prayer, the world could shift into a higher dimension state. We would peel away another layer of our onion. In fact, during some of our experiments when we took away some of our black boxes, once the focused-intention outcomes had been reached in the water, some of those high outcomes were still measurable by our instruments five years later.'

Blimey.

'And so when enlightened beings turn water to wine, this is what we have shown by focusing an intention to bring the pH up a point or down a point – we have changed its structure at its vacuum level. We now know that phenomena such as changing water to wine or oil and so on are possible in principle.'

I returned to my original questions and asked Bill about the visions of Mother Mary at Medjugorje. 'Is the area in which the visions appear a conditioned space?' I asked, 'or do the visions occur because thousands of people are there every day praying, sending out their intention for Mary to appear? And when Swamiji says he can stretch his subtle energy body across to Canada from India or wherever and seems to appear physically, is this his intention or that of the devotee who wants to see him?'

'It could be all of those things or a combination of them,' the Professor replied. 'Remember, once you create a sacred space to the point where the phenomena occurs, then this phantom effect can hang around for a long time. And because the people are praying daily it sustains the visions via the lattice structure. And before you ask me about the initial visions such as these, typically they tend to be experienced by children or adults who might be religious or who live in a religious country or community – and they might not be praying as such. They could just be walking anywhere and the vision appears. This I would describe then as the *unseen*, the spirit world or much higher dimensions *initiating* such an event. There is plenty of evidence to show that Spirit and other dimensions can definitely affect phenomena in this dimension. Masters of the self have 'inbuilt muscles', as it were, to do all this; they have a fully functioning acupuncture meridian chakra system. This is the core system that drives all the other systems in the physical body. If these systems are functioning properly then you are unlikely to become sick because my theory is that these systems work from the vacuum level, this magnetic level. And let's be clear that intention is not a vacuum – it is a quality. Consciousness is a quality. A vacuum is "simply" the space that remains when you remove all the physical particles that make up atoms and molecules.'

'And what about people like Jatinder [back in Chapter 9] and monks who can levitate ... how do they do that?'

'In this entire area there is obviously a lot of fakery ... but there is plenty of evidence to show that people in a coherent state can and do levitate, and we are now experimenting with conditioned spaces in regard to creating levitational forces. In the coming years people will have a more honed ability to create sufficient internal vacuum forces and they will simply levitate.'

'And does the brain have to be functioning in a coherent way to be able to effect what most people call miracles?'

'Pretty well, yes, and also the heart.'

Back to coherence. This reminded me of some research I had seen about the water at Lourdes. If you look at pictures of the crystalline structure of a snowflake, no two are the same – rather like us. Similar in many ways, but still unique. And if you melt a snowflake, and then allow it to re-freeze under natural conditions, it re-forms into a similar unique snowflake pattern. Water has a memory ... just as every atom and cell in our bodies has a memory. Water can also transfer frequency patterns and wavelengths carrying information. Biophysicist and homeopath Harry Oldfield was later to remind me that this is the basic theory of how homeopathy works.

And if you were to look at pictures of the ice crystals from Lourdes, they show beautiful, blue-tinged regular structures. The water at Lourdes is relatively coherent. So many truly sick people who go there pray and really want to be healed, and for the most part they truly believe in the water's magical powers – with all their hearts and minds, they literally 'love' the water, and so it loves them right back! The water transfers some of its coherence into the energy field of anyone who enters the waters, thus encouraging the body to heal itself. And after listening to Bill, I also realized that the area around Lourdes and many other places where miracles occur have become highly conditioned spaces.

My first chat with Bill had stretched to over two hours. It was time for a break – and anyway, I had the world-famous biologist Rupert Sheldrake coming for lunch the next day to talk about predicting the future, and I needed time to prepare. At least, I thought, as I went to bed that night, no one could ever accuse me of having a boring life!

Seeing the Future – and the Past

If we open a quarrel between the past and the present, we shall find that we have lost the future.

SIR WINSTON CHURCHILL

People always find it easier to be a result of the past rather than a cause of the future.

ANON

Can we really see the future or the past? And if, as a large body of scientific research and documented evidence shows, we are indeed capable of such feats, is the information that we access 100 percent reliable? I would say the answer is both yes and no ... with many shades in between.

In the media I have read stories of people who claimed to have dreamed the winning lottery numbers and then won the jackpot a couple of days later; of people who have 'seen' horses winning – and again, they have laid their bets and gone on to win. Then there are the thousands of cases of prophetic dreams – and days, weeks or months later these dreams come true. Unfortunately, the only problem with prophetic dreams is that you don't know if they are genuinely prophetic until the predicted events actually happen!

Seven years ago, the spirit of Princess Diana had 'shared' with me that her death had been 'set in stone'. But did she mean set in stone for all time, or set in stone as part of her life plan when she agreed to come back into this lifetime? Or had she meant 'set in stone' from a long, long time ago?

Professor Gary Schwartz had told me that our future is basically pure potential until our thoughts, words and actions bring our reality into being. He had also told me that we are all made up of recycled atoms containing huge amounts of information – which have been recycling in and around us since the Big Bang some 10 to 15 billion years ago. In other words, that we have the potential to see our past by accessing the information within the atoms that are here today – that have always been here and will always be here.

What I had forgotten to consider in seeing the future is multiple realities. Could it be that our futures are just one big potential? On the other hand, what if certain events that happened a hundred or several hundred years ago set in motion a chain of events that began weaving a 'lattice' or 'grid' that holds intentions in place, as Professor Tiller had told me? And that certain intentions take somewhat longer to come to fruition … and therefore Diana's death had been set in stone, perhaps not for all time, but for quite a long time? This made sense to me, and it would also explain why great sages have often been able to predict correctly some events that have indeed transpired hundreds of years later.

And what about the past? When I had met physicist Russell Targ, one of the founding fathers of remote viewing, at a conference in late 2003, he had shared specific scientific research verifying that extremely experienced psychics can indeed access the past as well as the present and future.

The CIA funded much of Targ's experiments at Stanford Research International (SRI) over a period of more than 15 years, and for 10 of those Targ told us that they had spied on the Russians via remote viewing. The accuracy of the remote viewers' sketches of numerous military sites, later verified via satellite imagery, were remarkable. One experiment that caught my eye was when Targ requested one of his team of psychics, several of whom were also scientists, to go into a deep meditative state and with his mind 'travel' to specific map co-ordinates located in a remote area. To their astonishment, the remote viewer sketched the site exactly as it had looked some 50 years *earlier*, which was later verified through archive photographs. After what Bill Tiller shared with me, this made sense – that certain events, places and so on leave a phantom effect in a 'conditioned space' that can hang around in the vicinity, and that someone with a highly attuned sixth sense can pick up the information (or as Serena said, the video clip) from the energy being held in that conditioned space – by the 'lattice grid'. There are currently more than 100,000 websites on remote viewing, and Russell Targ's is one you can trust, on www.espresearch.com

July 5, 2004 – Henley on Thames, England

With these myriad possibilities rattling around in my head, I greeted Rupert Sheldrake, the world-famous biologist, to our home in Oxfordshire. Rupert is a true English gentleman, softly spoken, polite – and a brilliant scientist.

And as we sat down, I shared with Rupert that I was writing about the material physicist Bill Tiller and he exclaimed 'Good heavens, when I attended Bill's lectures, even as a scientist I was struggling to understand the physics ... *you are brave.*'

My self-esteem shot up from nil to 100 in five seconds flat. It just shows how a kind word or a compliment can make one's day – or in my case, make my month!

As we chatted, Rupert told me that he has carried out some groundbreaking research on intuition and psychic abilities in humans and animals. I asked him if he had ever studied premonitions.

'Yes,' he replied, 'in fact, I did an in-depth study of precognitive dreams after the World Trade Center disaster in 2001, as at the time it was the biggest disaster in recent history.'

Another 'synchronicity'; I had been in New York on September 11 for a meeting with Gayle King, Oprah Winfrey's right-hand executive. So many futures changed on that dreadful day, including mine. But I am one of the lucky ones – I lived to tell my tale.

'And how,' I enquired, 'did you find people who had experienced premonitions?'

'A colleague in New York put up posters for me in Union Square within days of the disaster and I ran advertisements in a local paper. In all I received about 75 detailed accounts from local people who had precognitive dreams during the few days prior to the event. I interviewed some of them to filter out possible crank information, and the most impressive stories were those in which the person had related the dream to someone else before the disaster. Quite a few had indeed done that.

'They fell into three categories. The first category was those who dreamed they were in low-flying planes – they had felt a sense of doom, and felt that they were going to crash into buildings somewhere near Manhattan. One man actually had specified the World Trade Center and he had made a note of his dream. Others had thought it was the Empire State Building or skyscrapers in other cities.

'The second category was people dreaming that they were trapped inside tall buildings that were on fire.

'The third category was people who dreamed not only of a great sense of foreboding, but some saw "white" clouds rolling down the streets. There were also several cases of artists who had depicted to varying degrees what happened several days before the event. And these pictures were dated and verified as having been done prior to the disaster. There is also the documented case of an artist who worked in the WTC who was killed on September 11 – yet several months earlier he had sculpted two giant figures with planes sticking out of them. I would say what they had seen was a possible future that came true.

'However, what research shows is that for all the people that claim visions, prophecies and so on, we tend to hear only about the ones that come true, but not the ones that don't. I myself have had strong premonitions, some of which simply did not come true.

'Science for now tells us that our future is basically made up of potential probabilities. But there are degrees of probability. For instance, if you walk to the top of a cliff and throw a stone off the edge; you know that in the next few seconds that stone will crash to the bottom. So in a sense that is knowing the future – even if only a few seconds ahead. You could also say that there is a probability that the sun will come up tomorrow – as for the next few million years this is what should occur – and so in this sense you are "seeing" way into the future. But if something completely off the wall were to happen, like the sun spinning off into space, then this presumption of the sun coming up each morning would change.

'You could also suggest that because many terrorists were involved with September 11 that their collective thoughts and actions accumulated a coherent energy imprint in the ether, or what Bill Tiller might refer to as a "lattice" or "energy grid" – not only around New York, but in other places around the globe, and so sensitive people picked up this potential probability. But I think that precognition is a more plausible interpretation of the facts, especially the dreams in which people reported seeing dust in the streets. Even the terrorists themselves could not have known that the Twin Towers would collapse, nor of the catastrophic melting of the steel girders which was unexpected even by structural engineers.'

'Therefore, in a more "perfect" world,' I surmised with Rupert, 'if a person had a dream that a train is going to crash – and in the dream they were given the exact location and date and time of that crash – and the next morning they called an open-minded police officer who acted upon this information, then with a bit of luck this "probability" could be averted?'

Rupert smiled. 'That would be great, and on occasion precise evidence does present itself. Unfortunately, the police or anyone else would find it hard to carry on with their everyday work if they acted upon every prophetic call.'

Now it was my turn to smile. During 1994 an astrologer who used to give readings to Princess Diana, had in one of her books correctly 'foretold' that Diana would perish in a car crash – and this same lady had sent me an email in November 2003, informing me that the House of Commons was going to be attacked very soon, in fact probably the next day, which happened to be the date of the State Opening of Parliament. In good faith I took her warning so seriously that I rang my old friend Lord Feldman and told him to be careful. Thank goodness, nothing happened – except I had egg all over my face …

When I had told my friend Dr Serena Roney-Dougal about my *faux pas*, she had laughed and said, 'Let's say you have 50,000 written predictions but only one comes true. That's a 1 in 50,000 chance. What the other 49,999 people *might* have done was picked up other potential probabilities that did not occur, or they might have been picking up some emotion from their own subconscious mind that threw up a particularly symbolic story to help that person clear whatever stuff they were dealing with in that moment. Or it could have been either/and/or a combination of the two.'

In fact, Serena had told me that around 80 percent of people who experience predictions tend to 'see' events that are going to occur within 24 to 48 hours, which is incredibly common. However, people accurately predicting a week or so ahead is much less common, and if you move into months and years, it becomes really rare.

'In other words,' she had said, 'what we have here is that precognition is like "remembering" the future.' For instance, she had asked me, 'What were you doing this time yesterday?'

'Typing!' came my speedy reply.

'Okay, now what were you doing at this exact moment a week ago?'

I had to think harder about that one.

'And a month ago?'

Unless I looked at my diary, I thought, I would not have had the faintest idea.

'Do you get it? Serena asked. 'Say if it had been your birthday a month ago, or you had taken a plane trip or something really special, you would have automatically remembered that date. But in general you would not. A big event casts a bigger shadow *backwards* – and then once it happens in our space/time, it also casts a shadow *forwards*, meaning it can affect our possible futures.

'Think about the assassination of John Kennedy in the 60s. Lots of people picked up his death as a probable potential future. And because not enough people called the police the FBI or whoever to say, "This will happen to President Kennedy at exactly this time, on this road, on this day," then JFK died. Yes, several people reported that something might happen, as the people who organized his death were setting events in motion, but the police or the FBI or anyone else cannot deal with every "might" that is reported. Again, there are multiple realities. But if enough people could have "pre-seen" this event and reported exact details to the police, maybe JFK could have been saved in that particular instance.

'In the meantime, it's important for people to know that seeing the future on an everyday level happens to people *all the time*. For instance, a couple of weeks ago I had a dream in which I was changing the plug of a Hoover vacuum cleaner. The next morning I was helping out at local assembly rooms and the vacuum cleaner, a Hoover, had no plug on it, which made me laugh. Such simple phenomena are a part of everyday life, but we only tend to hear *en masse* about the big predictions.

'We think,' she added, 'of time as linear. But if you were to get a really long piece of paper and then write on it various dates starting on the left-hand side of the paper at say 10,000 BCE, to 5000 BCE, to 2000 BCE then write today's date in the centre – and continue writing dates out towards the right-hand side as, say, 2010 CE , then 3000 CE and so on into the future until you reach the end of the paper, and take a look at what you have done, you'll see the present day is in the middle of the future and the past. And as you look at that long piece of paper you can "look at" dates in the future and in the past. *Time can go forwards or backwards from where you are now* …'

'But what if,' I asked, 'you then tape the long piece of paper together at either end? Then wherever you had put today's date on that paper, you would always be in the middle, in the present?'

'You've got it. The long piece of paper laid out flat would represent linear time, but once you made it into a circle or an oblong or whatever, then wherever you are *in the present*, represented by your date written on the circle, will always be in the middle – that's the "now". Time as we currently understand it is simply our long-established method of separating events without having everything happen at once, which would be rather chaotic. But in fact the only real time is now. To understand this concept further, you could try crumpling up the long piece of paper so that every bit of time connects with every other bit of time, irrespective of the past or future.'

As I had sat with Serena, I recalled how everything back in 1998 had begun spinning. The energies within me and the air around me had felt like an increasingly large circle which kept expanding and spinning. But whenever I had become more aware of the spinning and paid attention to it, the energy circle would become smaller and smaller and faster and faster until it stopped dead somewhere deep within me – and all reality as I knew it ceased to exist; there was no time, there was absolutely nothing but being in that single tiny dot of nothingness that contained everything. I had felt like I had come from the beginning of time right through to the end of time. And in the myriad spaces in between, I had been able to see hundreds of potential futures and parts of our past – and hearing Spirit, healing, seeing through people and so on, had been for brief moments literally child's play.

Serena also mentioned a feature called 'Retroactive Prayer' in the spring 2004 edition of *The Journal of the Scientific and Medical Network* by Dr Brian Olshansky and Dr Larry Dossey which suggests that we have the potential to go back and change the past and therefore our potential futures. For details see www.scimednet.org And from what I knew in that heightened state in 1998, which truly enlightened beings have known for eons, is now beginning to be understood by science. To access more of Serena's work, log on to www.psi-researchcentre.co.uk

Returning to the present on July 5, after lunch I asked Rupert for his thoughts on telepathy.

'In my research I have found that telepathy is more common when people have an emotional link or a close bond, and distance is immaterial in such cases – like a mother knowing that something is wrong with her child, or an affectionate animal "knowing" that its owner is on their way home. The commonest kind of telepathy in the modern world happens in connections with phone calls. Many people have found that they start thinking about someone for no apparent reason and soon afterwards that person calls. Some people even say the phone sounds different when a particular person is ringing. And many people have had someone respond to their call by saying, "That's amazing, I was just thinking about you."

'My surveys show that about 80 percent of the population has had seemingly telepathic experiences with phones. Sceptics dismiss this by saying we think of other people all the time and only remember the cases when someone rings soon afterwards. But they have no evidence to back up this speculation. I have now done hundreds of experiments to find out if telephone telepathy really happens. In these tests, the subject names four people they might be telepathic with, and they give us their numbers. For each trial, the subject sits beside a phone (a land line, with no caller ID system) and is videotaped continuously to make sure they are not receiving any other calls or emails. We then pick one of the four callers at random by throwing a dice and we ring them up and ask them to call. When the subject's phone rings, he or she has to guess which of the four callers is on the line, before picking up the receiver. By chance people would be right one time in four, or 25 percent of the time. We have completed more than 800 of these trails and the average success rate is 42 percent. People are certainly not right every time, but they are right much more than they would be by chance. This result is statistically very significant.

'We have now done a similar experiment involving emails, in which the subjects have four emailers and again we pick one at random. The subject has to guess who is about to email them one minute before the email is sent. In 600 trials the average success rate is 45 percent – again, very significantly above the chance level of 25 percent. I now have an online version of this telepathy test which anyone can try for themselves at my website at www.sheldrake.org.'

You can imagine that as soon as Rupert told me this I had a go at his test – and failed. So much for my telepathic abilities!

Russell Targ had told us that the men and women who took part in more than 15 years of experiments with the SRI were highly trained and highly focused psychics; in other words, their brains had become more coherent and they had gained access to the vacuum level of energy – where possibilities are limitless.

After Rupert had left, I was so keen to ask Professor Tiller for his interpretation in science as to how we can see the future or the past that in my haste I completely forgot the eight-hour time difference between the UK and California. Let's just say in that moment Bill wished he had not given me his home number.

After profuse apologies, I related what Rupert and Serena had shared with me and, most importantly, I asked him about Princess Diana telling me from Spirit that her death had been set in stone.

'Let's talk about the future,' he began, 'which we are creating all the time. There are major patterns and there are minor patterns. Let's say that a major pattern was "fixed" in place on the grid lattice structure that had been set as a sustained focused intention hundreds of years ago. Remember what I told you, that once an intention reaches a certain magnitude plateau of space conditioning, then it becomes fairly "set" in place for some time, which can be years or possibly centuries.

'Or think of one lifetime as a unique wave. Diana was riding a specific wave that was right for her, in the great divine scheme of things. On an everyday level she still had free will to say and eat what she wanted, and so on, but at a deeper level she had come with a specific purpose that could indeed have been set long ago. Therefore yes, certain events could have been set in place long ago … and great seers can access possible major events by accessing specific wavelengths at the deeper levels of the vacuum.'

This was amazing to hear from such an eminent scientist. 'Well' I asked, 'does this mean with everything that Serena, Rupert, Gary and you have told me, that *if* sufficient numbers of people are living in fear of a terrorist attack, and such thoughts are in their subconscious minds, then they can actually help bring such an event to our reality?'

'Right now this whole subject remains an open question … it could be either/and/or people's actual thoughts and physical actions, or it could be their subconscious thoughts actually creating what they think about the most, or a combination of both … but from all our experiments of placing an intention in a box which in time creates a specific reality, we can surmise that if enough people are thinking something, even at a subconscious level, then this too could indeed be imprinting the invisible lattice structure that we talked about before, which in turn can imprint itself on the "terrorists" minds when they "suddenly" have an idea of attacking a certain place. You could even include the media in this equation – after all, we are constantly bombarded by more negative than positive news. This is sustained and therefore I would theorize that it adds to the "lattice", which "conditions" our world space. Edgar Cayce, perhaps the world's major psychic of the last century, warned us about this kind of thing – that thoughts are things and, if strongly focused upon, can participate in their materialisation into physical reality.

'You need to keep in mind that your subconscious mind can access about 50 million "bits" of the five physical senses type of information every second. But the conscious mind can only access less than 50 bits per second. And if a person suddenly had access to *all* the information, it would hugely affect their mental and physical functioning. The subconscious gathers information; it manipulates it, it edits information and eventually generates small kernels of information which it then feeds to the conscious mind. But it only feeds the information to the conscious mind that the conscious mind has said is meaningful to it. All the rest is thrown away. So it is the subconscious mind connecting to the energy within the vacuum that facilitates remote viewing, prophetic dreams and so on.

'Whatever the outcome that we eventually show in science, there is now no doubt that every thought counts at every level ... the means we use to gain the ends we wish to achieve in our life collectively create the future we must live in. So even if we have good goals, if we don't use the proper means to achieve those goals, we will probably end up with a future that we, our children and our grandchildren will not like to live in.'

A wonderful, magical man. Before we finally said goodbye, Bill added an apt postscript: 'Einstein once said, *"People like us, who believe in physics, know that the distinction between past, present and future is only a stubbornly persistent illusion"* – and he was right.'

Think about it.

16

Diana's Surprise Party

To imitate a saint is to ask for real trouble
ROBERT SVOBODA

Before I share with you the truly remarkable events that took place in Westport, Connecticut, in June 2004 I need to clarify a few points and set the scene for the unique gathering that the spirit world organized, not only for this book, but also for all of you who are open-minded.

The last time I saw Princess Diana in person was in late June 1995, at a small charity lunch party in her private apartments at Kensington Palace just before her birthday on July 1.

In *Divine Intervention*, I made it very clear that I definitely had not been a friend of Diana's; I was simply someone whom she had met on a few occasions along the way. But during that particular lunch, we had chatted about hearing spirit guides and afterwards, as Diana had walked me down to a waiting taxi, she had looked wistful and said she hoped that one day she would 'hear' her guides too. And as we had said goodbye, I prayed that she would. Neither of us knew then, in the grand scheme of things, that her days in this dimension were numbered. She was a lovely lady. At least I had found her so.

At this point sceptics might well say, 'Oh for God's sake, get real. A journalist who just 'happened' to have some weird experience in Harrods in 1998, who then 'happened' to claim that she could 'hear' messages from one of the most famous women in history? Why could she not simply have heard from her mother or her deceased aunt Nellie?' Why indeed.

To answer this question, consider why most major charities are constantly seeking a really famous celebrity to represent their cause in the media. Obviously, the answer is because it brings specific charities to people's attention and donations increase; more research is done, and more people benefit. Therefore, if I had experienced a spirit 'walk in' by my mother or auntie, who would have taken the slightest notice of what they had to say? No one.

When *Divine* first appeared, media flak virtually destroyed my reputation as an alternative health columnist almost overnight. My credibility – and an excellent salary – were gone. Initially, on TV and radio I was accused of writing my story for the money, but when people read the enormity of what I had gone through they understood my motives and soon realized that in monetary terms I had lost far more than I had gained.

I might have won the spiritual lottery, which no amount of money can buy, but in doing so I had paid a high earthly price. Yet, as the months passed, I received hundreds of wonderful, heartfelt letters from spiritual individuals who resonated to varying degrees with my experience. And every one of those letters was positive.

Neither, I should add, was I ever obsessed by the Princess. Sure, I would have loved to have been her friend, but so would millions of other people. I never considered her to be a saint, just a magical young woman and mother who was truly doing her best under, at times, very stressful and difficult circumstances. And she did make a huge difference. For those who judged her, could you have done better?

Today in my home, I happily admit to treasuring the few photographs that were taken of myself with the Princess, plus the letter she wrote to me after our lunch in 1995. The only other tangible memories I have of her are a copy of Earl Spencer's speech that he gave at her funeral, which he signed for me, plus a photograph of Diana from Althorp.

Therefore, what I and many others believe is happening, is that departed souls like Diana have agreed to act as famous spokespeople for the higher realms. The spirit world is desperate to let us know that life goes on, and to prove it through science. And this cause is fast gathering momentum.

In November 2003 I had interviewed renowned psychic researcher Montague Keen at his home in north London – who had spent more than 50 years investigating paranormal phenomena. As a member of The Society for Psychical Research, 'Monty', as he was known to his friends, liked to remain completely impartial until he had thoroughly investigated and verified any events claimed to be linked to the spirit world. In fact, it was Monty who had investigated the Christine Holohan case that I have featured in this book and, along with scientists such as David Fontana, Professor of Transpersonal Psychology at John Moores University in Liverpool, plus the late Professor Arthur Ellison from City University in London, Monty also investigated the Scole experiments that had taken place over a two-year period in the mid-1990s at a farmhouse in Norfolk. The Scole Group, as it became known, was a circle of experienced mediums who began 'sitting' in the basement of one of the medium's homes. Within weeks, light phenomena began to appear during séances, later followed by discarnate 'hands' that the sitters could grasp and feel. Objects appeared from nowhere and when pictures were taken in the room, *with the camera lens covers still on*, fascinating faces and scenes appeared. Voices were recorded that again came from thin air, and so on.

Professors Fontana and Ellison, along with Monty, were invited to take part in these sittings on numerous occasions to test for 'faking'. At one point a famous magician, James Webster, a member of the inner magic circle, who had investigated certain phenomena for over 50 years, was also asked to check the Scole Group for any possible fraud.

All the investigators concluded that there was absolutely no question of duplicity, and the Scole investigation – which took Monty and his colleagues two years to finish – remains the most complete scientific investigation of reported paranormal phenomena to date.

The reason I'm telling you this story here is because in January 2004, during a debate at the Royal Society of Arts in London, Monty collapsed and died. He and his wife, Veronica, who you may recall had effected my introduction not only to Professor Gary Schwartz but also Rupert Sheldrake, had a longstanding pact – that whichever one of them 'died' first, in spirit that partner would do their utmost to attempt to contact the other with personal messages, therefore proving once and for all that life after death is a reality.

The plot thickens.

Veronica claims to have seen and spoken to her husband on several occasions. And since Monty's 'passing', numerous mediums from around the world, some of whom did not know him in life, have received unusual messages from him that he asked to be passed to his dear wife. And through various means, she has received them. Each message on its own meant very little, but when Veronica began placing them together they told a bigger story that made sense to her. And when a medium told Veronica, 'Monty knows royalty in spirit,' she had been perplexed – until, during a later séance, Monty had told how he had met Diana in the spirit world.

This phenomena is fast becoming known as the Montague Keen 'cross correspondences', and Veronica is planning a book on all the phenomena that have happened and continue to happen almost daily since her husband's passing.

Sunday, June 27, 2004

Veronica invited me and many of Monty's oldest friends, colleagues and renowned researchers to join her for a day of remembrance at The Royal Society – in the very same room in which Monty had died of a heart attack back in January. Gary Schwartz presented some of his most recent and exciting research results, whilst Rupert Sheldrake shared with the audience the results of his research into 280 people who had 'seen' ghosts. Thirty-eight percent had 'seen' the person in spirit, 25 percent had heard their dearly departed speaking, 20 percent felt a touch, 22 percent had felt a presence and 14 percent smelled the person. Most importantly Rupert told the audience that 74 percent had said their various forms of contact had given them great comfort. Others shared their memories of Monty, who must have been a wonderful man. I had only met him once and he seemed like a true gentleman.

The highlight of the day came when Veronica played a tape recording that she told us had been recorded during a séance in May 2004, in which Monty's voice purportedly came through (all the details will be shared in Veronica's forthcoming book). In the meantime, 150 people or more sat spellbound as a voice claiming to be Monty – sounding like the tape I have of Monty – began speaking via the larynx of a trance medium, who had been gagged before the séance began to prevent him speaking with his own voice. This phenomenon is known as 'direct voice', and is quite rare.

The voice that came through the medium on the tape introduced himself as Montague Keen, and he gave the date as being May 2004 (five months after he had died). He then asked all the other people attending the séance to agree the date, and that this was really happening. They duly did so.

The speech from 'Monty' lasted about ten minutes, and it was very moving. However, it has yet to be scientifically tested and verified as being truly Monty's voice. Monty himself would have wanted no less. Shortly, you will understand the relevance of direct voice-spirit tapes and why I mention this incident.

Montague Keen was well known in psychic circles during his lifetime, but in death he is fast becoming a larger celebrity. Diana, however, is already world famous – and remains so. Virtually every day, stories about her appear in the media. Recent ones have told how interest has waned to such a degree that Earl Spencer may one day close his wonderful exhibition in memory of Diana at Althorp, and that he hopes the exhibition will move to Kensington Palace, which I believe would be a huge success.

Worldwide TV coverage showed the opening of a fountain in her memory by Her Majesty the Queen on July 6; and on July 16 2004, the media reported that the inquest into Diana's death may be seen live on television by millions of people. By the time you read this, I know that many more stories on Diana will have appeared in the press.

Sure, after seven years, interest in her life may be falling away naturally, but if there was a tape of Diana talking now, or if she miraculously appeared during a live TV show – which could be scientifically verified – then this would certainly make the news – rather than my dear old Mum or my auntie Nellie! In the case of Monty, there is no shortage of scientists, friends and colleagues who can verify the messages that are being received. In the case of Diana, verification becomes extremely complicated. I'll return to this subject in a moment.

There is now a huge body of evidence to show that human consciousness survives physical death. All you have to do is look it up and read it. And if, for instance, a medium claims contact with, say, Winston Churchill, Freddie Mercury, John Lennon or George Harrison, which many do, this would be fascinating, but you don't tend to read about these people regularly in the press. However, Diana remains a global icon and from the numerous alleged 'contacts' with her that are now being reported, it would appear that, along with deceased spirits like Monty, Diana and the spirit world are now piling on the pressure. They want us to take notice – big time. There is no disrespect meant to anyone's individual family here – and keep in mind that no one forces a spirit to come through. It is the spirit's choice. They are in control in these situations, not us.

In the meantime, in this dimension the plot thickens a whole lot more. During the several months that I have sat writing, researching and checking this book, I have often looked at Diana's picture on my desk and chatted away jokingly, saying, 'I could really use a strong ending for this book – but it needs to be based on science.' Little did I know that Diana and the spirit world were listening. In life, I believe she loved giving people surprises – but by this point I really wasn't expecting any more. In fact, the biggest surprise of all had been saved to the last …

Whilst Veronica Keen was busy keeping up with the various claims of contact from her dearly departed husband, which were coming in from all over the world, at the University of Arizona Professor Schwartz received a call out of the blue from a production company who were making a documentary about a British medium, Sally Morgan, whom the TV company researchers claimed was first class; as good, they said, as medium John Edward, whom Gary had tested at his lab on several occasions and knew was 'the real thing'. Filming was taking place in Westport, Connecticut, during June 2004, where she works for three months a year, and the production team were looking for a scientist who might be able to test Sally's mediumistic and psychic abilities as being fake – or real. They had found details of Gary's research projects on the internet.

Gary was invited to fly to Westport and test Sally under stringent conditions. Gary's curiosity was aroused and he agreed to take part – on his terms. He asked for no further facts on Sally. He explained that not only Sally, but also the entire production crew, would have to remain 'blind' as to the identity of the sitter and the person in spirit, whom Gary would select as participants in the research.

Gary called me in early June and asked if I would be by a phone on June 6, 2004, a Sunday evening.

'What else is there to do,' I had joked, 'on a Sunday evening, other than to be at my desk?' I was so busy when he called that I paid scant attention when he told me something about a medium he would be testing over that weekend. I simply wrote the date in my diary with a question mark beside it.

Unbeknown to me, Gary was going to attempt an experiment with Sally Morgan to see if Princess Diana might come through once again, but this time under double-blind conditions.

'Double-blind' means that the medium does not know the identity of the sitter or the deceased. Gary explained, 'It means that the sitter is not present when the reading is done, so that she or he can later score the data from the medium's reading that has been mixed with data from readings of other sitters. And she or he does not know which information belongs to which readings. It turned out as you will see that the evidence from the double-blind reading was so obvious that subsequent blind scoring was not necessary.

On Saturday, June 5, Gary began his tests and on that day he and his research fellow, Dr Julie Beischel, had set an intention that only Gary and Julie knew – that Montague Keen would come through with messages for Veronica, his widow, via the medium, Sally (and I am sure that Veronica will tell what happened in her forthcoming book).

Meanwhile, during that afternoon in a filming break, Gary chatted with Sally the medium, who told him that she has many famous clients in the UK. Gary, of course, has heard such claims many times before.

'Like who?' he asked casually.

Nervously Sally shared a few names, and then conspiratorially she dropped a metaphorical 'bombshell' in Gary's lap.

'She told me,' recalls Gary, 'that for four years one of her clients was Diana, Princess of Wales. At this point the sceptics will say, "This is ridiculous"; and yet, out of all the mediums in the world (and there are many thousands of mediums) I had been asked to test a medium who had actually known Diana. The odds of this happening by "chance" were virtually off the scale. Sally had only ever previously mentioned her association with Diana to her closest family and friends. Sally has never sold or told her story. I did not know this fact previously. And in the tests we could have been looking for Winston Churchill, Gandhi or anyone. The synchronicity was truly astonishing. And as we stood in the kitchen I acted politely surprised, but did not in any way share with Sally who we were hoping might come through on the Sunday. Only myself and Julie knew that fact.'

The plot at this point turns into a soup! By now, I trust you are on the edge of your seat …

Sunday, June 6, 2004 – Westport, Connecticut

Allow me to once more clarify who is where and doing what on this date.

Professor Gary Schwartz is in Connecticut with the medium Sally Morgan and the film crew. He and Sally met for the first time on Friday, June 4, 2004.

Dr Julie Beischel, a research scientist, joins the party on the phone from Gary's lab in Arizona. Julie is acting as a proxy sitter for me. It is Julie who gives Sally precise instructions as to what is required.

Sally Morgan is the nervous British medium who has no idea who is the true sitter (me), nor who in the spirit world Gary and Julie are hoping to hear from. Sally has never met Dr Beischel. In other words, Sally is totally 'blind' in this experiment. Moreover, I was not present at the reading; in other words, I was blind to the experiment too. Hence the term 'double-blind',

Me – Hazel Courteney. At my desk in Oxfordshire in the UK, blissfully unaware of what was unfolding thousands of miles away. I had never heard the name Sally Morgan – had never spoken to, nor seen nor met her. But we were due to speak on the phone at 7pm that evening.

Keep in mind that there are six billion people alive today – and that Sally was being asked to give details about a total stranger somewhere on this planet to Dr Bieschel, who was 'sitting' on my behalf. And for those of you who think that Sally may have 'read' Julie's mind during this reading – or that Julie knows all about me – at that moment on June 6, Julie and I had also never met, nor ever spoken on the phone. Neither had Gary been to my home in the UK; he was due to arrive in the UK later in June.

The cameras began rolling.

Dr Julie Beischel began the test by telling Sally, 'There is an absent sitter expecting to hear from someone specific, but for this section, we'll just try to get any information we can about anyone related to that sitter.'

Sally: 'Yeah. Okay. Do you want me to start?'

Julie: 'Go ahead.'

Sally: 'The first thing that I pick up is two women. I'm picking up the sitter as being a woman and the person in the spirit world as being a woman. Okay?'

Julie 'Mm.'

Sally: 'What do you want me to start with?'

Julie: 'Whatever you are getting.'

Rather than continue in this highly formal manner – as the transcripts are lengthy – I'll give you the edited highlights.

Sally firstly talked about a 'mother' in spirit, and then mentioned the name Helen. (Diana had a personal assistant called Helena Roach, and people often call me Helen rather than Hazel). She also mentioned the name Penny – and the only Penny I know is Penny Thornton, who was one of Diana's astrologers for a time in the 1980s. The scenario then became very unclear for a couple of sentences until Sally talked of a woman standing by a dark-coloured car ...

She goes off on a tangent about an older lady talking about the 1950s, and mentions a young man who had killed himself who had something to do with the family of the deceased. (In May 2004 I recalled a story in the media about a young man – a member of the Shand Kydd family – who had died from a suspected drugs overdose.) It's evident that Sally is extremely nervous and has not the faintest idea who she is looking for ... but suddenly, she seems to settle down and becomes calmer.

'I think the sitter (she is referring to me – Hazel) is on a quest ... but there's a lot of love here. I'm looking at bags of clothes here, it's like a laundry bag full of clothes. This is not dirty laundry. I think the person in spirit watched her daughter do this... Whoever the woman is in the spirit world, she wants to communicate with this person – it's as if she is saying to the sitter, "I'm taking care of everything, you needn't worry about a thing."

'... This woman is spirit is *everywhere*, she's watching everything. It's really bizarre, but I feel like I'm up a tree! It would be interesting to know if anyone in this family fell off a tree. Whether somebody used to climb up this tree and get through a window ...

'I have definitely got the sitter and I have definitely got a lady in spirit – and they connect. I mean maybe we could be looking at twins ... but it's like – it's almost as if – wow – they are like – they fit together. They are like part of a whole.'

When I read this transcript for the first time, I was amazed that Sally picked up so much correct information so quickly.

At this point, Dr Beischel asks Sally to try to concentrate on the deceased spirit with any messages for the sitter (me) – and Julie tells Sally that the sitter's name is Hazel. So, from here on in this became a single-blind experiment.

Sally chats on about 'a mother' in spirit. Later that day, when I finally spoke to Sally on the phone, which I'll come to shortly – I told Sally that Diana's mother Frances Shand-Kydd had died on Thursday June 3. According to Sally, she had not known this – as they had been working intensely and she had not seen any news on TV. Could it be, I wondered, that the bags of clothes might have referred to the items that Diana's mothers and sisters removed from Kensington Palace after Diana's death? It's a thought.

'And she (the spirit) has come in ... she is looking at two little boys on the earth plane. And she's saying to me, "they're my sons ... they're my boys." She is standing by a car. Maybe this person died in a car accident ... this woman has blond hair ... she is happy where she is, but she's sad because she misses her sons ... her two little boys. This would have been a very sudden death. This is quite unexpected. This is not a death that, I feel, anybody expected ... because she is saying, "One minute I was there, the next I'm here. But I'm home ..." She is whispering, "He knows I'm here ..."

Sally then adds, 'I think there are certain people in this lady's family that are quite terrified that she might appear in the spirit world. They miss her terribly, but they're worried she could appear. They are scared ... now the woman in spirit is saying, "I wasn't prepared for any of this ..."'

At this point in the proceedings a new and strange voice whispers, '*Why?.. why?*' on the speakerphone that Sally is using for her conversation with Julie, plus a couple of other words that were inaudible, and Sally shouts excitedly, 'Did you hear that?' to the TV recording people and a female voice in the background says ' I heard it' ... Sally was later to tell me this was one of the film crew.

At this point Gary reports that Sally's hair is almost standing on end, and she is visibly shaken. And like the TV crew and Gary, I'm praying that the 'voice on the phone' can be heard, just as I was later to hear Monty on June 27 on the TV crew's equipment ... the implications, of course, are phenomenal. In fact, Professor David Fontana says, 'This type of phenomena, where voices appear as if from nowhere, is now fairly common. In my research we have examined results such as this that have been obtained under carefully controlled conditions, and there seems little doubt that the paranormal explanation is the most appropriate. And if you would like more information on David Fontana's research, read *Is There an Afterlife?* (John Hunt).

Back in Connecticut, Sally mentions a few more names and facts – and then Gary interrupts to ask Sally to concentrate on the person in spirit.

'I don't know exactly why, she doesn't like noise,' continues Sally, 'because when she died there was a terrific amount of noise.'

Dr Julie Beischel then tells Sally that she is going to ask more detailed questions about the deceased in the hope that Sally might identify her. First, Julie asks the spirit to describe herself as she was in life.

'Well,' says Sally, 'I mean, this is a good-looking woman. This was a woman that took care of herself. I also think she worked hard. I think she was someone who was very proud of her existence. She could hold her own in a room of people …'

'Okay – and can you get what age she is?' asks Julie.

'She was only maybe … maybe 38 …'

'Okay, what were your (the spirit's) hobbies?'

'Well, she had young children, and what I'm sensing her asking is, "Did I have time for hobbies?" She socialised a lot, she had friends all over … she's showing me telephone work …

'She's just sorry. That it had to be how it was. Because she says, "No one will ever forget, will they?" This lady died in a tragedy. She is showing me complete and utter chaos, like, um, a war zone … could be 9/11.' (Sally was later to tell me that in the days preceding this experiment she had done several readings for widows who had lost their husbands in 9/11 in 2001.)

'You need to tell this lady (the sitter Hazel) that she is saying she never knew a thing … the noise is what she remembers. Like a roar. If you can imagine the biggest roar … it's massive – and then … like it just … and then, bang.'

Julie then enquires about the birth date of the spirit and Sally states that the person was a Gemini. In fact Diana was Cancer, which runs from June 23 to July 23 (her birthday was July 1) – but Gemini is close, from May 22 to June 22.

I can quite understand why at this point a sceptic would ask, 'Well if Sally was really hearing Diana, how come Diana did not just say, "July 1". The truth is that I don't know why. Also, keep in mind that the medium can only relate what they are told by Spirit. I know from my own experience that Spirit need certain conditions to contact us directly and clearly. As Diana had told me back in 1998, for Spirit to contact us feels to them like 'swimming through treacle'. Like a poor telephone connection, some things are clearer than others. You miss some words, you hear others, you think that you hear the caller saying one thing, but they may actually have said something else. It happens on my mobile all the time!

Perhaps Diana used to think of herself more as a Gemini personality type – but only her friends and family would know this. This is the crux in this whole field. The fact that this experiment took place may well receive publicity – but it is *verification* that is needed. Sally came up with a considerable amount of specific information under very controlled circumstances – just as Allison and Laurie had done back in Arizona during October 2003.

When I had written *Divine Intervention*, I had several meetings with Sarah, Duchess of York, and in that book she agreed to go on the record stating that she had believed my story and what I had told her. During May 2004 I once again contacted her office to ask if she might consider reading all the information that had come through from Allison and Laurie. I was not surprised when she declined this time around, as the Royal family have at long last welcomed Sarah back into their circle, and anyway, Sarah has come through a considerable amount of controversy in her life – and I believe that she doesn't need any more.

Back in 1999 I had naively tried to pass messages to Prince Charles via my friend Lord Feldman, and through another intermediary I also attempted to set up a meeting with Patrick Jephson – Diana's ex equerry, and of course Paul Burrell, all to no avail.

Before the session with Sally ended, Julie asked Sally to describe where the spirit said she had lived at the time she had passed.

And her reply really made me take notice.

'Well, I lived in a house, but I might have been staying in an apartment or vice versa. So, it's like she is saying, "Which one do you want me to tell you about?" And she is saying, "At weekends, I could go to a much bigger place..."'

Sally then mentions a man who passed with the spirit and there is talk of an eye patch …

Gary returns to the question of the cause of this woman's death and Sally replies, 'Trauma, tremendous trauma. Rubble, smoke, chaos and noise – then total silence.'

Finally, before closing the reading Julie asks the spirit if she has anything more to say to anyone. Messages to her family follow and she closes on, 'How are they coping? Their mummy is still around them. You have to let them know. And that – this is the bag of clothes that I spoke about – that just to keep a few items of my clothing for them.' Oh – and her wedding dress …

By the end of the morning, they were all drained and Gary said, 'Sally never saw the face of the deceased until she was on the phone with Hazel. It's as though Diana did not want to identify herself until the single-blind part of the study, thus preserving the scientific integrity of the previous double-blind reading. In other words, if Sally had recognized Diana early on in the double-blind reading, the experiment would have been worthless, as then any information she might have picked up could have been from Sally's memory.

'There was *no* indication to Sally from the deceased that she lived with wealth, or was royalty. Sally did *not know* who the deceased was. I pressed her several times quite hard on tape to ask her if she could guess the identity of the deceased. Sally had looked and behaved totally perplexed. Clearly, much of the information reported by Sally fitted Princess Diana. And yet, obvious details were left out – *apparently by the deceased* – that would identify her. The question is, why? This question was to be answered when we called Hazel at 7pm her time. Hazel recorded what followed.

And this is the point at which I joined the party. Gary simply explained what a double-blind trial was and he told me where and who all the characters were and their names. Also, he clarified the test was now single-blind as they had told Sally my first name and they had called me a 'friend' of the deceased. Most crucially Gary told me that neither Sally nor the TV crew had the faintest idea of who the deceased was.

Very quickly he gave me a few of the 'facts' that Sally had picked up and I understood instantly that she was indeed hearing from Diana. Gary informed me he would pass the phone to Sally and I could ask what I liked, but that I must not *tell her* who the deceased was.

Sally and I basically said 'Hi,' and I must confess I was rather at a loss as to what Gary wanted me to ask. Sally related some of what had happened and she said that a friend of mine had come through. She asked if I had any questions as 'she (the spirit) had come in again.'

'Do you have any idea who she is?' I asked.

'Do you know,' Sally said slowly, 'I think I might have known her.'

It was as if she knew but was too nervous to tell me. As if she was about to make some huge mistake. Trying to be nonchalant, I replied with a non-communicative 'Umm' – not knowing, at this point, that Sally used to read for Diana. I presumed by this time that if Sally had realized it was Diana, she would have 'known' facts about Diana from the media, as we all did.

'Well, what I am getting is that she is pleased to be able to talk to you – and *also to me* – which seems strange ... Was she quite well known?' asked Sally, remaining cautious.

'Yes.'

'Did you go to school with her?'

'No.'

'Well I'm seeing a country house, it could be like a school or it could be a home ... Edwardian, in a park, and she walks with you there ...'

This was spot on. My current home is Edwardian – and stands in a large garden, surrounded by park-like farmers' fields. And when I have time to wander around the garden, I have often sensed that Diana might be with me.

I asked, 'Is there any way that you could tell me what my relationship was with her?'

'Were you her hairdresser – as her hair was very important to her? And, do her family know that we are discussing this?'

'No they don't,' I replied.

There was a long pause before Sally reluctantly asked: '*Is this the Princess of Wales?*'

I must say that I was impressed. In the parts of the transcript that I have shared, on reading this you could think, 'Well, she must have known it was Diana straight away', but there was plenty of other information in between not included here that may or may not have applied to Diana. It could have been any woman. Sally got a fair bit wrong ... but she also got an awful lot right.

Sally began telling me on the phone that she had seen Diana earlier, but because she used to read for her, Sally thought she somehow had 'crossed communications', as she could hardly believe that a Professor from Arizona was wanting to hear from Princess Diana.

Sally then said something fascinating. 'In my head I first saw Diana's face walking in that park with you – and then I totally *knew* who it was ... it was like she was saying, "You (Hazel) are my lookalike" ... and so when she turned in the park to face me, it was as though she had teased me enough and I could hear her saying, "Say, say it, say it" ... urging me to say her name to the people around me.'

As Sally said this I was flattered that Diana might consider me 'a lookalike'. Let's say that was a loose description! I happen to be Diana's height, and blonde, but thinner and older – with bags under my eyes.

For the record, Gary says, 'The sceptic will be quick to question whether fraud was involved here'; and of course, this was my first question, too.

Could Sally have somehow figured out that we were after Diana, or on the previous day Monty Keen; and on the Sunday acted like she didn't know who the deceased was during the double-blind portion, and then faked her shock in the single-blind portion?

'Though this is highly improbable, as we had kept Hazel's original test results from October 2003 very quiet, it is not impossible. As a scientist, what counts to me is the total pattern of information over the two days, plus the absolute integrity of Dr. Beischel and myself – as our afterlife research is called The International Veritas (truth) Project, to emphasize our focus on the truth, whatever it is, concerning mediumship and survival of consciousness after death.

'What these readings indicate is that the deceased individuals act like people who are alive, thoughtful, and who want this research not to be misinterpreted by sceptics or researchers alike. They want us to know that they are as alive as we are, and that they have important information and guidance to share with us – if we are willing to listen.

'Only a rabid disbeliever would dismiss our two complete sets of readings over that weekend as anything less than extraordinary and inspiring. This particular double-blind experiment is, to my mind, extraordinarily good – further confirmation that Diana, Montague Keen and others are keen to let the world know that life after death is real – and they want to assist in this research. As a scientist, I would also add that from meeting Hazel, and through the three experiments I have carried out on her to date in regard to her association with Diana, the evidence points to Hazel's story concerning her contact with Diana in the spirit world as being real.'

Thanks, Gary. For a well-respected and highly qualified scientist to stand on such a parapet takes courage. Sadly, however, we still had no verifiable proof. Yes, on the tapes Sally had described my unusual 'relationship' with Diana during 1998 in truly accurate terms when she had said we 'could be twins', and so on – that's how it had felt during April, May and June – as though Diana was inside me, we were as one. So for me this experiment was again great personal verification.

July 14, 2004, Surrey, England

On a wet and dismal rainy day in London I drove out to meet Sally Morgan just to check the facts one more time – I would not receive the transcripts of events from June 6 from Gary's office until Friday July 16, and I wanted to look into her eyes to see if I believed in her integrity. As the deadline for finishing the book approached, it seemed as though everything was indeed happening at once!

Sally and her husband John are both in their mid-fifties, extremely down to earth and without a shred of ego between them. Their home is comfortable but not pretentious, and Sally made me feel at ease with cups of tea and biscuits. Before we got to know each other, I asked Sally to give me a personal reading, as apart from the Diana connection and our telephone conversation, she knew virtually nothing about my life. The information she gave me was astonishingly accurate. She told me of emotions that were in my heart on that day, gave me intimate messages that could have only come from my dear Mum that no one else knew, especially regarding my daughter. Like Gary, I concluded that Sally Morgan is the 'real deal'.

On the subject of Diana, Sally is fairly tight-lipped, and I admire her for not telling or selling her story. But she did tell me that she was introduced to Diana by an immediate member of Diana's family. I know the name, but Sally asked me to withhold this information. A year before Diana's death, Sally had foretold to this family member what would happen – only Sally had thought that Her Majesty the Queen was going to die. She had 'seen' a woman lying in a road being given heart massage.

Because of this tape, at the time of going to press Sally is being interviewed by the police investigating the Paris crash. Diana had warned Sally on several occasions to be careful and to leave notes of all that Sally knew in a bank vault. This Sally has done.

After Diana's death, the relative had called Sally and asked her how she felt about the accident. Sally told me, 'I *knew* that for some higher reason I had to lie and I said it had been an accident,' and the relative said, "Thank you Sally, we'll always keep it like that, won't we?" Obviously it was what was *not* said that was important here. It made me reconsider that what I had seen a year earlier, during a reading for this relative, had in fact been Diana's death — a Queen of Hearts.'

In Sally's opinion, Diana was never meant to be in the car with Dodi on that fateful night. Sally believes that whoever caused their deaths was after Dodi — not Diana. She felt that the establishment wanted to scare Diana sufficiently that she would never flaunt a lover to such a degree again.

And therefore, according to Sally, Diana's death had in one sense been an accident. During my experience Diana had said over and over again that her death had been an accident and now, thanks to Sally, I was seeing things in a new light. Maybe it was an accident and maybe it wasn't. That is not for me to decide, that's for a coroner and the police to decide. What is vitally important here is that members of Diana's immediate family know that the spirit of Diana lives on and is 'out there', keen to communicate. But they may never publicly admit such a fact. I pray that one day they may change their minds.

In the meantime, if you would like to contact Sally, her website is at www.psychicsally.com

July 7, 2004 – Hyde Park, London

In the previous Sunday papers I had read a truly scathing article describing the memorial fountain to Diana as looking like 'a concrete trench'. For months, as I had watched the fountain take shape on my long walks through the park every week, I had always thought it would be a totally inappropriate memorial. Surely, I had thought, Diana would prefer a children's hospice, or something similar.

On the night of July 6, I had dreamed vividly of Diana – which is a really rare event. In my dream, I saw her walking towards me with some children, and as they got closer one of the young African girls, ran towards me and grabbed my leg. She was desperate to be picked up and as I pulled her up, her little arms clung round my neck and the intense feeling of love that she was transferring was awesome and humbling. Then Diana handed a lifeless baby into my arms. And as Diana walked away from me, she said, 'There are so many desperate for love – please help them when and where you can.'

The emotion was so intense that I woke at 5.30am with a jolt. Now, I'm not even the type that likes children a whole lot … I call them screamers. But, this was different. It was the pure love I had felt from the child in the dream that had touched me to the core.

It may sound ridiculous, but it was as though Diana was calling me. I got out of bed, quietly put on an old tracksuit and headed out across the park. A handful of early joggers and dog walkers were already about their business as the new day began. The sun struggled to break through the threatening sky over the Serpentine and the air was cool. The fountain area on the previous day had been thronged with thousands of people, including the Queen and Diana's family for the official opening – but on that morning it was virtually deserted.

I walked all around the fountain, which is more a granite ' trench' – but the granite sparkles and it undulates into varying widths and depths. I walked across one of the flat bridges over the fountain and into the midst of the fountain's grassy centre. The wind whispered through the trees. Underfoot, the grass was damp, but it didn't matter. I sat to listen to the water singing its multitude of sounds and flowing at different speeds, and an overwhelming feeling of peace and healing flowed through me. It was as if she was saying, 'Thanks Hazel, you have come through. It's okay, it's okay.' Tears pricked my eyes. It was very moving. Only when a group arrived later with two small children was the moment shattered when one of the young children asked her mother, 'Who was Princess Diana?' Like millions of others I firmly believe that a statue of Diana in the centre of that fountain, paid for by the people who admired her, would help her to remain as a 'Queen of Hearts' and a true 'Princess of the People' for generations to come.

And as I slowly made my way back towards my home and another busy day, I knew that I had done my best. That's all anyone can do.

Epilogue: The Way Forward

As human beings, our greatness lies not so much in being able to remake the world – more in being able to remake ourselves.

MAHATMA GANDHI

The synchronicities that have occurred during the writing of this book – even to someone as open-minded as myself – have at times left me speechless with amazement. In my original concept, I wanted to write about being part of an orchestra, and wondered how I would explain in science who the conductor is. I had also thought that Diana might warrant a paragraph or three. But as events unfolded, it quickly became evident that Diana and the spirit world had become the entire trumpet section.

There are many people who might say that connecting with the spirit world is a 'sin' and yet the word religion, from *religiere*, means 'to connect again'. In fact, what many organized religions have done for thousands of years is to *disconnect* us from the ultimate truth. What, you may wonder, are they so afraid of? Jesus and all the other truly enlightened beings have always taught that God, the Guiding Organizing Designer is within you, and it is now time to truly understand this statement – for it is an inescapable and awesome truth.

To my mind, reconnecting is what this book is all about. But before you can reconnect, you need to be clearer on what or whom you are connecting to. Much help is obviously available from the higher realms, and yet all the scientists who have shared morsels of their considerable knowledge have reminded me time and again that before the higher dimensions can become involved in a *reciprocal* relationship, you first need to know or at least believe and acknowledge their existence, and then to ask for their help in a positive and loving way.

Even then, we still have a choice as to whether we take up the torch of truth, the eternal knowledge, that the higher realms are now offering to every one of us who is prepared to grasp it. Again I remind you that knowledge is neutral – it's how we use it that counts.

During the 'swinging 60s' I was a naive, selfish teenager. I loved the concept of a 'New Age' that encouraged 'free love' and flower power, and invited us all to love each other. Unfortunately, with light also comes dark: and so this era also triggered a greater lack of respect for any authority. Drugs that made you feel good became the new rock 'n' roll, which back in the 1950s had seemed so daring to the post-war generation.

But the 1960s also left a bitter legacy that now, in many respects, has gone way out of balance. Children learn from example, and if no one sets boundaries or gives sensible discipline, then they will continue to push the boundaries to their ultimate conclusion. Today this is what we are experiencing and witnessing throughout society, especially in the West.

During my profound spiritual awakening back in 1998, I had to the depths of my being totally understood Gandhi's phrase, 'An eye for an eye leaves everyone blind.' A deep knowing had enveloped me, that if I were to hurt someone intentionally then the universe would act like a mirror – and at some point, it would reflect back to me what I had sent out. And I knew that in hurting others we ultimately hurt ourselves.

Religious fanatics and die-hard sceptics tend to proclaim that everything in life is either black or white – they leave no room for the hundreds of shades of grey in between. Imagine, then, how life on this planet could change if everyone, not just a handful of enlightened men and women, could fully comprehend the staggering ramifications of an eternal life, plus cause and effect at every level.

For a start, we could all stop rushing so much. Back in 1998, I often sang the famous lyrics 'We've got all   the time   in the world ...' from the James Bond film *On Her Majesty's Secret Service*. I knew that I could leave my physical body through the rebirth of physical 'death', return home, then after discussion and deliberation with my guides, be recycled and continue to reincarnate time after time until I no longer had any need to incarnate. If someone had put a gun to my head, whilst I was in that heightened state it would not have bothered me in the least, as any sense of attachment had left me. Fear, at times, simply became a word without meaning – and without fear, I became free. And if, upon my return to this dimension, I did not achieve everything that I had wanted to in this lifetime, I knew that I could try again in the next.

Until I got it right.

Having read the evidence I have offered on survival of consciousness and reincarnation, how do you feel about death now? Does it hold less fear for you? I hope so. As, like Gary and many others, I no longer believe that physical death is the ultimate end that most people have considered it to be for thousands of years.

And if we could all accept reincarnation and life after death as a reality, then with this acceptance would surely come a greater sense of self-responsibility? For instance, in environmental disaster films such as *The Day After Tomorrow* we are reminded by Hollywood of the ultimate price we may have to pay for mistreating our planet so badly.

Global consciousness is changing. Like a huge giant waking from a very long sleep. There is no longer any doubt about this. Huge amounts of people are fascinated by miracles, life after death and paranormal phenomena. Concepts that even 10 years ago were considered by many to be 'cranky' are now accepted as being normal. Acupuncture and healing, for instance, are offered in many hospitals, and *Star Trek* energy medicine is becoming more widely available. Sadly, there is also a growing element of intolerance, bigotry and religious differences that daily spill over into physical death. Remember, everything has two sides. And those two sides simply need to come back into balance.

To achieve this, the easiest way is to begin with yourself. There are thousands of health books out there to help you. Eat one healthy meal a day, reduce the amount of refined junk foods you eat, get some exercise, learn to breathe deeply, drink more clean water, and as much as possible be happy. After all, this life is so short. Learn to meditate, which will not only help you to be healthier but also help you to connect to the higher realms. Find your passion in life. Do what you can, where you can to make a positive difference. Make one other person smile every day. If you are concerned about the environment then start recycling – even running less water when you are cleaning your teeth and flushing the loo less frequently will make a huge difference. Using environmentally friendly products and organic foods also helps. Every one of us can help to make things better; all you need to do is start today. Always keep in mind that what goes around, comes around – and science now agrees.

Professor Schwartz and others before him have told me that our physical bodies are all simply recycled atoms, going around and around. And when Bill Tiller had shared his profound evidence and conclusions drawn from 35 years' painstaking research, that every single one of us is creating our reality at every level through our thoughts, words and actions, then finally I felt as though my own personal beliefs as to who we really are and why we are here were verified.

And if after reading this book you want to learn more, there are thousands of great books and websites to choose from. If, for instance, you wanted to know more about coherent water and see pictures of coherent crystals then log on to Dr Masuru Emoto's website on www.masaru-emoto.net and find details of his books.

Once you ask for help and guidance on your journey from the higher realms, believe me they will not leave you idle for long. And if what one person says doesn't resonate with you, then move to another. Find your own truth in your own way – that's free will.

Recently whilst chatting with a girl friend she jokingly said, 'You must have learned so much in writing this book – you should suggest a new list of commandments,' we had laughed. But as I sat with her, I started with humility making a few suggestions. And here they are...

Learn to listen to the supreme universal intelligence that is within you and without you.

Think positively as much as you can – watch your thoughts.

Learn to forgive and forget – yourself and others – and then move forward.

Don't ram your personal beliefs down anyone else's throat.

Don't intentionally harm or judge others – live in peace.

Control your ego.

Begin to understand how special you really are.

Look in the mirror every day and say, '*I love you.*' And then look again, and ask, 'Who am I?' And then, without ego, say, 'I am the Guiding Organizing Designer'. Finally, you may ask, 'Who is the conductor?' At an ultimate level you are; we all are. And then say, 'We are all one. *We are everything and no-thing. And so it is.*'

For me this book has become far more than finding my own personal truth. There is great wisdom in these pages, from many learned people – who know far more than I.

Whatever you believe in your heart, I hope some of my journey will resonate with you and help you on your way. Above all, I wish you peace and happiness on your own journey, as I now leave you to continue my own.

Hazel Courteney
www.hazelcourteney.com
October 2004

Other books by Hazel Courteney include:

Divine Intervention (Cico Books)

This courageous book tells the riveting story of Hazel's near-death experience and spiritual emergency during 1998. It has inspired thousands of people since its publication and is now available with a new foreword by Professor Gary Schwartz

500 of the Most Important Heath Tips You'll Ever Need (Cico Books)

Since its publication, this book has become a 'must have' home reference book. It has now been revised, updated and greatly expanded. Covering everything from Acid Stomach and Bronchitis to Leaky Gut and new conditions such as MRSA. *Dr Gillian Mckeith* says **'A great book for anyone who is serious about their health'**.

500 of the Most Important Ways to Stay Younger Longer (Cico Books)

Written in a clear A–Z format, covering topics from Absorbtion to Alzheimers, the Brain in Ageing, to Liver Function, Cancer and Chelation – this highly authoritative book covers more than 100 conditions relating to ageing. **Robin Morgan, Editor of the** *Sunday Times Magazine* **says 'Forget the fads and fashions – the key to living a younger life for longer is knowledge and nobody knows better then Hazel Courteney'**.

You can also visit Hazel's website at **www.hazelcourteney.com**